HEALING THE SHAME
THAT BINDS YOU

HEALING THE SHAME
THAT BINDS YOU

New York Times bestselling author
JOHN BRADSHAW

Expanded and Updated Edition

Health Communications, Inc.
Deerfield Beach, Florida

www.bcibooks.com

Library of Congress Cataloging-in-Publication Data

Bradshaw, John, 1933–
Healing the shame that binds you / John Bradshaw.—Expanded and updated ed.
    p. cm.
Includes bibliographical references.
ISBN-13: 978-0-7573-0323-4
ISBN-10: 0-7573-0323-4
1. Shame. 2. Psychotherapy. I. Title.

RC455.4.S53B73 2005
616.89'14—dc22

2005052577

HCI, its logos and marks are trademarks of Health Communications, Inc.

Publisher: Health Communications, Inc.
           3201 S.W. 15th Street
           Deerfield Beach, FL 33442-8190

Cover design by Andrea Perrine Brower
Inside book formatting by Dawn Von Strolley Grove

To Karen, my extraordinary wife, whose golden smile
can wither away the darkest shame
and who loves me unconditionally.

To my longtime friends (who used to be my children)
Brad, Brenda and John. Forgive me for all the times
I've transferred my shame to you.

To my father, Jack. Toxic shame took your life
and robbed us of our time.

Contents

Acknowledgments

I want to thank Silvan Tompkins for his groundbreaking work on shame. I want to thank Gershan Kaufman for his book *Shame,* which has been a major resource in my understanding Tomkins's work and in naming the demon I call toxic shame. My book was deeply enriched by Kaufman's pioneering efforts.

I'm also indebted to the anonymous writer of the Hazelden publication entitled *Shame* for my understanding of healthy shame as that which signals our essential human limitation and of the more-than-human/less-than-human polarity of toxic shame.

Several other people have been important to my understanding of the dynamics of shame. Dr. Donald Nathanson has further helped me understand Tompkins's theory of the affects as the primary motivators of human behaviors. Others who have helped me greatly are Carl D. Schneider, Charles Darwin, Havelock Ellis, Vladimir Soloviev, Max Scheler, Marilyn Mason, Merl Fossem, Sheldon Kopp and my colleague at the Meadows Treatment Center, Pia Mellody.

Kip Flock, my friend and cotraining therapist in Los Angeles, was extremely helpful in my developing the concepts in my first book. Kip and I have spent countless hours discussing and clarifying the concept of shame.

I want to thank my colleagues at the Center for Recovering Families in Houston (especially Mary Bell, may she rest in peace).

I thank my best friends, my brother Richard, George Pletcher and Rev. Mike Falls, for sharing their pain and vulnerability with me. Their non-shaming acceptance has allowed me to share my toxic shame with them. Together we've reduced the power of toxic shame in our lives.

Thanks to my publishers, Peter Vegso and Gary Seidler, for their continued commitment and total support of my work. I'm grateful to the entire production staff at Health Communications.

My publicist Diane Glynn and her able associate Jodee Blanco went far beyond the call of duty in promoting the first edition of this book.

My original book would not have been possible without the incredible patience of Barbara Evans, who diligently typed and retyped my manuscript (at all hours of the day and night). Thanks to my associate Barbara Bradshaw, whom many of you have come to love. Thanks to my brilliant wife, Karen, who read and advised me on this new edition and who knows all about computers!

And lest I forget (which I too often do), my greatest gratitude goes to my Higher Power, whose grace has saved me from my toxic shame.

Preface to the Revised Edition

It's been sixteen years since I wrote the first edition of *Healing the Shame That Binds You*. At that time the material on shame was tremendously helpful to me personally, but I had no idea of its impact on the public. The response has been a joy to me, and I want to thank you for your continuing letters of appreciation. The book is now in ten languages and has sold more than 1.5 million copies in the United States and more than one hundred thousand copies abroad. I was most amazed when it hit the *New York Times* best-seller list. That is an honor my toxic shame had never let me dream could happen.

In the intervening years I've enriched my understanding of the importance of healthy shame in forming our sense of identity, in guarding our honor and dignity, in safeguarding our spirituality and in forming our conscience. I'll be completing a new book in 2006 on the unique kind of moral intelligence that is the source of virtue and ethical sensitivity. Without healthy shame, moral behavior and ethical responsibility are impossible.

In researching my book on family secrets, I found many writings concerning shame that I had not known about when I first wrote *Healing the Shame That Binds You.*

Thanks to the psychiatrist Donald Nathanson and his fine book *Shame and Pride,* I learned that the first scholarly treatise on shame, entitled *Two Dialogues of Shame,* went back to a Renaissance genius named Annibale Pocaterra, who wrote it in 1592.

Pocaterra clearly understood shame was an innate feeling that could be internalized as a destructive identity.

I further came to realize that Charles Darwin, writing three hundred years later, found blushing and the mother of blushing, shame, to be the emotion that distinguishes humans from all other animals. At the turn of the century, Havelock Ellis produced his extensive studies, *The Psychology of Sex,* the first part of which he called "The Evolution of Modesty," an essay on shame and blushing that supports Darwin's discussion. In Russia, a great

xi

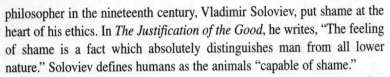

philosopher in the nineteenth century, Vladimir Soloviev, put shame at the heart of his ethics. In *The Justification of the Good*, he writes, "The feeling of shame is a fact which absolutely distinguishes man from all lower nature." Soloviev defines humans as the animals "capable of shame."

I wrote my master's dissertation on the work of the German philosopher Nietzsche and quoted his statements on shame "as the source and safeguard of spirituality" in the first edition. Nietzsche delved deeply into the meaning of shame in his attempt to understand what it means to be human. I will expand on Nietzsche's understanding of the relationship between shame and spirituality in the new Part III of this book, where I expanded Chapter Twelve of the original edition into three separate chapters.

I've come to see that one of the most profound aspects of healthy shame is its role in forming, directing and fulfilling the sex drive and in forming mature and soulful sexuality. I'm indebted to Carl D. Schneider, in his book *Shame, Exposure and Privacy,* for presenting the work of the German philosopher Max Scheler. Scheler wrote his German treatise, entitled *Über Scham ünd Schamgelfühl,* in the mid-twentieth century. Unfortunately, this work has been translated only into French, under the title *La Pudeur.* I'm completely indebted to Schneider for his presentation of this important material in English. I have put this material in the new Chapter Twelve, entitled "Spirituality and Sexuality." In this chapter, I outline how healthy shame forms, directs and fulfills the development of healthy sexuality.

I've added my own interpretations to Scheler's work, and I take full responsibility for the final product. With shameless pornography grossing more money than ABC, NBC, CBS and cable networks combined, Scheler's work is most relevant.

The most important enrichment in my understanding of healthy and toxic shame has come directly from reading the work of Silvan Tompkins, called the "American Einstein" by Donald Nathanson. Both Gershan Kaufman, who was a constant guide in the first edition of *Healing the Shame That Binds You,* and Donald Nathanson, who helped clarify many issues in this new edition, are directly indebted to Silvan Tompkins for their own works. This is not to take anything away from each man's originality, but it is something that both generously acknowledge.

Tomkins's work is highly clinical and often hard to read and understand. But it seems clear he is presenting a new and original theory of the primacy of human affects as the essential motivating force in human behavior. Affects, according to Tompkins, are biological mechanisms that unfold according to precisely written scripts. When an affect is named, the word "feeling" is used. The word "feeling" implies that the person has some level of awareness that an affect has been triggered. When Tompkins speaks of an affect as an emotion, he implies some biographical experience has taken place, since a triggered affect (feeling) always happens in the context of some situation or interaction that is encoded in our memory as a scene.

Tompkins thus describes an emotion as the complex combination of an affect with those memories that record their original occurrence and with the affects that the emotion may further trigger. When I use the words "affect," "feeling" or "emotion" in this book, I will be using them in the sense I've just described.

For example, if I told you I was *angry* with my dad because of his continued broken promises, you would go to your own scenes (your memories of being angry at your dad if he broke his promise to you), but you would not know exactly what my emotion of anger is referring to. I would have to describe in sensory-based detail what I meant by anger. In my case the scene(s) involved my dad promising me every month for two years that he would take me to play golf. On the day we were finally going to play he said he had to go downtown to his office on Franklin Street in Houston, Texas, in order to get his paycheck. We didn't have a car so we carried our golf clubs on the bus and went downtown. I can remember standing at 504 Franklin Avenue while my dad went up to his office. He was gone twenty-five minutes, which is an eternity to an anxious twelve-year-old. When he finally came down he told me that he had to go back to work—that an emergency had come up. I knew he was lying and that he was going out to drink with his pals. My dad was a serious alcoholic. I was too cowed and too desperate for his love to confront his lie. So I took my golf clubs and got back on the bus. Shortly after I got on the bus I felt intense hurt, anger and shame. I went into an hysterical state—crying, sobbing and yelling at the bus driver to open the window next to my seat. I intended to throw my golf clubs out of the window. They were brand new, a gift from my grandfather. I was in such a state of panic that the bus driver stopped the bus and a group of people on the bus tried to console me. This triggered an even stronger feeling of shame as humiliation.

As you read this scene, it may trigger some scene you experienced and feelings that go with your scene, or you may have felt your own feelings of anger at my father and sadness for me. In any case, you now can understand and get a visual picture of the scene that embodies my emotion of anger at my father for his broken promises.

Tompkins discovered nine innate affects in his research. The nine affects are excitement, pleasure, startle, distress (sadness), fear and anger, shame, dissmell and disgust. In the case of the latter three, shame is an affect auxiliary, which is like a natural boundary governing excitement and pleasure. If excitement or pleasure go on too long or are excessive, the feeling of shame kicks in to stop them. I will expand on this throughout the text.

The feelings of "dissmell" and "disgust" are drive auxillaries that originally monitored hunger and thirst. These feelings have become more complex and abstract. Dissmell is a feeling that is present in prejudice and operates poignantly in sexual relations. Think of the billions spent on perfumes and genital deodorants. Disgust is related to anger and shame. There is much disgust displayed during many divorce proceedings. There is also great disgust in relation to sexual violation and rejection. Rapists frequently have their sex drive fused with anger and disgust.

For Tompkins, the primary blueprint for cognition, decision and action is provided by the affect system. This means that for Tompkins, affects (feeling) are forms of thinking and are integrally related to decision and action. The neuroscientist Antonio Damasio supports Tompkins's position in his book *Descartes' Error.* He has proven that when there is damage to the part of the brain that controls feelings, the damaged person cannot make decisions.

Tompkins sees the affect system as one of our bodily systems, like the nervous system or the immune system. For Tompkins, Freud was wrong in viewing libido (sexual energy) as the motivating energy of human behavior. Tompkins writes:

> *I see affect or feeling as the primary innate biological motivating mechanism, more urgent than drive deprivation and pleasure and more urgent than physical pain.*

He goes on to say that without feeling, nothing matters, and with feeling, anything can matter.

Current trends and conclusions in modern neuroscientific studies support Tompkins's overall position. The work that follows is also predicated on Tompkins's theory of the primacy of affect.

The Affect of Shame

The subject of this book is the affect of shame. No affect is more important to our sense of self or our identity, dignity and honor. And no affect is more important for our ethical and spiritual life. The affect shame as toxic is a source of most of the neurotic and character-disordered behaviors that we now understand. It is also the source of violence to self and others.

I've modified some of the chapters from the original edition. I've deleted the sections on dreams, the NLP technique of building a new self-image and some of the material on tracking down toxic voices. The feedback I've gotten is that those exercises and strategies were not found by many readers to be useful.

I've expanded Part III to include chapters on spirituality and sexuality, and healthy shame as revelatory and revolutionary in terms of finding our true selves, spiritual destinies and callings. And the final chapter outlines seven major blessings that come from healthy shame.

I want to thank all of you in the United States and abroad who read the first edition of *Healing the Shame That Binds You.* You have honored me beyond my wildest expectations. My hope is that you find this new edition worthy of its revision.

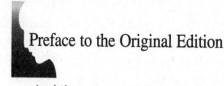

Preface to the Original Edition

And they were not ashamed.

—Genesis

Ten years ago I had one of those life-jolting discoveries that significantly changed everything. I named the core demon in my life. I named "shame." This means that I became aware of the massive destructive power shame had exerted in my life. I discovered that I had been bound by shame all my life. It ruled me like an addiction. I acted it out; I covered it up in subtle and not-so-subtle ways; I transferred it to my family, my clients and the people I taught.

Shame was the unconscious demon I had never acknowledged. In becoming aware of the dynamics of shame, I came to see that shame is one of the major destructive forces in all human life. In naming shame I began to have power over it.

In itself, shame is not bad. Shame is a normal human emotion. In fact, it is necessary to feel shame if one is to be truly human. Shame is the emotion that gives us permission to be human. Shame tells us of our limits. Shame keeps us in our human boundaries, letting us know we can and will make mistakes and that we need help. Our shame tells us we are not God. Healthy shame is the psychological foundation of humility. It is the source of spirituality.

What I discovered was that *shame as a healthy human emotion can be transformed into shame as a state of being. As a state of being shame takes over one's whole identity. To have shame as an identity is to believe that one's being is flawed, that one is defective as a human being. Once shame is transformed into an identity, it becomes toxic and dehumanizing.*

Toxic shame is unbearable and always necessitates a cover-up, a false self. Since one feels his true self is defective and flawed, one needs a false self that is not defective and flawed. *Once one becomes a false self, one ceases to exist psychologically.* To be a false self is to cease being an authentic human being. The process of false self formation is what Alice

xvii

Miller calls "soul murder." As a false self, one tries to be more than human or less than human. Toxic shame is the greatest form of learned domestic violence there is. It destroys human life. Toxic shame is the core of most forms of emotional illness. Gershen Kaufman writes in *Shame*:

> *Shame is the affect which is the source of many complex and disturbing inner states: depression, alienation, self doubt, isolating loneliness, paranoid and schizoid phenomena, compulsive disorders, splitting of the self, perfectionism, a deep sense of inferiority, inadequacy or failure, the so-called borderline conditions and disorders of narcissism.*

Toxic shame so destroys the function of our authentic selves that clear syndromes of shame develop out of the false self cover-ups. Each syndrome has its own characteristic pattern. Toxic shame becomes the core of neurosis, character disorders, political violence, wars and criminality. It comes the closest to defining human bondage of all the things I know.

The Bible describes shame as the core and consequence of Adam's fall. In Hebrew, Adam is equivalent to mankind. Adam symbolizes all human beings. The Bible suggests that Adam was not satisfied with his own being. He wanted to be more than he was. He wanted to be more than human. He failed to accept his essential limitations. He lost his healthy shame. The Bible suggests that the origin of human bondage (original sin) is the desire to be other than who we are . . . to be more than human. In his toxic shame (pride), Adam wanted a false self. The false self led to his destruction.

After Adam alienated his true being, he went into hiding. "And the Lord God called unto Adam . . . where art thou?" And Adam said, "I heard thy voice in the garden and I hid myself" (Genesis 3:9–10). Before the fall, the man and the woman were both naked and "were not ashamed" (Genesis 2:25). Once they chose to be other than what they were, they became naked and ashamed.

Nakedness symbolized their true and authentic selves. They were who they were, and they were okay with it. There was nothing to hide. They could be perfectly and rigorously honest.

This symbolic and metaphorical description of Adam and Eve is a description of the human condition. Unconditional love and acceptance of self seems to be the hardest task for all humankind. Refusing to accept our "real selves," we try to create more powerful false selves, or we give up and become less than human. This results in a lifetime of cover-up and secrecy. This secrecy and hiding is the basic cause of human suffering.

Total self-love and acceptance is the only foundation for happiness and the love of others. Without total self-love and acceptance, we are doomed to the enervating task of creating false selves. It takes lots of energy and hard work to live a false self. This may be the symbolic meaning of the Biblical statement that after the fall the man and the woman would suffer in their natural activities: the woman in childbirth, the man in his work.

How do we heal this shame that binds us? Wherein lies our hope? This is the concern of this book. In what follows I'd like to share with you my own journey in healing shame. This journey has been the most important issue in my life. Toxic shame is everywhere. Toxic shame is cunning, powerful and baffling. Its power resides in its darkness and secretiveness.

In Part I, I try to bring shame out of hiding by examining its many faces and exposing its origins and major cover-ups. I show how shame creates hopelessness and spiritual bankruptcy.

Part II offers every way I know for reducing toxic shame and transforming it back into healthy shame. My most sincere hope is that every reader who is bound by the ties of toxic shame will use this book to free himself from this menacing enemy.

PART I

The Problem— Spiritual Bankruptcy

We have no imagination for Evil, but Evil has us in its grip.

—C. G. Jung

Introduction: Shame as Demonic (The Internalization Process)

As I've delved deeper into the destructive power of toxic shame, I've come to see that it directly touches the age-old theological and metaphysical discussion generally referred to as the problem of evil. The problem of evil may be more accurately described as the mystery of evil. No one has ever explained the existence of evil in the world. Centuries ago in the Judeo-Christian West, evil was considered the domain of the Devil, or Satan, the fallen angel. Biblical scholars tell us that the idea of a purely evil being like the Devil or Satan was a late development in the Bible. In the book of Job, Satan was the heavenly district attorney whose job it was to test the faith of those who, like Job, were specially blessed.

During the Persian conquest of the Israelites, the Satan of Job became fused with the Zoroastrian dualistic theology adopted by the Persians, where two opposing forces, one of good, Ahura Mazda, the Supreme Creator deity, was in a constant battle with Ahriman, the absolute god of evil. This polarized dualism was present in the theology of the Essenes and took hold in Christianity where God and his Son Jesus were in constant battle with the highest fallen angel, Satan, for human souls. This dualism persists today only in fundamentalist religions (Muslim terrorists, the Taliban, the extreme Christian Right and a major part of evangelical Christianity).

The figure of Satan and the fires of hell have been demythologized by modern Christian biblical scholars, theologians and philosophers.

The mystery of evil has not been dismissed by the demythologizing of the Devil. Rather, it has been intensified in the twentieth century by two world wars, Nazism, Stalinism, the genocidal regime of the Khmer Rouge in Cambodia, and the heinous and ruthless extermination of Tibetans and Tibetan Buddhism by Pol Pot. These reigns of evil form what has been called a collective shadow, and it has been shown how naïve and unconscious the people of the world have been in relation to these evils.

The denial of evil seems to be a learned behavior. The idea of evil is always subject to denial as a coping mechanism.

Evil is real and is a permanent part of the human condition. "To deny *that evil is a permanent affliction of humankind," says the philosopher Ernst Becker in his book* Escape from Evil, *"is perhaps the most dangerous kind of thinking." He goes on to suggest that in denying evil, humans have heaped evil on the world. Historically, great misfortunes have resulted from humans, blinded by the full reality of evil, thinking they were doing good but dispensing miseries far worse than the evil they thought to eradicate. The Crusades during the Middle Ages and the Vietnam War are examples that come to mind.*

While demons, Satan and hellfire have been demythologized by any critically thinking person, the awesome collective power of evil remains. Many theologiams and psychologists refer to evil as the demonic in human life. They call us to personal wholeness and self-awareness, especially in relation to our own toxic shame or shadow, which goes unconscious and in hiding because it is so painful to bear. These men warn against duality and polarization. "We must beware of thinking of Good and Evil as absolute opposites," writes Carl Jung. Good and evil are potentials in every human being; they are halves of a paradoxical whole. Each represents a judgment, and "we cannot believe that we will always judge rightly."

Nothing can spare us the torment of ethical decision. In the past, prior to the patriarchies of Hitler, Stalin and Pol Pot, it was believed that moral evaluation was built and founded on the certitude of a moral code that pretended to know exactly what is good and what is evil. But now we know how any patriarchy, even religious ones, can make cruel and violent decisions. Ethical decision is an uncertain and ultimately a creative act. My new book on moral intelligence calls these patriarchies "cultures of obedience," and presents an ethics of virtues as a way to avoid such moral totalism. The Jews who killed their Nazi guards or SS troopers coming to search their homes are now considered ethically good, no matter what the absolutist moral code says about killing. There is a structure of evil that transcends the malice of any single individual. The Augustinian priest Gregory Baum was the man I first heard call it "the demonic."

It can begin with the best of intentions, with a sincere belief that one is doing good and fighting to eradicate evil, as in the Vietnam War—but it ends with heinous evil. "Life consists of achieving Good, not apart from Evil, but in spite of it," says the psychologist Rollo May. There is no such thing as pure good in human affairs. Those who claim it are seriously deluded and will likely be the next perpetrators of evil.

As I pointed out in the preface to this revised edition, the affect shame has the potential for the depths of human evil or the heights of human good. In this regard shame is demonic. "The daimonic," says the psychologist Steven A. Diamond, "is any natural function which has the power to take over the whole person." Shame is a natural feeling that, when allowed to function well, monitors a person's sense of excitement or pleasure. But when the feeling of shame is violated by a coercive and perfectionistic religion and culture—especially by shame-based source figures who mediate religion and culture—it becomes an all-embracing identity. A person with internalized shame believes he is inherently flawed, inferior and defective. Such a feeling is so painful that defending scripts (or strategies) are developed to cover it up. These scripts are the roots of violence, criminality, war and all forms of addiction.

What I'll mainly describe in the first part of this book is how the affect shame can become the source of self-loathing, hatred of others, cruelty, violence, brutality, prejudice and all forms of destructive addictions. As an internalized identity, toxic shame is one of the major sources of the demonic in human life.

The Healthy Faces
of Shame (HDL Shame)

Everyone needs a sense of shame,
but no one needs to feel ashamed.

—Frederick Nietzsche

Because of its preverbal origins, shame is difficult to define. It is a healthy human feeling that can become a true sickness of the soul. Just as there are two kinds of cholesterol, HDL (healthy) and LDL (toxic), so also are there two forms of shame: innate shame and toxic/life-destroying shame. When shame is toxic, it is an excruciatingly internal experience of unexpected exposure. It is a deep cut felt primarily from the inside. It divides us from ourselves and from others. When our feeling of shame becomes toxic shame, we disown ourselves. And this disowning demands a cover-up. Toxic shame parades in many garbs and get-ups. It loves darkness and secretiveness. It is the dark, secret aspect of shame that has evaded our study.

Because toxic shame stays in hiding and covers itself up, we have to track it down by learning to recognize its many faces and its many distracting behavioral cover-ups.

SHAME AS A HEALTHY HUMAN FEELING

The idea of shame as healthy seems foreign to English-speaking people because we have only one word for shame in English. To my knowledge, most other languages have at least two words for shame (see Figure 1.1).

FIGURE 1.1
The Languages of Shame

DISCRETION Before an Action HDL SHAME		DISGRACE After an Action LDL SHAME	
Latin	*Pudor* *Verecundia*	Latin	*Foedus* *Macula*
Greek	*Entrope* *Aidos*	Greek	*Aischyne*
French	*Pudeur*	French	*Honte*
German	*Scham*	German	*Schande*

ANNIBALE POCATERRA

The earliest treatise on shame was written by Annnibale Pocaterra, born in 1562. My awareness of Pocaterra's book, *Two Dialogues on Shame,* came from Donald Nathanson's comprehensive book *Shame and Pride.* According to Nathanson, Pocaterra wrote his book on shame at age thirty. His book was the only scholarly work on shame until Darwin wrote about it three hundred years later. Pocaterra died a few months after publishing his book. Only thirty-eight copies are known to exist today. Nathanson owns one of them, and I'm indebted to him for what follows (see *Shame and Pride,* pages 443–445).

In the beginning of his book, Pocaterra tells us that "in the end shame is a good thing, a part of everyday existence." Shame, according to Pocaterra, makes us timorous, humble and contrite and causes outrage against the self.

When we are attacked by shame, Pocaterra says we "would like nothing better than to run and hide from the eyes of the world." He also describes shame as the "fear of infamy," which can lead a person to attack his enemy with passion. Shame is thus capable of both cowardice and bravery. Long before Silvan Tomkins's treatise on shame, Pocaterra posited that our emotions are innate and that "they are only good or evil as the end to which they are used." There is an innate and a learned component to all emotion. "Therefore," Pocaterra writes, "there must be two shames, one natural and free from awareness and the other acquired."

Pocaterra understood shame to be our teacher. He thought the shame of children was like a seed that will become a small plant in youth and leads to virtue at maturity. Pocaterra looked at blushing as the external sign of shame and believed that blushing was both the recognition of having made a mistake as well as the desire to make amends. Three hundred years later Darwin would posit blushing as that which distinguishes us from all other animals. Darwin knew that the mother of the blush was shame. For Darwin, shame defines our essential humanity. Silvan Tomkins views shame as an innate feeling that limits our experience of interest, curiosity and pleasure.

SHAME AS PERMISSION TO BE HUMAN

Healthy shame lets us know that we are limited. It tells us that to be human is to be limited. Actually, humans are *essentially* limited. *Not one of us has, or can ever have, unlimited power.* The unlimited power that many modern gurus offer is false hope. Their programs calling us to unlimited power have made them rich, not us. They touch our false selves and tap our toxic shame. We humans are finite, "perfectly imperfect." Limitation is our essential nature. Grave problems result from refusing to accept our limits.

Healthy shame is an emotion that teaches us about our limits. Like all emotions, shame moves us to get our basic needs met.

EGO BOUNDARIES

One of our basic needs is structure. We ensure our structure by developing a boundary system within which we safely operate. Structure gives our lives form. Boundaries offer us safety and allow more efficient use of energy.

There is an old joke about the man who "got on his horse and rode off in all directions." Without boundaries we have no limits and are easily confused. We go this way and that, wasting a lot of energy. We lose our way or become addicted because we don't know when to stop; we don't know how to say no.

Healthy shame keeps us grounded. It is a yellow light, warning us of our essential limitations. *Healthy shame is the basic metaphysical boundary for human beings.* It is the emotional energy that signals us that we are not God—that we will make mistakes, that we need help. Healthy shame gives us permission to be human.

Healthy shame is part of every human's personal power. It allows us to know our limits, and thus to use our energy more effectively. We have better direction when we know our limits. We do not waste ourselves on goals we cannot reach or on things we cannot change. Healthy shame allows our energy to be integrated rather than diffused.

THE DEVELOPMENTAL STAGE OF HEALTHY (HDL) SHAME

Figure 1.2 gives an overview of how the feeling of shame expands and grows over our lifetime. The chart is epigenetic, meaning that each stage builds upon and retains the previous stage.

We need to know from the beginning that we can trust the world. The world first comes to us in the form of our primary caregivers. We need to know that we can count on someone to be there for us in a humanly predictable manner. If we had a caregiver who was mostly predictable, and who touched us and mirrored all our behaviors, we developed a sense of basic trust. When security and trust are present, we begin to develop an interpersonal bond, which forms a bridge of empathic mutuality. Such a bridge is crucial for the development of self-worth. The only way a child can develop a sense of self is through a relationship with another. We are "we" before we are "I."

In this earliest stage of life, we can only know ourselves in the mirroring eyes of our primary caregivers.

FIGURE 1.2
Developmental Stages of Healthy (HDL) Shame

TRANSCENDENCE	Shame as **WISDOM,** knowing what is valuable and what is not worth your time.
	Older Age Shame as the experience of the **NUMINOUS SACRED HOLY & KNOWING A HIGHER POWER.** Shame as the source and safeguard of spirituality.
INTER-DEPENDENCE	*Adult* **EXPERIENCE OF LIFE'S LIMITS—SUFFERING AND DEATH.** Shame as knowing you don't know it all—openness to novelty/creativity.
	Young Adult New secure attachment figure—**LOVE AS EXPOSING YOUR VULNERABLE SELF**. Shame as modesty.
INDEPENDENCE	*Puberty* **SHAME EXPERIENCED AS LIMITS TO SELF-IDENTITY.** Shame limits mental curiosity—*studiasitas* (temperance of the mind).
	Puberty Emergence of the sex drive experienced as awesome. Healthy shame monitors sex drive. Shame is dominant in peer group acceptance.
	8–Puberty Shame as **INFERIORITY** experienced as limits to one's abilities—social shame related to ethnicity, gender, status.
	8–Puberty Shame as **EMBARASSMENT** coming from making mistakes, especially neighborhood social play—juvenile sex play—social shame as related to belonging.
	3.5–8 Years **GUILT** as moral shame, the internalized parental rules and voices that form conscience. Early sexual curiosity—manners and modesty.
COUNTER-DEPENDENCE	*18 Months–3.5 Years* **FULL AFFECT OF SHAME** experienced as limits put on child's autonomous need to separate and do things his or her own way.
	6–18 Months Shame as limits to curiosity and interest—when children get into trouble they often **HIDE THEIR EYES.**
INTERPERSONAL BRIDGE ESTABLISHED CODEPENDENCE	*6 Months* Once securely attached—shame as **SHYNESS** appears as a response to being exposed to strange faces.

THE INTERPERSONAL BRIDGE

The relationship between child and caregiver gradually evolves out of reciprocal interest, along with shared experiences of trust. Actually, trust is fostered by the fact that we come to expect and rely on the mutuality of response. As trust grows, an emotional bond is formed. The emotional bond allows the child to risk venturing out to explore the world. This bond becomes an interpersonal bridge between child and caregiver. The bridge is the foundation for mutual growth and understanding. The interpersonal bridge is strengthened by certain experiences we have come to accept and depend on. The other person, our primary caregiver, becomes significant in the sense that that person's love, respect and care for us really matter. We allow ourselves to be vulnerable in that we allow ourselves to need the other person.

SHAME AS SHYNESS

Once basic trust has been established, the child's feeling of shame emerges. The first appearance of the feeling of shame usually occurs at about six months. At that age, a child has become familiar with his or her mother's face. When a strange face (maybe a relative seeing the baby for the first time) appears, the infant experiences shame as shyness in looking at the strange face.

Some children are temperamentally shy and withdrawn. But all of us experience some shyness in the presence of what is unfamiliar.

SHAME AS A LIMIT TO CURIOSITY: THE DEVELOPMENT OF HEALTHY SHAME

SIX MONTHS TO EIGHTEEN MONTHS

At about six to eighteen months of age, a child begins to develop musculature. He needs to establish a balance between "holding on and letting go." The earliest muscle development focuses on crawling and then gaining balance when standing up and walking. This triggers the desire to roam and explore, and in order to roam and explore, the child needs to separate from his primary caregivers. The early exploratory stage is characterized by touching, tasting and examining the many fascinating aspects of the environment. Children lack coordination and knowledge. My grandson Jackson loved to dunk his head into the toilet at this stage. When he was stopped from doing something (like throwing his train into the TV) he hid his eyes. Six- to eighteen-month-olds are magical in their thinking. When Jackson hid his eyes, we disappeared. In his magical mind, *if he couldn't see us, then we couldn't see him.* Hiding the eyes is characteristic of shame because shame guards against overexposure. When we are exposed without any way to protect ourselves, we feel the pain of shame. If we are continually overexposed, shame becomes toxic.

EIGHTEEN MONTHS TO THREE AND A HALF YEARS

The psychologist Erik Erikson says that the psychosocial task at this stage of development is to strike a balance between autonomy and shame and doubt. This stage (eighteen months to three and a half years) has been called "the terrible twos" because children begin to explore by touching, tasting and testing. Two-year-olds are in a counterdependent stage. They need to separate and are stubborn. They want to do it their way (always within eyesight of their caregiver). When two-year-olds are thwarted (like every three minutes), they have intense anger and temper tantrums. At this stage the child needs to take possession of things in order to test them by purposeful repetition. The world is brand new—sights, sounds and smells all have to be assimilated through repeated experience.

THE CHILD'S NEEDS

This stage has also been referred to as "second" or "psychological" birth. The child is beginning to separate. Saying "no" and "it's mine" and throwing temper tantrums are the first testing of boundaries. What a child needs most is a firm but understanding caregiver, who in turn needs to have her own needs met through her spouse and her own resources. Such a caregiver needs to have resolved the issues in her own source relationships and needs to have a sense of self-responsibility. When this is the case, such a caregiver can be available to the child and provide what the child needs. No parent is perfect and none can do this perfectly. They simply need to be "good enough."

MODELS

The child needs good modeling of healthy shame and other emotions. The child needs the caregiver's time and attention. Above all, the child needs the caregiver to model good boundaries. A child needs to have a caregiver available to set limits and express anger in a nonshaming way. Outer control must be firmly reassuring. Dr. Maria Montessori found that a "prepared environment" takes the heat off the parents. The prepared environment is developmentally geared to the child's unique needs at each stage of development. These needs were called "sensitive periods" by Dr. Montessori. The child needs to know that the interpersonal bridge will not be destroyed by his new urge for doing things his own way—his new urge toward autonomy. Erikson writes in *Childhood and Society*:

> Firmness must protect him against the potential anarchy of his yet untrained sense of discrimination, his inability to hold on and to let go with discretion.

If a child can be protected by firm but compassionate limits, if he can explore, test and have tantrums without the caregiver's withdrawal of love, i.e., withdrawal of the interpersonal bridge, then the child can develop a healthy sense of shame. It may come as the child's embarrassment over his normal human failures, or as timidity and shyness in the presence of strangers, or as the beginning feeling of guilt as the child internalizes his parents' limits on excitement and pleasure. This sense of shame is crucial and necessary as a balance and limit for one's newfound autonomy. Healthy shame signals us that we are not omnipotent.

Our shyness is always with us as we encounter strangers or strange new experiences. The stranger, by definition, is one who is "un-family-iar." The stranger is not of our family. The stranger poses the threat of the unknown. Our shyness is our healthy shame in the presence of a stranger. Like all emotions, shyness signals us to be cautious, to take heed lest we be wounded or exposed. Shyness is a boundary that guards our inner core in the presence of the unfamiliar stranger.

Shyness *can* become a serious problem when it is rooted in toxic shame.

SHAME AS GUILT

Healthy guilt is *moral shame*. The rules and limits children have experienced from their caregivers or from the environment are internalized and become an inner voice that guides and limits behavior. Guilt is the guardian of conscience, and children begin to form their conscience during the preschool period.

SHAME AS EMBARRASSMENT AND BLUSHING

As preschool children grow older, they begin to explore their own bodies and their gender identity. Their healthy shame is the foundation for developing manners and a sense of modesty. A child's manners and modesty become a more sophisticated and complex guide that triggers shame as embarrassment and blushing. Preschool and school-age children become more social and have more occasion for unexpected exposure that leads to embarrassment and blushing.

In an embarrassing situation one is caught off guard—one is exposed when one is not ready to be exposed. One feels unable to cope with some situation in the presence of others. It may be an unexpected physical clumsiness, an interpersonal sensitivity or a breach of etiquette.

In such situations we experience the blush of healthy shame. Blushing manifests the exposure, the unexpectedness, the involuntary nature of shame.

In *On Shame and the Search for Identity* Helen Lynd writes, "One's feeling is involuntarily exposed; one is uncovered."

Blushing is the manifestation of our human limits. The ability to blush is a metaphor for our essentially limited humanity. With blushing comes the impulse to "cover one's face," "bury one's face," "save face," or "sink into the ground." With blushing we know we've made a mistake. Why would we have such a capacity if mistakes were not part of our essential nature? Blushing as a manifestation of healthy shame keeps us grounded. It reminds us of our core human boundary. It is a signal for us not to get carried away with our own excellence.

SHAME AS THE SOURCE OF CREATIVITY AND LEARNING

I once did a workshop with Richard Bandler, one of the founders of NeuroLinguistic Programming (NLP). It was a very powerful experience. I've never forgotten one aspect of that experience. Richard asked us to think of a time in our lives when we knew we were right. After a few seconds, I remembered an incident with my former wife. He asked us to go over the experience in our memory. Then he asked us to make a movie of the experience: to divide it into acts and to run it as a film. Then he asked us to run the film backward. Then we were to run the acts out of sequence: the middle act first, the last act in the middle, etc. Then we were to run through the experience again as we had done it the first time. We were to pay exquisite attention to the details of the experience and to the feeling of rightness.

By the time I reran the experience, it no longer had the voltage it had the first time. In fact, I hardly felt anything of the initial intensity. Richard was introducing us to a form of internal remapping called submodality work. But that was not important for me. What was important for me was a statement Richard made about creativity. For me, the greatest human power is the creative power.

HEALTHY INFERIORITY

Richard Bandler suggested that one of the major blocks to creativity was the feeling of knowing you are right. When we think we are absolutely right, we stop seeking new information. To be right is to be certain, and to be certain stops us from being curious. Curiosity and wonder are at the heart of all learning. Plato said that all philosophy begins in wonder. So the feeling of absolute certainty and righteousness causes us to stop seeking and learning.

Our healthy shame, which is a feeling of our core boundaries and limitedness, never allows us to believe we know it all. Our healthy shame is nourishing in that it moves us to seek new information and learn new things. Inferiority can be experienced as a healthy limit to our abilities.

SHAME AS THE BASIC NEED
FOR COMMUNITY—SOCIAL SHAME

There is an ancient proverb that states, "One man is no man." This saying underscores our basic human need for community, which underscores our need for relationships and social life. Not one of us could have made it without someone being there for us. Human beings *need help*. Not one of us is so strong that he does not need love, intimacy and dialogue in community.

We will need our parents for another decade before we are ready to leave home. We cannot get our needs met without depending on our primary caregivers. Our healthy feeling of shame is there to remind us that we often need help. No human being can make it alone. Even after we have achieved some sense of mastery, even when we are independent, we will still have needs. We will need to love and grow. We will need to care for another, and we will need to be needed. Our shame functions as a healthy signal that we need help, that we need to love and be in caring relationships with others.

Without the healthy signal of shame, we would not be in touch with our core dependency needs.

SCHOOL AGE

Social shame emerges as the school-age child becomes aware of social difference and the culture's norms for beauty and success. Financial status, ethnicity, intelligence, popularity, physical appearance, athletic ability and talent all contribute to a person's sense of shame. Many of our cultural norms become occasions for toxic shame. But if children have a good, loving home with parents who model spiritual values, they can sift through the social garbage.

PUBERTY—SEXUAL SHAME

As the sex drive fully emerges, the feeling of shame becomes more activated than at any other time in the life cycle. The initial experience of sexuality is one of awe and strangeness. Today we have lost what the ancients called the phallic and vaginal mysteries. Thomas Moore writes poignantly about the mystery of sexuality in his book *The Soul of Sex*. In our *shameless culture,* sex has been depersonalized. It has become a fact, not a sacred value. Parents need to model and teach an awe and reverence for their own and their children's sexuality.

SHAME AS AN AFFECT AUXILLARY

In the new preface I mention that the foundation for this book is Silvan Tompkins's theory of the affect system and shame as an affect auxillary. This means that shame monitors excitement and pleasure. Nature has made the sexual experience the most exciting and pleasurable of all our experiences. Nature wants us to mate and procreate. Sex and shame go hand in hand because we need our sense of shame as a boundary for our sexual desires.

Adolescence is the time when the major biological transformation from child to adult is taking place. It is the time a person feels most exposed. Embarrassment is so excruciatingly painful in adolescence that teenagers are diligently on guard to protect themselves while projecting on others.

Belonging to the peer group is paramount. One's whole sense of identity is coming together in adolescence. If one has a good foundation prior to adolescence, the sense of self can be preliminarily defined. Identity is always social—one's sense of self needs to be matched by others: one's friends, teachers and parents. Adolescence is the time the brain (frontal lobes) is reaching full maturity. It is a time of ideals, of questioning and projecting into the future. An adolescent needs to have the discipline of mind the philosopher Thomas Aquinas called *studiasitas*. Studiasitas is a disciplined focus on studies and thinking, a kind of temperance of the mind. Its opposite is *curiositas,* a kind of mental wandering all over the place without limits.

Healthy shame at this stage is the source of good identity, a disciplined focus on the future and on studious limits in pursuing intellectual interests.

LOVE (ATTACHMENT)

The power of the interpersonal bridge, along with a sense of identity, form the foundation for a healthy adult love relationship. A toxically shamed person is divided within himself and must create a false-self cover-up to hide his sense of being flawed and defective. You cannot offer yourself to another person if you do not know who you really are.

CONNECTING BEHAVIOR

Having a secure attachment with one's source figures, and having developed a sense of self-worth, a person feels he is loveable and wants to love another. A securely attached person with a solid sense of self is capable of *connecting* with another in an intimate relationship. Intimacy requires vulnerability and a lack of defensiveness. *Intimacy requires healthy shame.*

Most people have a way to go in terms of developing intimacy and connecting skills when they get married or enter a long-term relationship. But the great thing about a committed relationship is that the *relationship itself is a form of therapy.* If both partners are committed, most of their differences can be worked out and even appreciated. Shame as the root feeling of humility allows each partner to appreciate and accept the other's foibles and idiosyncrasies. Knowing and accepting my own limitations allows me to accept my perceptions of my partner's limitations. Giving and receiving unconditional love is the most effective and powerful way to personal wholeness and happiness.

CREATIVITY AND GENERATIVITY

It has been said that creative people see more in any given reality than others see. The more they have healthy shame as the core of humility and modesty, the more they know that what they know is a tiny fraction of what there is to know. A person with humility shame is open to new discovery and learning. When a person with curiosity and interest has discipline available to him, he has the right formula for creativity. The philosopher Nietzsche spoke of the creative act as involving both Dionysian and Apollonian elements. The Dionysian represents the passionate interest and desire to learn. The Apollonian represents the form and structure that must guide any truly creative act. Music is limited by the diatonic scale, and poetry is limited by words and the forms of poetic cadence. The world is full of people with good ideas and fantasies that never come to fruition because they don't have disciplined limits.

GENERATIVITY

A person need not write music or poetry in order to be generative. Caring parents are generative; planting flowers and trees and caring for all life forms are generative behaviors. Being in a business that makes useful products that enhance the quality of life is generative work.

Toxically shamed people tend to become more and more stagnant as life goes on. They live in a guarded, secretive and defensive way. They try to be more than human (perfect and controlling) or less than human (losing interest in life or stagnated in some addictive behavior).

SHAME IS AWE AND REVERENCE

Healthy shame is the source of awe and reverence when experiencing the immensity and mystery of life. Life is a mystery to be lived. Whether it be looking out at the immensity of space on a starry night, or experiencing the phallic and vaginal mysteries, or experiencing your own offspring being conceived, born and growing in their own unique way, or marveling at the mysteries of scientific discovery or the unexplained miracles that occur throughout our lives—all of this gives us pause and moves us to experience our own littleness in the face of the enormity of reality.

SHAME AS THE NUMINOUS

Shame as awe and reverence leads directly to what the theologian Rudolf Otto called the idea of the holy. Otto studied the theophanies (the appearances of God) in all the sacred books of the world's religions. He defined the experience of holy God as the uncanny, and he called the uncanny a numinous experience, which he described as "the mysterium tremendum et fascinans"—the mystery that attracts us with passionate fascination but which is fearful at the same time. Anyone who has nurtured healthy shame and experienced awe and reverence for the immensity of life must acknowledge the numinous. "Woe to them who speak of God," said St. Augustine, "yet mute is even elegant." We cannot experience our own finite limitations without questioning the meaning and purpose of life. And we cannot escape the common sense conclusion there are many higher powers that shape our lives. Many people call their higher power God. The great Lutheran theologian Paul Tillich suggested that because personal love and intimacy is the highest form of creaturely life, then the creator cannot be less than personal.

SHAME AS THE SOURCE OF SPIRITUALITY

In *The Farther Reaches of Human Nature,* Abraham Maslow, the pioneering third force psychologist, once wrote:

> The spiritual life is . . . part of the human essence. It is a defining characteristic of human nature . . . without which human nature is not full human nature.

Spirituality embraces the numinous (the holy). Spirituality has to do with an inner life of values and meaning. It also has to do with our finitude—our awe and reverence for the mysteries of life. Spirituality is about love, truth, goodness, beauty, giving and caring. Spirituality is about wholeness and completion. Spirituality is our ultimate human need. It pushes us to transcend ourselves and become grounded in the ultimate source of reality.

Our healthy shame is essential as the foundation of our spirituality. By reminding us of our essential limitations, our healthy shame lets us know that we are not God. Our healthy shame points us in the direction of some larger meaning. Our healthy shame is the psychological ground of our humility.

2

The Toxically Destructive Faces
of Shame (LDL Shame)

*The affect of shame is important
because no affect is more disturbing to the self,
none more central for the sense of identity.*

—Gershan Kaufman

All human powers, affects and drives have the potential to encompass our personalities. In the introduction to Part I, I referred to this potential for absolutizing as the "demonic." Any emotion can become internalized as an identity. We say that someone is an "angry" person, or we call someone a "sad sack." They are predictably melancholy and negative. Someone else can be called a "fearful" person. Their whole identity seems to be dominated by fear. A person with a severe overeating disorder can be called a "hunger" addict. People can be possessed by their sex drive and become sex addicts.

The feeling of shame has the same demonic potential to encompass our whole personality. Instead of the momentary feeling of being limited, making a mistake, littleness, or being less attractive or talented than someone else, a person can come to believe that *his whole self is fundamentally flawed* and defective. Such a person does not have his healthy guilt (moral shame) available to him. Healthy guilt would say, "I made a mistake or a blunder, and I can repair that blunder." When a person's guilt has become neurotic, it becomes an "immorality shame."

A person says, "I *am* a mistake—everything I do is flawed and defective." The demonic potential of shame can lead to the most destructive emotional sickness of self a person can have. Internalized shame is like LDL cholesterol. It is destructive and if unchecked can ultimately kill us. Internalized or toxic shame lethally disgraces us to the point where we have no limits or boundaries. With LDL shame, we are no longer perfectly imperfect—we are totally imperfect.

How does healthy shame become a destructive identity that threatens our lives and makes us feel hopeless? I will spend the rest of this chapter describing the destructive faces of shame. Chapter Three describes in greater detail how shame becomes internalized and absolutized. In Chapter Four I'll outline the various defenses or defending scripts (strategies of behavior) that a shame-based person uses to hide from the awful and excruciating feeling of being a flawed human being.

THE DEVELOPMENTAL STAGES OF TOXIC (LDL) SHAME

Figure 2.1 gives you an overall view of the various faces that destructive shame puts on. I will briefly outline each.

INFANCY

Any form of faulty or traumatic attachment sets a person up for toxic shame. One of my clients' mother was pregnant with her when she married. The mother was a strict evangelical fundamentalist whose family insisted that she marry the guy who got her pregnant. The guy's family agreed and pressured him to marry her. She felt ashamed and angry. When her child (my client) was born, the child took on her mother's shame and anger (really repressed rage). No matter how much my client's mother repressed her feelings they were still present.

In my book *Family Secrets,* I show how secrets (in this case, unexpressed and concealed feelings) operate destructively in the interpersonal relationships in the family.

CARRIED FEELINGS

My colleague at The Meadows, Pia Mellody, has shown how damaging the attachment bond can be when the parent or source figure has hidden feelings, thoughts and fantasies. The child who is bonded to the parent will take on, or "carry," the parent's disowned or unexpressed feelings, thoughts or fantasies. Pia Mellody describes healthy shame as a "gift from God" and emphasizes the fact that *our healthy shame cannot hurt us.* What hurts is our carried or induced shame.

FIGURE 2.1
Developmental Stages of Toxic (LDL) Shame

NEUROTIC OR CHARACTER DISORDERED SYNDROMES	***Spiritual Bankruptcy*** Religiosity • God as a drug • Atheism • Misanthrope Self-contempt • Judgmental • Cynical about life • Religion as an addiction
	Older Adult Active addiction in late stages • Severe depression
	Adult STAGNATION Homeless • Jobless • Job as conformity and boredom or job success as a cover-up for feeling of being flawed and defective
	Young Adult ISOLATION Inability to connect • Intimacy dysfunction • Love as enmeshment
	Late Puberty Addiction • Codependency • Enmeshed marriage • Frequent divorce • Identity confusion • False self-Split self • Multiple selves • Borderline personality • Narcissistic personality • Paranoia personality • Psychopathic disorder
	Puberty Beginning of compulsive addictive disorders • Sexual dysfunction • Sex drive fused with shame • Sexual compulsivity • Sexual promiscuity
CARRIED AND INTERPERSONAL TRANSFER (INDUCED) SHAME	***8–Early Puberty*** Conforming to group • Either smart and popular or delinquent DEVELOPMENT OF GOVERNING SCRIPTS AS STRATEGIES TO DEFEND AGAINST TOXIC SHAME
	8–Puberty Development of defending scripts: Being perfect, controlling, rageful, critical or being helpless or dysfunctional • Polarization of the self and others—people are all good or all bad
	3.5–8 Years Neurotic guilt • Immorality shame • Sex is shameful • The need to defend and hide • Emotional illiteracy NEED SHAME BINDS
	18 Months–3.5 Years Overexposed • Severe limits to autonomy • Punishments • Spankings "Breaking the child's will • No boundaries PURPOSE SHAME BINDS • PLEASURE SHAME BINDS • ANGER SHAME BINDS
	6–18 Months Shame as apathy • Child is fearful • Severe limits to curiosity INTEREST OR CURIOSITY SHAME BINDS
	0–6 Months—Infancy Faulty or traumatic attachment • Failure to form the interpersonal bridge "BEING" SHAME BINDS

An immature parent with unresolved issues and repressed shame can also transfer his or her shame to us. This interpersonal transference of shame is referred to as "induced shame."

BEING SHAME BINDS

My client's mother became more and more depressed as her young husband turned out to be a very bad alcoholic. Deep down, my client's mother felt her life had been ruined by having a child. While her mother never expressed her disappointment out loud, my client was constantly verbally shamed by her mother. My client's infancy was characterized by a lack of touching and holding. She was schedule fed and was left alone for long periods of time during which she cried endlessly and experienced great fear. This information was given her by her two favorite aunts who were living in the same household with her. My client experienced a "being shame bind." She was what I'll refer to in the next chapter as a "Lost Child." She was never told she was unwanted or that her mother was enraged at her for her very existence, but she felt it and knew it with the intelligence that governs affects in the nondominant hemisphere of the brain.

My client was acutely shy. As she grew she played in her room alone for hours at a time, trying not to be seen or to bother her mother. Her cover-up isolation was a plea to be allowed to live.

SIX MONTHS TO EIGHTEEN MONTHS

In the early toddler, the affect of curiosity/interest and excitement goes into full swing unless a child has not formed a solid emphatic mutuality or strong and healthy attachment to his source figure. Feelings of excitement and curiosity become bound in shame, and the child's courage and enthusiasm are severely limited.

Toxic shame takes on the face of apathy or cowardice at this stage. Describing the impact of her father's incest, the poet Mary Oliver writes in her poem "Rage": "And you see how the child grows—timidly, crouching in corners."

EIGHTEEN MONTHS TO THREE AND A HALF YEARS

Toddlerhood is the time a child stands on her own two feet and starts walking. Toddlers are developing their musculature and their ability to "hold on" and "let go." They are beginning their psychological or "second birth." Nature urges them to separate and begin the journey toward their own selfhood. Spiritual traditions, as well as evolutionary biologists, tell us that we each have a true self (soul) and an inner core that cannot be destroyed by those around us. This is good news, and we'll return to it in Part III of this book.

In the past, Western families were dominated by the structure of patriarchy and the religious belief in original sin. Spanking and shaming were thought to be viable methods of child rearing and used to discipline children. It was also believed that the stain of original sin predisposed a person toward evil and that the child's will should be crushed at an early age. The assertiveness of the toddler who is beginning to exercise his own will, as evidenced by temper tantrums, saying "no" and "it's mine," are the natural behaviors of separation and personal boundary building. In the past they were thought to be manifestations of the human propensity for sin. We now know that these behaviors are perfectly normal.

Crushing the toddler's autonomy and purposeful will *is the most damaging form of shaming that can be done.* When autonomy is crushed, toxic shame is manifested either as total conformity or rebellion against authority. Once willpower, anger and purpose are bound in shame, a child's selfhood and personal power are severely wounded. His drive for separateness and autonomy are bound by shame. This has been called a "purpose shame bind."

THREE AND A HALF YEARS TO EIGHT YEARS

With the child already shame-based, the feeling of discouragement takes over the whole personality. As the shame-based child forms her primitive conscience, shame becomes immorality or neurotic guilt. The conforming child believes he can do nothing right, and the rebellious child believes that whatever she does is right and everyone else is to blame. This is the beginning of either a neurotic or character-disordered lifestyle.

Ages three and a half to eight is a time when a normal child endlessly asks questions. Their curiosity begins to extend to their identity, which includes their sexual identity as well as what they want to be when they grow up (their vocation). The normal child also begins to experience his or her needs for structure, gender identity and challenge. Gay, lesbian and trans-gendered children are not even accounted for in the psychological literature during this (or any other) developmental stage. Every gay or lesbian child I know in any depth was born gay or lesbian. Some are born transgendered (they are a girl in a boy's body or vice versa). These children are the most viciously shamed and oppressed in our society, mostly by homophobic reli-gions (especially the white supremacists and many Christian denominations, especially the evangelical fundamentalists). Common sense would tell us that no one would choose to be ridiculed, condemned to hell, and risk being viciously beaten or killed if being gay, lesbian or transgendered were a choice. It is also absolutely certain that gayness and lesbianism exist in the animal kingdom and hence being gay or lesbian is not against nature. Also, the same percentage of people have been gay and lesbian since the begin-ning of recorded history. There is good clinical data showing that the gay brain is different from the heterosexual brain (see Chapter Eleven).

Gays, lesbians and transgendered people are toxically shamed from the get-go. The churches and people who shame them should be ashamed.

Any child who reaches preschool with a shame-based foundation (no secure attachment and constant overexposure) will experience her needs as selfish and her sexuality as shameful and bad.

EIGHT YEARS TO PUBERTY

As the shame-based child enters school she will become polarized, as either a conformist or a rebellious ruffian or bully. Bullies shame other chil-dren the way they themselves have been shamed.

During school age, the bright, shame-based child will attempt to develop *inhuman* ego defenses or defending scripts, such as perfectionism, blaming, criticizing, righteousness or being judgmental. The character-disordered try to be more than human. Since being grounded in healthy shame is the per-mission to be human, the toxically shamed become polarized trying to be more than human or giving up and becoming less than human. If you look at Figure 2.2, you can see the polarization split. Either side of the polarity is *shameless*. The more-than-human have to be perfect to cover up their feelings of being flawed and defective. The less-than-human feel flawed and defective and act accordingly.

FIGURE 2.2
Polarization Split Synthesis

SHAMEFUL ACTING OUT	NATURAL SHAME POLARITY LIMITS	SHAMELESS ACTING IN
Less than Human Compulsivity Obsessive	Core of Finitude	More than Human Compulsivity Obsessive
Slob/Failure	Permission to Be Human	Perfectionistic
Out of Control	Natural Boundary	Controlling
Self-Blame	Adequate Amount of Shame Forms	Blame
Sinfulness Intimacy Dysfunction	Development of Identity and Intimacy	Righteousness Intimacy Dysfunction
Rage	Sense of Dignity	Passive/Aggressive
Self-Judgment Gluttony Self-Contempt	Brings a Sense of Awe, Reverence and Modesty	Judgment Self-Deprivation Criticism/Contempt Disgust
Erroneous or Lax Conscience No Conscience	Critically Examined Conscience	Rigid, All-Knowing Conscience or Puritanical, Scrupulous Conscience

PUBERTY

By puberty the toxically shamed feel inherently flawed and/or at war with themselves. They conform to a peer group that can be a delinquent gang, the athletic club, the good-looking popular ones or the nerds.

The other extreme is the teenager who feels isolated and alone and cannot seem to fit in anywhere. This group is fertile ground for fostering serious criminals.

Sexual confusion goes hand in hand with identity or role confusion.

I was a troubled teenager. I was fatherless and ran with other fatherless guys from broken homes. My group frequented brothels as early as the eighth grade. This is often referred to as the *Summer of '42* syndrome from the movie in which the young teenager has sex with an older woman. Young teenagers of either gender are not equipped to handle sex with adults.

I was also stalked and sexually abused by a Catholic priest in high school. This was very shaming for me, as I had no father as a male role model.

When I ended adolescence I decided to be a celibate priest. In my state of identity confusion and toxic sexual shame, my celibacy amounted to more-than-human sexual anorexia.

YOUNG ADULT

When I left the seminary, I left in deep shame. I had an uncle tell me that he knew I didn't have the guts to make it. Catholic families feel honored if one of their children becomes a priest or nun. To leave is to let the co-dependent family down.

I felt as if I were a failure and went through a series of dysfunctional love addictions. Having no real sense of a true self, I led with my defensive false self: the good guy, a people-pleasing, overfunctioning caregiver.

When I finally married, I married a fine person, but one who had been sexually abused in much the same way I had been. We married out of need and became codependently enmeshed, filling up the holes in each other's psyche.

Even though I was married, I was isolated and alone. I never really felt connected to my wife, and I had no connecting skills. Toxic shame is experienced in this developmental stage as loneliness and isolation.

LATER ADULTHOOD

I had begun to get some therapy about the time of my marriage, and I did not move on to stagnation and despair as one who has not dealt with their toxically shamed identity would naturally do. Although I was spiritually bankrupt when I married, the good news is you can recover, uncover and discover your true self and your personal power.

But you must be willing to come out of hiding and embrace your toxic shame. If you refuse to admit your powerlessness and the unmanageability of your life you cannot find the inner strength you've been covering up because you feel flawed and defective.

I'll discuss this recovery of our self and discovery of our true self at some length in Part II. The failure to take action leads to stagnation and the development of neuroses, character disorders, loneliness and addictions.

Hell, in my opinion, is never finding your true self and never living your own life or knowing who you are. This is the fate that lies at the end of the journey of ever-deepening toxic shame.

TOXIC SHAME AS THE CORE OF NEUROSES AND CHARACTER DISORDERS

Scott Peck describes both neuroses and character disorders as disorders of responsibility. In *The Road Less Traveled,* Peck writes:

> The neurotic assumes too much responsibility; the person with a character disorder not enough. When neurotics are in conflict with the world, they automatically assume that they are at fault. When those with character disorders are in conflict with the world, they automatically assume the world is at fault.

All of us have a smattering of neurotic and character disordered personality traits. The major problem in our lives is to decide and clarify our responsibilities. To truly be committed to a life of honesty, love and discipline, we must be willing to commit ourselves to reality. This commitment, according to Peck, "requires the willingness and the capacity to suffer continual self-examination." Such an ability requires a good relationship with oneself. This is precisely what no shame-based person has. In fact, a toxically shamed person has an adversarial relationship with himself. Toxic shame—the shame that binds us—is a core part of neurotic and character disordered syndromes of behavior.

NEUROTIC SYNDROMES OF SHAME

Toxic shame, the shame that binds us, is experienced as the all-pervasive sense that "I am flawed and defective as a human being." Toxic shame is no longer an emotion that signals our limits; it is a state of being, a core identity. Toxic shame gives you a sense of worthlessness, a sense of failing and falling short as a human being. Toxic shame is a rupture of the self with the self.

It is like internal bleeding—exposure to oneself lies at the heart of toxic shame. A shame-based person will guard against exposing his inner self to others, but more significantly, he will guard against exposing himself to himself.

Toxic shame is so excruciating because it is the painful exposure of the perceived failure of self to the self. In toxic shame the *self becomes an object of its own contempt,* an object that can't be trusted. As an object that can't be trusted, one experiences oneself as untrustworthy. Toxic shame is experienced as an inner torment. Toxic shame is paradoxical and self generating.

There is shame about shame. People will readily admit guilt, hurt or fear before they will admit shame. Toxic shame is the feeling of being isolated and alone in a complete sense. A shame-based person is haunted by a sense of absence and emptiness.

Toxic shame has been studied very little. It is easily confused with guilt, and guilt is generally misunderstood. Guilt is the affect shame as further developed. Guilt can either be the guardian of conscience or the neurotic, tormenting voice that judges every behavior as inadequate. In the first edition of this book I did not fully understand that guilt is a later development of the shame affect.

SHAME AS AN IDENTITY (THE INTERNALIZATION PROCESS)

Any human emotion can become internalized. When internalized, an emotion stops functioning as an emotion and becomes an identity.

Internalization involves at least three processes:

1. Identification with unreliable and shame-based models (faulty attachment bonding), which is the source of "carried" shame.
2. The trauma of abandonment, which severs the interpersonal bridge and the binding of feelings, needs and drives with shame.
3. The interconnection of memory imprints, which forms collages of shame.

As our developmental Figure 2.1 shows, internalization is a gradual process and happens over time. Every human being has to contend with certain aspects of this process. Internalization takes place when all three processes are consistently reinforced.

IDENTIFICATION WITH SHAME-BASED MODELS

Identification is one of our normal human processes. We always have the need to identify. Identification gives a sense of security. By belonging to something larger than ourselves, we feel the security and protection of the larger reality.

The need to identify with someone, to feel a part of something and belong somewhere, is one of our most basic needs. With the exception of self-preservation, no other striving is as compelling as this need, which begins with our caregivers or significant others and extends to family, peer group, culture, nation and world. It is seen in lesser forms in our allegiance to a political party or our rooting for a sports team. Our team provides a way to experience the powerful emotions of winning or losing.

This need to belong explains the loyal and often fanatic adherence people display to a group . . . their group.

When children have shame-based parents, they identify with them. This is the first step in the child's internalizing shame because the children *carry* their parent's shame.

ABANDONMENT: THE LEGACY OF
BROKEN MUTUALITY

Shame is internalized when one is abandoned. Abandonment is the precise term to describe how one loses one's authentic self and ceases to exist psychologically. Children cannot know who they are without reflective mirrors. Mirroring is done by one's primary caregivers and is crucial in the first years of life. Abandonment includes the loss of mirroring. Parents who are shut down emotionally (all shame-based parents) cannot mirror and affirm their children's emotions.

Since the earliest period of our life was preverbal, everything depended on emotional interaction. Without someone to reflect our emotions, we had no way of knowing who we were. Mirroring remains important during our entire lives. Think of the frustrating experience, which most of us have had, of talking to someone who is not looking at us. While you are speaking, they are fidgeting around or reading something. Our identity demands a significant other whose eyes see us pretty much as we see ourselves.

In fact, Erik Erikson defines identity as interpersonal. In *Childhood and Society* he writes:

> The sense of ego identity is the accrued confidence that the inner sameness and continuity . . . are matched by the sameness and continuity of one's meaning for others.

Besides lack of mirroring, abandonment includes: neglect of developmental dependency needs, abuse of any kind and enmeshment into the covert or overt needs of the parents or the family system. Abandonment induces shame in the child who is utterly dependent on the parents. Abuse causes the interpersonal transfer of shame (*induced* shame.)

FEELING, NEED AND DRIVE SHAME BINDS

The shame binding of feelings, needs and natural instinctual drives is a key factor in changing healthy shame into toxic shame. *To be shame-bound means that whenever you feel any feeling, need or drive, you immediately feel ashamed.* The dynamic core of your human life is grounded in your feelings, needs and drives. When these are bound by shame, you are shamed to the core.

THE INTERCONNECTION OF MEMORY IMPRINTS THAT FORM COLLAGES OF SHAME

As shaming experiences accrue and are defended against, the images created by those experiences are recorded in a person's memory bank. Because the victim has no time or support to grieve the pain of the broken mutuality, his emotions are repressed and the grief is unresolved. The verbal (auditory) imprints remain in the memory, as do the visual images of the shaming scenes. As each new shaming experience takes place, a new verbal imprint and visual image form a scene that becomes attached to the existing ones to form collages of shaming memories.

Children record their parents' actions at their worst. When Mom and Dad, or stepparent or caregiver, are most out of control, they are the most threatening to the child's survival. The child's amygdala, the survival alarm center in their brain, registers these behaviors the most deeply. Any subsequent shame experience that even vaguely resembles that past trauma can easily trigger the words and scenes of the original trauma. What are then recorded are the new experiences and the old. Over time, an accumulation of shame scenes is attached. Each new scene potentiates the old, sort of like a snow-ball rolling down a hill, getting larger and larger as it picks up snow.

As the years go on, very little is needed to trigger these collages of shame memories. A word, a similar facial expression or a scene can set it off. Sometimes an external stimulus is not even necessary. Just going back to an old memory can trigger an enormously painful experience. Shame as an emotion has become frozen and embedded into the core of the person's identity. Shame is deeply internalized.

SHAME AS SELF-ALIENATION AND ISOLATION

When one suffers from alienation, it means that one experiences parts of one's self as alien. For example, if you were never allowed to express anger in your family, your anger becomes an alienated part of yourself. You experience toxic shame when you feel angry. This part of you must be disowned or severed. There is no way to get rid of your emotional power of anger. Anger is self-preserving and self-protecting energy. Without this energy you become a doormat and a people-pleaser. As your feelings, needs and drives are bound by toxic shame, more and more of you is alienated.

Finally, when shame has been completely internalized, nothing about you is okay. You have the sense of being a failure. There is no way you can share your inner self because you are an object of contempt to yourself. When you are contemptible to yourself, you are no longer in you. To feel shame is to feel exposed in a diminished way. When you're an object to yourself, you turn your eyes inward, watching and scrutinizing every minute detail of behavior. This internal critical observation is excruciating. It generates a tormenting self-consciousness that Kaufman describes as "creating a binding and paralyzing effect upon the self." This paralyzing internal monitoring causes withdrawal, passivity and inaction.

The severed parts of the self are projected in relationships. They are often the basis of hatred and prejudice. The severed parts of the self may be experienced as a split personality or even multiple personalities. This happens often with victims who have been through traumatic physical and sexual violation.

To be severed and alienated within oneself also creates a sense of unreality. One may have an all-pervasive sense of never quite belonging, of being on the outside looking in. The condition of *inner alienation and isolation is also pervaded by a low-grade chronic depression.* This has to do with the sadness of losing one's authentic self. Perhaps the deepest and most devastating aspect of neurotic shame is the rejection of the self by the self.

SHAME AS FALSE SELF

Because the exposure of self to self lies at the heart of neurotic shame, escape from the self is necessary. The escape from self is accomplished by creating a false self. The false self is always more or less than human. The false self may be a perfectionist or a slob, a family Hero or a family Scapegoat. As the false self is formed, the authentic self goes into hiding. Years later the layers of defense and pretense are so intense that one loses all conscious awareness of who one really is. However, as we'll discuss in Chapter Twelve, the true self never gets away.

It is crucial to see that the *false self* may be as polar opposite as a super-achieving perfectionist or an addict in an alley. Both are driven to cover up their deep sense of self-rupture, the hole in their soul. They may cover up in ways that look polar opposite, but each is still driven by neurotic shame. In fact, *the most paradoxical aspect of neurotic shame is that it is the core motivator of the superachieved and the underachieved, the star and the scapegoat, the righteous and the wretched, the powerful and the pathetic.*

SHAME AS CODEPENDENCY

Much has been written about codependency. All agree that it is about the loss of selfhood. Codependency is a condition wherein one has no inner life. Happiness is on the outside. Good feelings and self-validation lie on the outside. They can never be generated from within. I have come to define codependency as "a dis-ease of the developing self that does not manifest fully until one is in an adult relationship." There is no significant difference in that definition and the way I have described internalized shame. It is my belief that internalized shame is *the essence of codependency*, since toxic shame is a rupture of the authentic self that necessitates developing a false self. With a false self, intimacy is impossible.

SHAME AS BORDERLINE PERSONALITY

Kaufman sees many of the categories of emotional illness that are defined in *DSM* (the diagnostic manual used to define emotional illnesses) as rooted in neurotic shame. It seems obvious that some of these disorders are related to syndromes of shame. These include dependent personality, clinical depression, schizoid phenomena and borderline personality. My own belief is that toxic shame is a unifying concept for what is often a maze of psychological definitions and distinctions. While I realize there is clinical and psychotherapeutic value in the kinds of detailed etiological distinctions offered by accurate and precise conceptualizing, I also think some of it is counterproductive.

My own study of James Masterson's work on borderline personalities, as well as my experience watching his working films, convinces me that there is minimal difference in the treatment of many toxically shame-based people and his treatment of the borderline personality. I'm convinced that Masterson's borderline personality is a syndrome of neurotic shame. It is described in *Borderline Adolescent to Functioning Adult: The Test of Time* as a syndrome of these roughly related complaints:

1. Self-image disturbance.
2. Difficulty identifying and expressing one's individuated thoughts, wishes and feelings and autonomously regulating self-esteem.
3. Difficulty with self-assertion.

SHAME AS THE CORE AND FUEL OF ALL ADDICTION

Neurotic shame is the root and fuel of all compulsive/addictive behaviors. My general working definition of compulsive/addictive behavior is "a pathological relationship to any mood-altering experience that has life-damaging consequences."

The drivenness in any addiction is about the ruptured self, the belief that one is flawed as a person. The content of the addiction, whether it be an ingestive addiction or an activity addiction (such as work, shopping or gambling), is an attempt at an intimate relationship. The workaholic with his work and the alcoholic with his booze are having a love affair. Each one alters the mood to avoid the feeling of loneliness and hurt in the underbelly of shame. Each addictive acting out creates life-damaging consequences that create more shame. The new shame fuels the cycle of addiction. Figure 2.3, which I have adapted from Dr. Pat Carnes's work, gives you a visual picture of how internalized shame fuels the addictive process and how addictions create more shame, which sets one up to be more shame-based. Addicts call this cycle the squirrel cage.

I used to drink to solve the problems caused by drinking. The more I drank to relieve my shame-based loneliness and hurt, the more I felt ashamed. Shame begets shame. The cycle begins with the false belief system shared by all addicts: that no one could want them or love them as they are. In fact, addicts can't love themselves. They are an object of scorn to themselves. This deep internalized shame gives rise to distorted thinking. The distorted thinking can be reduced to the belief, "I'll be okay if I drink, eat, have sex, get more money, work harder, etc." The shame turns one into what Kellogg has termed a "human doing," rather than a human being.

Worth is measured on the outside, never on the inside. The mental obsession about the specific addictive relationship is the first mood alteration, since thinking takes us out of our emotions. After obsessing for a while, the second mood alteration occurs. This is the "acting out" or ritual stage of the addiction. The ritual may involve drinking with the boys, secretly eating in one's favorite hiding place or cruising for sex. The ritual ends in drunkenness, satiation, orgasm, spending all the money or whatever.

What follows is shame over one's behavior and the life-damaging consequences: the hangover, the infidelity, the demeaning sex, the empty pocketbook. The meta-shame is a displacement of affect, a transforming of the shame of self into the shame of "acting out" and experiencing life-damaging consequences. This meta-shame intensifies the shame-based identity.

"I'm no good; there's something wrong with me," plays like a broken record. The more it plays, the more one solidifies one's false belief system. The toxic shame fuels the addiction and regenerates itself.

FIGURE 2.3
The Compulsive/Addictive Cycle Fueled by and Regenerating Shame

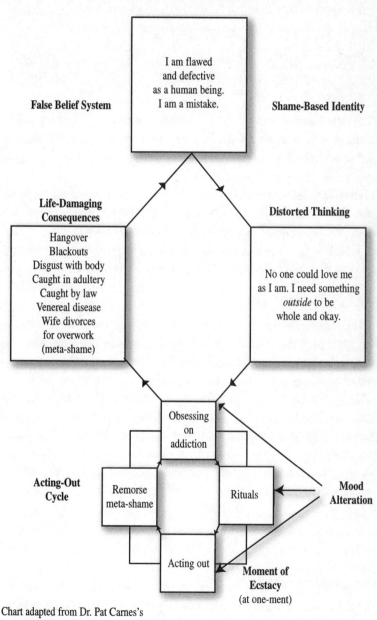

False Belief System

I am flawed
and defective
as a human being.
I am a mistake.

Shame-Based Identity

Life-Damaging Consequences

Hangover
Blackouts
Disgust with body
Caught in adultery
Caught by law
Venereal disease
Wife divorces
for overwork
(meta-shame)

Distorted Thinking

No one could love me
as I am. I need something
outside to be
whole and okay.

Obsessing
on
addiction

Acting-Out Cycle

Remorse
meta-shame

Rituals

Mood Alteration

Acting out

Moment of Ecstacy
(at one-ment)

Chart adapted from Dr. Pat Carnes's
book *Out of the Shadows*

CHARACTER DISORDER SYNDROMES OF SHAME

NARCISSISTIC PERSONALITY DISORDER

According to James Masterson in *The Narcissistic and Borderline Disorders,* the main clinical characteristics of the narcissistic personality disorder are:

> Grandiosity, extreme self-involvement, and lack of interest and empathy for others, in spite of the pursuit of others to obtain admiration and approval.

The narcissist is endlessly motivated to seek perfection in everything he does. Such a personality is driven to the acquisition of wealth, power and beauty and the need to find others who will mirror and admire his grandiosity. Underneath this external facade there is an emptiness filled with envy and rage. The core of this emptiness is internalized shame.

PARANOID PERSONALITY

The paranoid defense is a posture developed to cope with excessive shame. The paranoid person becomes hypervigilant, expecting and waiting for the betrayal and humiliation he knows is coming. The paranoid person interprets innocent events as personally threatening and constantly lives on guard.

Harry Stack Sullivan described the paranoid as "feeling hopelessly defective." The sources of the paranoid's own sense of deficiency are found elsewhere. It's as if the inner eyes of shaming, contempt and disdain are projected outward. Wrongdoings, mistakes and other instances of personal failure cannot be owned by the paranoid-type personality. They are disowned and transferred from the inner self to others.

OFFENDER BEHAVIOR

CRIMINALITY IN GENERAL

Alice Miller has shown convincingly that much criminal behavior is "acting out" behavior. Acting out is also called "reenactment." What this means is that a criminal offender was once victimized in much the same way he criminalizes. Children from violently abusive families or children from families where high-voltage abandonment takes place suffer terrible victimization. They generally either take on a victim role and reenact it over and over again, or they identify with their offender and reenact the offense on helpless victims (as they once were). This reenactment is called "repetition compulsion."

In Miller's book, *For Your Own Good,* she outlines in detail the reenactments of a teenage drug addict and a child murderer. While no one can prove that every criminal is acting out his own abandoning shame, I believe there is enough data to support the hypothesis that this is most often the case. Surely no one has offered any effective solution to the everlasting problem of crime and criminality. Without any doubt, criminals feel like social outcasts and bear enormous toxic shame.

PHYSICAL ABUSE

The physical offender was once a victim who was powerless and who was humiliated. Parents who physically humiliate and abuse their own children were typically abused when they were young. They have never resolved the internalized shame in their own lives. Their own childhood traumas are embedded in a series of interrelated memories. These original scenes become reactivated by their own children and compel reenactment like a Pavlovian trigger. Kaufman suggests:

> Parents who are about to abuse their own children are simultaneously reliving scenes in which they were also beaten, but they relive the scene from the perspective of their own parents as well. They now play their parents' role.

Why would parents, who were once abused and beaten children, want to play their parents' role? This answer lies in the dynamic of identification. Offender identification was clearly defined by Bettelheim with the phrase "identification with the aggressor." When children are physically hurt and in psychological pain, they want out of it as quickly as possible. So they cease identifying with themselves and instead identify with their shaming oppressor in an attempt to possess that person's power and strength. In forming the identification with the parent, one becomes at once the weak, bad child and the strong transgressor parent. The internal image of the abusive parent triggers the old scene and mediates the process. Physical abuse can trigger compulsive reenactment of the abuse either toward oneself or one's spouse or one's children. Internalized shame maintains the process. It compels the reenactment.

The victims of physical violence may also remain victims. Martin Seligman has done extensive studies on what is called "teamed helplessness." In essence, arbitrary, random and unpredictable beatings create a state of passivity in which the victim no longer feels there is anything that she can do. A negative belief system is adhered to. The person no longer believes she has a choice.

A simpler explanation for the bonding to violence is the fact that as one is beaten more and more, one is shamed more and more. The more internalized the shame, the greater the belief in oneself as defective and flawed. The more one believes one is defective and flawed, the more one's choices diminish. Internalized shame destroys one's boundaries. Without boundaries one has no protection.

SEXUAL ABUSE

Sexual abusers are most often sex addicts. Sometimes they are reenacting their own sexual or physical violation. Sexual abuse generates intense and crippling shame, which more often than not results in a splitting of the self. Incest and sexual abuse offenders are fueled by internalized shame. Kaufman writes:

> The perpetrator of the assault or violation also is shame-based. Such acts are acts of power and revenge, born of impotence and fueled by shame. . . . that scene of forcible violation is a reenactment, a transformation of a scene of equal powerlessness and humiliation experienced by the perpetrator at the hands of a different tormentor. . . . The victim, the target of revenge, is confused with the source of the perpetrator's shame. By defeating and humiliating the victim, the perpetrator is momentarily freed of shame.

The victimization could be incest, molestation, rape, voyeurism, exhibitionism, indecent liberties or phone calls, cybersex or pornography. In every case there is an acting out of shame and a victimization of the innocent.

GRANDIOSITY—THE DISABLED WILL

Toxic shame also wears the face of grandiosity. Grandiosity is a disorder of the will. It can appear as narcissistic self-enlargement or wormlike helplessness. Each extreme refuses to be human. Each exaggerates: one is more than human; the other is less than human. It's important to see that the less-than-human, the hopeless one, is also grandiose. Hopelessness says that nothing and no one could help me. "I'm the sickest of the sick. . . . I'm the best/worst there ever was."

Grandiosity results from the human will becoming disabled. *The will is disabled primarily through the shaming of the emotions.* The shamed and blocked emotions stop the full integration of intellectual meaning. When an emotional event happens, emotions must be discharged in order for the intellect, reason and judgment to make sense out of it. Emotions are a form of thinking, and blocked emotions bias thinking. As emotions get bound by shame, their energy is frozen, which blocks the full interaction between the mind and the will.

The human will is intensity of desire raised to the level of action. The will is an appetite. It is dependent on the mind (reasoning and judgment) for its eyes. Without the mind, the will is blind and has no content. Without content the will starts willing itself. This state of disablement causes severe problems, some of which are:

1. The will wills what can't be willed.
2. The will tries to control everything.
3. The will experiences itself as omnipotent or, when it has failed, as "wormlike."
4. The will wills for the sake of willing (impulsiveness).
5. The will wills in absolute extremes—all or nothing.

TOXIC SHAME AS SPIRITUAL BANKRUPTCY

The problem of toxic shame is ultimately a spiritual problem. It has been called "spiritual bankruptcy." I suggested earlier that spirituality is the essence of human existence. We are not material beings on a spiritual journey; we are spiritual beings who need an earthly journey to become fully spiritual.

Spirituality is that which enhances and expands life. Therefore, spirituality is about growth and expansion, newness and creativity. Spirituality is about being. Being is that victorious thrust whereby we triumph over nothingness. Being is about why there is something, rather than nothing. Being is the ground of all the beings that are.

OTHERATION AND DEHUMANIZATION

Toxic shame, which is an alienation of the self from the self, causes one to become "other-ated."

"Otheration" is the term used by the Spanish philosopher Ortega Y. Gasset to describe dehumanization. He says that man is the only being who lives from within. To be truly human is to have an inner self and a life from within. Animals live in constant hypervigilance, always on guard, looking outside themselves for sustenance and guarding against danger. When humans no longer have an inner life, they become otherated and dehumanized.

Toxic shame, with its more-than-human, less-than-human polarization, is either inhuman or dehumanizing. The demand for a false self to cover and hide the authentic self necessitates a life dominated by doing and achievement. Everything depends on performance and achievement rather than on being. Being requires no measurement; it is its own justification. Being is grounded in an inner life that grows in richness.

"The kingdom of heaven is within," says the Scripture. Toxic shame looks to the outside for happiness and validation, since the inside is flawed and defective. Toxic shame is spiritual bankruptcy.

SHAME AS HOPELESSNESS—THE SQUIRREL CAGE

Toxic shame feels irremediable: If I am flawed, defective and a mistake, then there is nothing that can be done about me. Such a belief leads to impotence. How can I change who I am? Toxic shame also has the quality of circularity. Shame begets shame. You saw in Figure 2.3 how addicts act out internalized shame and then feel shame about their shameful behavior. Remember, though, toxic shame only *feels* irremediable; it can be remedied.

FUNCTIONAL AUTONOMY

Once internalized, toxic shame is functionally autonomous, which means that it can be triggered internally without any attending stimulus. One can imagine a situation and feel deep shame. One can be alone and trigger a shaming spiral through internal self-talk. The more one experiences shame, the more one is ashamed, and the beat goes on.

It is this dead-end quality of shame that makes it so hopeless. The possibility for repair seems foreclosed if one is essentially flawed as a human being. Add to that the self-generating quality of shame, and one can see the devastating, soul-murdering power of neurotic shame.

The reader can begin to see how dramatic it was for me to discover the dynamics of shame. By being aware of the dynamics of shame, by naming it, we gain some power over it.

The Major Sources of Toxic Shame

*She learned to her dismay that
she only felt loved when she wasn't being herself.*

—Joel Covitz

*Children will invest as much energy as is needed to
ensure the preservation of family harmony,
even if it means sacrificing themselves to do so
by developing psychological disorders.*

—Joel Covitz
Emotional Child Abuse

THE FAMILY SYSTEM

Toxic shame is primarily fostered in *significant* relationships. If you do not value someone, it's hard to imagine being shamed by what he says or does. The possibility of toxic shame begins with our source relationships. If our primary caregivers are shame-based, they will act shameless and pass their toxic shame onto us. There is no way to teach self-value if one does not value oneself.

Toxic shame is multigenerational. It is passed from one generation to the next. Shame-based people find other shame-based people and get married. As each member of a couple carries the shame from his or her own family system, their marriage will be grounded in their shame-core. The major outcome of this will be a lack of intimacy. It's difficult to let someone get close to you if you feel defective and flawed as a human being. Shame-based couples maintain nonintimacy through poor communication, nonproductive circular fighting, games, manipulation, vying for control,

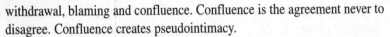

withdrawal, blaming and confluence. Confluence is the agreement never to disagree. Confluence creates pseudointimacy.

When a child is born to these shame-based parents, the deck is stacked from the beginning. The job of parents is to model. Modeling includes how to be a man or woman; how to relate intimately to another person; how to acknowledge and express emotions; how to fight fairly; how to have physical, emotional and intellectual boundaries; how to communicate; how to cope and survive life's unending problems; how to be self-disciplined; and how to love oneself and another. Shame-based parents cannot do any of these. They simply don't know how.

Children need their parents' time and attention. Giving one's time is part of the work of love. It means being there for the child, attending to the child's needs rather than the parent's needs.

For example, I used to spend lots of time with my son. Often it consisted of my watching a football game while my son played in the room. If he made too much noise, I scolded him. We spent time together, but it was quantitative rather than qualitative.

Part of the work of love is listening. Children are clear about what they need and will tell us in no uncertain terms. We need to listen to them. This requires a fair amount of emotional maturity. To listen well, one must have one's own needs met. If one is needy, it's hard to listen. Our neediness is like a toothache. When we are shame-based, we can only focus on our own ache.

Needy, shame-based parents cannot possibly take care of their children's needs. The child is shamed whenever he or she is needy because the child's needs clash with the parents' needs. The child grows up and becomes an adult. But underneath the mask of adult behavior there is a child who was neglected. Needy children are insatiable. They have a hole in their soul created by unresolved grief and developmental dependency deficits. This makes them adult children. They can never get enough as adults. Healthy adults are satisfied with what they get and work harder to get more the next time. An adult child can't get enough because it's really a child's needs that are in question.

For example, in my beginning relationships I always went too far and wanted too much. If I met a girl and we hit it off, I immediately began talking about her in terms of marriage—*even after one date!* Once she was in love with me, I expected her to take care of me like a mother. Needy children need parents, so adult children turn lovers into parents, someone to take care of their needs.

The bottom line is that shame-based, needy marriages that receive no treatment create shame-based, needy families. The children grow up in the soil of shame rather than the nurturing arms of love.

Shame-based families operate according to the laws of social systems. When a social system is dysfunctional, it is rigid and closed. All the individuals in that family are enmeshed in a kind of trancelike frozenness. They take care of the system's need for balance, rather than their own needs for growth.

Children go to school, church or synagogue and grow up to live in society. Each of these social systems adds its own unique contribution to the toxic shame induction process.

MAX'S STORY*

Max was perhaps the most tragic figure I encountered over a twenty-year period of counseling. He came to me at age forty-four. I liked him instantly. Everyone seemed to like him. His problem was one I had never heard of before. Max ran away. He had done it nine times. At certain points in his life, most often when he was doing very well and the pressures of success were mounting, he would just pack up his car with a few necessities and start driving. He would leave everything: clothes, furnishings, family and job. Max was a sales engineer.

The running away was a form of hiding. Max would reach a point where his boundaries were so weak that he could not handle the exposure and just run away. Max had five children. Three children were from his first marriage, the fourth from his second, and the fifth from his third. As I talked to Max, the deep hurt and pain of his life was apparent. His shame was more apparent. In fact, Max's life was a metaphor of internalized shame.

He embodied many of the faces of shame and was the product of the major sources of shame. He also acted out many of the major cover-ups of shame.

---

*Max is a composite symbol—a sort of "everyman of toxic shame." I have taken bits and pieces from the tragic lives of actual shame-based people. One of them is now dead—a tragic victim of toxic shame.

He broke eye contact continually when he talked. He frequently blushed. He was painfully self-conscious and hypervigilant. Sometimes he would defiantly look me in the eyes and make matter-of-fact statements about the things he had done, severely condemning himself. And then he would follow this with long, delusional descriptions of how he had been responsible and successful. When I gently confronted his denials, he would become energetically reactive and defensive and sometimes go into a rage. What became clear was his despair, his desperate loneliness and his shame-based hopelessness. Although he was gifted intellectually and evidently a skilled salesman and engineer, he would subject himself to the most menial jobs during his runaways. He had been a janitor, a dishwasher, a garbage man's helper, a lumberjack, a stagehand, a short-order cook, and on his last "trip," as he referred to it, he collected and sold aluminum cans.

Max, although quite attractive to women, always stayed alone and celibate on his trips. He was six feet, three inches tall and handsome. By the time he saw me, he was impotent. This was partly due to years of isolation, marijuana abuse and sexualizing. Max was what Pat Carnes, in his book *Out of the Shadows,* calls a Level I and II sex addict.

Level I sexual addiction involves:

- multiple affairs or sex partners
- compulsive masturbation with or without pornography
- chronic homosexual or heterosexual cruising, fetish behavior, beastiality, and prostitution

Level II involves:

- voyeurism
- exhibitionism
- indecent liberties
- lewd phone calls

Carnes also speaks of Level III sexual addiction which includes:

- incest
- rape
- molestation

The levels refer to the level of victimization and legal punishment accompanying the sexual act. Levels II and III always have a victim and are punishable by law.

In Max's case he had multiple affairs during his three marriages. During the early part of his second marriage he had engaged in voyeurism. He described the voyeurism with a great feeling of degradation and shame. On one occasion he hid in the branches of a tree for three hours to get a two-minute glimpse of a young woman in her bra and panties.

Max also cruised shopping malls, engaging in subtle forms of indecent liberties. By the time Max came to me for counseling, he had completely given up any relationship with women. He was isolated and without any real relationships of any kind. He had resigned himself to a menial job as a bookkeeper in a hardware store.

Max's children were all addicts. His oldest was already in her second marriage at twenty-six years of age. She was a severe caretaker codependent who confused love with pity. She found men who were down and out and nourished them back to health. Her second husband was a European ex-drug dealer who had served time for drug dealing in France. Max's two sons and the daughter from his second marriage were all serious drug addicts and had major problems with sex and relationships. The youngest, a male child from his third marriage, had been arrested and jailed several times for violent alcohol- and drug-related behavior by age thirteen.

I saw Max off and on for almost seven years. Just when I thought we were making progress, Max would quit (run away from me). I became more involved with Max than any counselor should. Max hooked my own shame and codependency. I wanted to help Max so much that I was overly invested in the outcome of our work. In September of 1974, Max died at the age of fifty-two. This was the exact age his own father had died.

Max had a grandiose melodramatic quality to his personality. At the same time, there was true generosity and nobleness about him. His compassion for the suffering of others was boundless. He died of emphysema in the back ward of a public county hospital. At his funeral, I wept in a way I could not have imagined.

Max represented all of us shame-based people. I said he died of emphysema. What he really died of was toxic shame. His internalized shame was the source of his codependency and chemical and sex addictions. His life, from beginning to end, illustrated the sources and the demonic power of toxic shame.

I shall use the elements of Max's life to outline these sources of toxic shame: his dysfunctional family of origin, his shame-based parental models, his multigenerational family history, his abandonment issues, his schooling, his religious background and the shaming culture we all share with him.

DYSFUNCTIONAL FAMILIES

Toxic shame originates interpersonally, primarily in significant relationships. Our most significant relationships are our source relationships. They occur in our original families.

As Judith Bardwick says so well in *Transition*:

Marriage and thus family are where we live out our most intimate and powerful human experiences. The stuff that family is made of is bloodier and more passionate than the stuff of friendship, and the costs are greater, too.

Our families are where we first learn about ourselves. Our core identity comes first from the mirroring eyes of our primary caretakers. Our destiny depends to some extent on the health of our caretakers.

In Max's case, his father, Jerome, was a full-fledged alcoholic and womanizing sex addict. Jerome was shame-based. He had been abandoned by his own father and was raised by an emotionally incestuous alcoholic mother, Felicia. Max's description of his grandmother was frightening.

By the time Max was eight, his mother had divorced his father. From eight years on, Max was neglected emotionally and financially. His older brother, Ralph, took over the role of being Max's father. His older sister, Maxine, also took on a parenting role. They were his Little Parents.

Max's mom and dad married at ages seventeen and eighteen respectively. They married because they were pregnant with Max's older sister, Maxine. Felicia came from a staunchly Christian family. The family demanded that Jerome marry Felicia. Felicia was extremely prudish and shut down emotionally. She carried her mother's repressed sexuality. Her mother had been sexually violated by her own father (also an alcoholic) and two of her nine brothers.

Felicia's mother had never dealt with her incest issues and carried them as her shame secret. Felicia, while ostensibly proper and prudish, had "acted out" the sexual shame of her mother by getting pregnant at seventeen. Felicia had also been sexually violated by her maternal grandfather.

Felicia was her father's emotional spouse. She became his Little Woman and confidante after her mother withdrew with hypochondria.

Jerome was also the emotional caregiver of *his* mother. He was her Little Man and became her Surrogate Spouse. Both of Max's parents were Surrogate Spouses. Because each one's parents had unresolved sexual issues, their surrogate spousing had sexual overtones. Both were severely shame-based. When parents who have unresolved sexual issues become enmeshed with one of their children, that child is more often than not covertly seduced by their parent's unresolved sexuality. There are no toxic *shame* secrets in families, only denial. The secrets get acted out by one or more of the children. Both of Max's parents were covert incest victims, codependent and addicted. Max's mother was dutiful but cold and nonsensual. Max was born five years after Jerome and Felicia were married. He was not planned and not really wanted. He was an accidental pregnancy. Max was what is called the Lost Child in family systems theory.

FAMILIES AS SOCIAL SYSTEMS

You noticed that I've capitalized the words "Lost Child," "Surrogate Spouse," and "Little Parents." I capitalize these words to show that they are rigid roles necessitated by the needs of the family system. In my book *Bradshaw On: The Family,* and my PBS series by the same name, I outlined a newly emerging understanding of families as social systems.

Families are social systems that follow organismic laws. The first law of social organisms is that the whole is greater than the sum of its parts. A family is defined by the interaction and interrelationships of its parts, rather than the sum of its parts.

A way to illustrate this holistic principle is to think of the human body. Our body is a whole organic system composed of many subsystems. We have a nervous system, a circulatory system, an endocrine system, etc. The human body as an organism is not the sum of its parts, but rather the interrelationship of the parts. My body is not my body if it is cut into parts. For example, if you cut my legs from my body, you'd hardly look at them and think of me. In a system every part is related to every other part. Each part is wholly a part and partly a whole.

In a family, the whole family as an organism is greater than any individual in the family. The family is defined by the relationship between the parts, rather than the sum of the parts. As social systems, families have components, rules, roles and needs that define the system.

CHIEF COMPONENT

The chief component in the family system is the marriage. If the marriage is healthy and functional, the family will be healthy and functional. If the marriage is dysfunctional, then the family will be dysfunctional.

In Max's case, his parents' marriage was extremely dysfunctional. When the chief component of a system is dysfunctional, the whole system is thrown out of balance. When the system is out of balance, another law comes into play: the law of dynamic homeostasis. This is the law of balance.

DYNAMIC HOMEOSTASIS

Dynamic homeostasis means that whenever a part of the system is out of balance, the rest of the members of the system will try to bring it back into balance.

I used a mobile on *my TV* series to illustrate this. If you touch one part of the mobile, the rest of it is affected. If one part moves, all the parts move. The mobile will always return to a state of rest. In a healthy, functional family, the mobile will be in gentle motion. In a dysfunctional family, the mobile will tend to become frozen and static.

The children in a dysfunctional family take on rigid roles necessitated by the family's need for balance. For example, if a child is not wanted, he or she will try to balance the family by not being any trouble, by being helpful, perfect, super-responsible or invisible. This is the Lost Child role. I capitalize it to show that it is a dysfunctional role.

Both Max and his older sister, Maxine, were Lost Children. Max's brother, Ralph, was a family Star or Hero, i.e., he superachieved to give his shame-based, alcoholic family a sense of dignity. Max's older brother and sister became Max's Little Parents.

As Jerome became more and more alcoholic, he abandoned all his children. Since the family system had no father, Ralph took on that role and became Max's Little Father. Since the family had no marriage (chief component), Ralph became Felicia's Surrogate Spouse. The system had no money earner, so Ralph and Maxine became superresponsible Caregivers.

As a child, Max was sheltered from his father's drinking by being taken to the homes of relatives. He was the protected one. He experienced this as abandonment. It's crucial to see that all these roles are cover-ups for toxic shame.

Ralph covered up his shame by playing his Star-Hero role. He also acted shameless toward Max by demanding that Max be perfect. He tried to overdiscipline Max, continually measuring him with shoulds and oughts. Ralph was a constant source of shame for Max. Max loved and admired his older brother. He willingly accepted his brother's interpersonal transfer of shame. Ralph was also extremely religious. He studied to be a Christian minister. He used religious righteousness as a cover-up for his shame and dumped it on Max by moralizing and making judgments of him.

When the fear, hurt and loneliness of the shame in a dysfunctional family reaches high levels of intensity, one person, often the most sensitive, becomes the family Scapegoat. The function of this role is to lessen the pain all the members are in. At first Maxine took on this role for Felicia. She became Mom's Scapegoat. Later Ralph became the Scapegoat due to his active alcoholism in his teenage years. Ralph repented and went into the ministry. This left the job for Max. Max started his drinking and running away at age fifteen. His first major disappearance was for four days, winding up on a beach in New Orleans. As his bizarre runaways continued, the family focused more and more on him. By discussing and obsessing on Max, everyone in the family system could avoid their own pain.

Max became like the sacrificial goat in the Jewish atonement ritual. In that ritual the goat is smeared with blood and sent into the desert. In this way the scapegoat atones for the people's sins. Max became the sacrificial goat. He literally went to his death carrying the shame of several generations of his family.

All of the roles in Max's family system were played as a way to control the distress of Jerome's alcohol addiction and Felicia's codependent addiction. In functional families the roles are chosen and are flexible. The members have the choice of giving up the roles. In dysfunctional families the roles are *rigid*. Figure 3.1 outlines the various roles in Max's family of origin. I've added a few I haven't mentioned. Notice that all the roles cover up the shame-based inner core. As each member of the system plays his rigid role, the system stays frozen and unchanging. Dysfunctional families are frozen in a trancelike state. The shame-core keeps the system frozen. Everyone is in hiding. The roles cover up each person's true and authentic self.

SHAME-BASED FAMILIES AND MULTIGENERATIONAL ILLNESS

One of the devastating aspects of toxic shame is that it is multigenerational. The secret and hidden aspects of toxic shame form the wellsprings of its multigenerational life. Since it is kept hidden, it cannot be worked out. *Families are as sick as their toxic shame secrets.* See my book *Family Secrets* for a full discussion of the dynamics of toxic shame secrets. Family secrets can go back for generations. They can be about suicides, homicides, incest, abortions, addictions, public loss of face, financial disaster, etc. All the secrets get acted out. This is the power of toxic shame.

The pain and suffering of shame generate automatic and unconscious defenses. Freud called these defenses by various names: denial, idealization of parents, repression of emotions and dissociation from emotions. What is important to note is that we can't know what we don't know. Denial, idealization, repression and dissociation are unconscious survival mechanisms. Because they are unconscious, we lose touch with the shame, hurt and pain they cover up. *We cannot heal what we cannot feel.* So without recovery, our toxic shame gets carried for generations.

I've already suggested that Max's mother and father had both come from shame-based families. Figure 3.2 gives you a visual picture of Felicia's genogram. Her mother came from an alcoholic, incestuous family. Felicia's mother was an untreated, shame-based codependent in acute stages of her addiction. She was agoraphobic and a hypochondriac. Felicia's father

FIGURE 3.1
Max's Dysfunctional Family of Origin

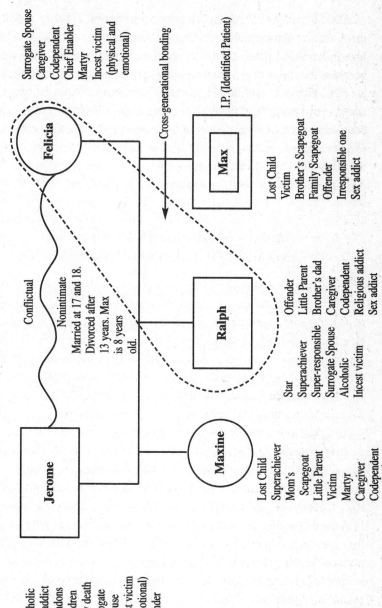

Jerome

Alcoholic
Sex addict
Abandons children
Early death
Surrogate Spouse
Incest victim (emotional)
Offender

Conflictual

Nonintimate
Married at 17 and 18.
Divorced after 13 years. Max is 8 years old.

Felicia

Surrogate Spouse
Caregiver
Codependent
Chief Enabler
Martyr
Incest victim (physical and emotional)

Cross-generational bonding

Maxine

Lost Child
Superachiever
Mom's
Scapegoat
Little Parent
Victim
Martyr
Caregiver
Codependent

Ralph

Star
Superachiever
Super-responsible
Surrogate Spouse
Alcoholic
Incest victim

Offender
Little Parent
Brother's dad
Caregiver
Codependent
Religious addict
Sex addict

Max   I.P. (Identified Patient)

Lost Child
Victim
Brother's Scapegoat
Family Scapegoat
Offender
Irresponsible one
Sex addict

enabled her mother's shame by allowing her to be sick. He also set Felicia up in the Surrogate Spouse role. Felicia was an untreated emotional and physical incest victim who repressed her sexuality and carried her mother's unresolved incest issues. She unconsciously acted it out by being seductive to both Ralph and Max. Ralph, as oldest son, became Felicia's Surrogate Spouse, which repeated her covert incest. Felicia idealized her dad and enabled his severe codependency and work addiction. Felicia's three sisters all married dysfunctional men. Each daughter carried her mother's unresolved sexualized disgust and rage.

Felcia's mother continually bad-mouthed men from her sick bed. Max reported that as a boy he remembered that one of her favorite sayings was, "Men only want one thing. They think with their penises." This statement, said in the presence of a young male, is sexually abusive. Ralph and Max were both victimized by Felicia's unconscious sexual rage, disgust and contempt for men.

When Felicia got pregnant, she was "acting out" her mother's unresolved sexual shame, as well as her own unresolved incest. Max reenacted Felicia's acting out by getting his first wife, Bridget, pregnant when he was seventeen. Ralph also married pregnant.

In Figure 3.3 I've outlined the major parts of Jerome's genogram. Jerome's mother saw her own mother burn to death when she was seven years old. She was abandoned by her father. He sent her to live with her two man-hating aunts. She rebelled against this situation by continually getting into trouble.

She acted out sexually at an early age. I always suspected that her promiscuity was acting out of some form of sexual abuse. Max had no data on her side of the family, so I was never able to verify this. Max greatly disliked his paternal grandmother and had never even seen his grandfather.

Jerome's mother first married at age sixteen. Her husband died a tragic death before age thirty. He was electrocuted while working at a power plant. Jerome's mother received a large amount of money as the surviving widow. She boozed and partied for the next few years. She was a full-blown genetic alcoholic.

She married Jerome's father pregnant, and after a stormy seven years, he divorced her. Jerome was eight years old. He only saw his father twice from that point on. Once he hitchhiked three hundred miles to see him, only to

FIGURE 3.2
Max's Mother's (Felicia) Genogram

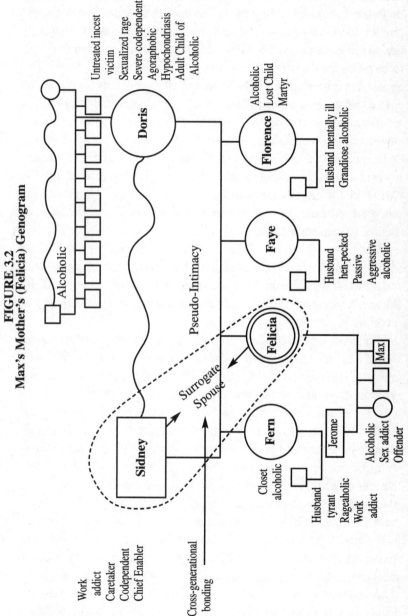

Daughters all prove that mother was right—"Men are no damned good"

be disappointed by being put on a bus and sent home. The other time was a chance run-in. Finally Jerome read of his father's death in a newspaper. He went to the funeral and was asked to leave, being told that it was too awkward for him to be there. His father had remarried and had three children by his second wife.

So Jerome grew up with no father and was enmeshed with his alcoholic, sex addict mother. He was her emotional incest victim. Max would *"act out" these multigenerational abandonment patterns in his runaways.* Both his parents, Jerome and Felicia, had been abandoned by their same-sex parents. Both were used for their parents' needs, rather than their parents being there for them.

Max met his first wife, Bridget, in college. She was an Adult Child of an Alcoholic (ACoA) and the apple of her dad's eye. An only child, she was beautiful and smart. She was the family star and was cross-generationally bonded with both her parents.

Max was the third child. Third children often carry the dynamics of their parent's marriage. Max literally reenacted his parents' pregnancy and early marriage. He later abandoned his children as his father had abandoned him. Max felt the loneliness and isolation his parents experienced in their marriage.

Bridget was the Caregiver in her family. She literally took care of her father's sadness, deep-seated isolation and depression. She did this by always being up and cheerful. She was a high school cheerleader. This role became so chronic, she lost any contact with her authentic self.

On one occasion Max asked me to see her because of their eldest daughter. I had suggested to Max that Bridget seemed to be in an enabling relationship with their daughter. She had bailed her out of jams on numerous occasions and was always giving her money she couldn't afford. When Bridget spoke to me, I had the uneasy feeling of not knowing who I was talking to. She had a parrotlike vocabulary and was "acting." The role was so sealed, she had no idea she was in an act.

Figure 3.4 gives you a visual picture of Max's own family system. The oldest child was clearly a Lost Child who gave her all to take care of everybody. Each of the other children was acting out the family system's shame. The middle sons were severely alcoholic. The fourth child was also alcoholic and hooked on pills. The youngest son was acting out Max's internalized rage in offender behavior.

FIGURE 3.3
Max's Father's (Jerome) Genogram

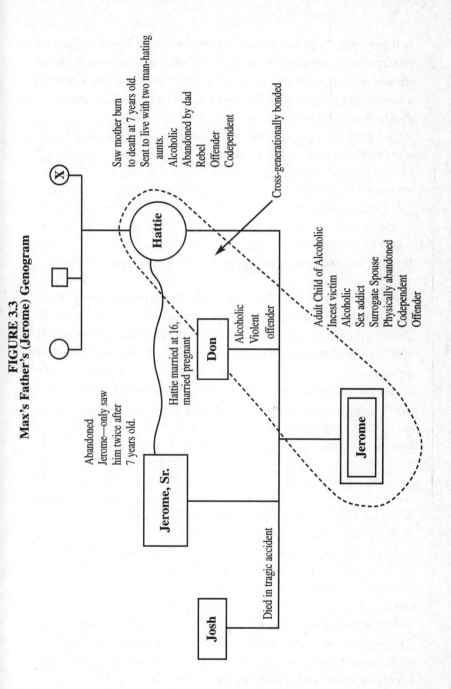

Saw mother burn to death at 7 years old.
Sent to live with two man-hating aunts.
Alcoholic
Abandoned by dad
Rebel
Offender
Codependent

Cross-generationally bonded

Adult Child of Alcoholic
Incest victim
Alcoholic
Sex addict
Surrogate Spouse
Physically abandoned
Codependent
Offender

Alcoholic
Violent offender

Hattie married at 16, married pregnant

Abandoned Jerome—only saw him twice after 7 years old.

Died in tragic accident

Hattie

Don

Jerome

Jerome, Sr.

Josh

In summary, I hope you can feel the power of the multigenerational patterns in Max's background. I hope you can see how Max reenacted those patterns and passed them on to his children. In Max's five-generation genogram there are five generations of alcoholism, physical and emotional abandonment, and codependency. There are four generations of sexual abuse and sexual addiction. There are early pregnancies, multiple marriages and divorces. Max was abandoned by his father, Jerome, at exactly the same age Jerome was abandoned by his father. Max died at exactly the same age his father died. Max's five-generation family map is not atypical of shame-based families.

SHAME-BASED MARRIAGE AND PARENTAL MODELS

It is obvious that a major source of toxic shame is the family system and its multigenerational patterns of unresolved secrets.

More specifically, these families are created by the shame-based people who find and marry each other. Each expects the other to parent the child within him or her. Each is incomplete and insatiable. The insatiability is rooted in each person's unmet childhood needs. When two adult children meet and fall in love, the child in each looks to the other to fill his or her needs. Since "in love" is a natural state of fusion, the incomplete children fuse together as they had done in the symbiotic stage of infancy. Each feels a sense of oneness and completeness. Since "in love" is always erotic, each feels "oceanic" in the sexual embrace. "Oceanic" love is without boundaries. Being in love is as powerful as any narcotic. One feels whole and ecstatic.

Unfortunately this state cannot last. The ecstatic consciousness is highly selective. Lovers focus on sameness and are intrigued by the newness of each other. Soon, however, real differences in socialization begin to emerge. The two families of origin rear their shame-based heads. Now the battle begins! Who will take care of whom? Whose family rules will win out? The more shame-based each person is, the more each other's differences will be intolerable. "If you loved me, you'd do it my way," each cajoles the other. The Hatfields and the McCoys go at it again.

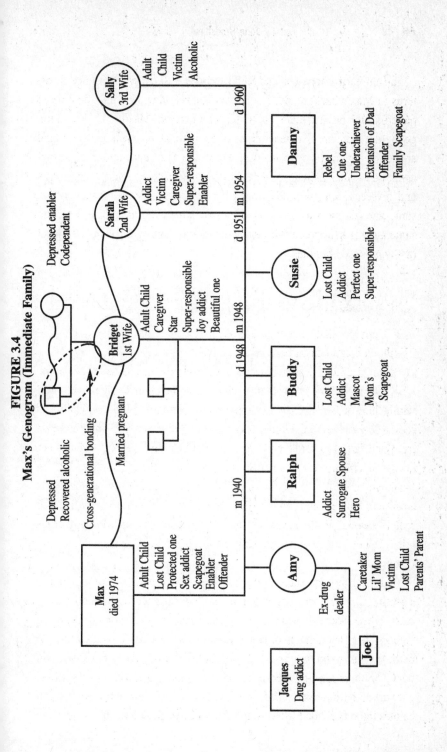

FIGURE 3.4
Max's Genogram (Immediate Family)

SHAME-BASED FAMILY RULES

Each family system has several categories of rules. There are rules about celebrating and socializing, rules about touching and sexuality, rules about sickness and proper health care, rules about vacations and vocations, rules about household maintenance and the spending of money. Perhaps the most important rules are about feelings, interpersonal communication and parenting.

Toxic shame is consciously transferred by means of shaming rules. In shame-based families, the rules consciously shame all the members. Generally, however, the children receive the major brunt of the shame. Power is a cover-up for shame. Power is frequently hierarchical. Dad can yell at anyone. Mom can yell at anyone but Dad. The oldest can yell at anyone but Mom and Dad, etc. The youngest tortures the cat!

THE DYSFUNCTIONAL FAMILY RULES

1. **Control or Chaos.** One must be in control of all interactions, feelings and personal behavior at all times—control is the major defense strategy for shame. In the less-than-human shameless marriage, both parents may be cocaine addicts or addicted in other ways. They may be dishonest criminals. The children experience chaos, as well as secrecy rules that guard their family's behavior.
2. **Perfectionism or Anomie.** Always be right in everything you do. The perfectionist rule always involves an imposed measurement. The fear and avoidance of the negative is the organizing principle of life. The members live according to an externalized image. No one ever measures up. In the less-than-human family, there are no rules—the children have no structure to guide them.
3. **Blame.** Whenever things don't turn out as planned, blame yourself or others. Blame is another defensive cover-up for shame. Blame maintains the balance in a dysfunctional system when control has broken down.
4. **Denial of the Five Freedoms.** The five freedoms, first enunciated by Virginia Satir, describe full personal functionality. Each freedom has to do with a basic human power: the power to perceive, to think and interpret, to feel, to want and choose, and the power to imagine. In

shame-based families, the perfectionist rule prohibits the full expression of these powers. It says you shouldn't perceive, think, feel, desire or imagine the way you do. You should do these the way the perfectionistic ideal demands.

5. **The "No Talk" Rule.** This rule prohibits the full expression of any feeling, need or want. In shame-based families, the members want to hide their true feelings, needs or wants. Therefore, no one speaks of his loneliness and sense of self-rupture.

6. **The "No Listen" Rule.** Everyone is so busy using their energy to defend themselves or play their rigid roles, no one really hears anything from the other's true self.

7. **Don't Make Mistakes.** Mistakes reveal the flawed, vulnerable self. To acknowledge a mistake is to open oneself to scrutiny. Cover up your own mistakes, and if someone else makes a mistake, shame him.

8. **Unreliability.** Don't expect reliability in relationships. Don't trust anyone, and you will never be disappointed. The parents didn't get their developmental dependency needs met and will not be there for their children to depend on. The distrust cycle goes on.

9. **Don't Trust.** Since no one feels validated or listened to, and there is unpredictability and unreliability on the part of the source figures, no one develops basic trust in themselves or others.

These rules are not written on the refrigerator door. However, they are the operative principles that govern shame-based families in their interpersonal relationships. They continue the cycle of shame for generations.

The parenting rules used in most Western world families create massive shame. Add alcoholism, incest and physical abuse to these systems, and you get major dysfunctionality. Alice Miller has summed up these rules under the title *"Poisonous Pedagogy"* in her book *For Your Own Good.* These rules state:

1. Adults are the masters of the dependent child.
2. They determine in godlike fashion what is right and what is wrong.
3. The child is held responsible for the parents' anger.
4. The parents must always be shielded.
5. The child's life-affirming feelings pose a threat to the autocratic adult.

6. The child's will must be "broken" as soon as possible.

7. All this must happen at a very early age so that the child "won't notice" and will therefore not be able to expose the adult.

Such beliefs about the parent's absolute power stem from the time of monarchs and kings. They are predemocratic and pre-Einsteinian. They presuppose a world of eternal laws, a *deus ex machina* view of the world. This was the world of Newton and Descartes. Such a worldview has been refuted many times over.

The poisonous pedagogy justifies highly abusive methods for suppressing children's vital spontaneity: physical beatings, lying, duplicity, manipulation, scare tactics, withdrawal of love, isolation and coercion to the point of torture. All of these methods are toxically shaming.

SHAME AS A STATE OF BEING

Let me expand here on the process whereby healthy shame is transformed into toxic shame. The process is called the "absolutizing" or "internalization" process. The healthy feeling of shame is lost, and a frozen state of being emerges, whereby a person believes himself to be flawed and defective as a human being. This transformation involves three dynamics:

1. The identification with shame-based models and the *carrying* of their unexpressed shame.

2. The trauma of abandonment and the shame binding all one's feelings, needs and drives.

3. The interconnection and magnification of visual memories or scenes, and the retaining of shaming auditory and kinesthetic imprints.

THE ABANDONMENT TRAUMA

The word abandonment, as used here, goes far beyond the ordinary understanding of that word. In naming our demons, we have to stretch the old meanings of our words.

I want to expand the meaning of the word abandonment to include various forms of emotional abandonment: stroke deprivation, narcissistic deprivation, fantasy bonding, the neglect of developmental dependency needs and family system enmeshment. My definition of abandonment also includes all forms of abuse.

Alice Miller, in her powerful book, *The Drama of the Gifted Child*, has described the paradoxical fact that many good, kind, devoted parents abandon their children. She also outlines the equally paradoxical fact that many highly gifted, superachieving and successful people are driven by a deep-seated chronic depression, resulting from their true and authentic selves being shamed through abandonment in childhood. I referred to this earlier as the "hole in your soul" phenomena. Alice Miller's work has expanded my understanding of the abandonment trauma. She does not use shame as a major organizing principle of her work. However, it is easy to see that the loss of authentic selfhood, with its accompanying depression, is another way to describe toxic shame.

When one is abandoned, one is left alone. This can happen through physical absence as well as physical presence. In fact, to be abandoned by someone who is physically present is much more crazy-making.

ACTUAL PHYSICAL ABSENCE

Max began his life with two strikes against him. He was not planned or really wanted. He was an accidental pregnancy in an ever-intensifying dysfunctional marriage. Jerome's drinking had escalated so that Felicia had attempted separation on several occasions in an attempt to control his drinking. Four separations occurred during Max's first eight years of life.

Max was also separated from his brother and sister during three of these separations. He and Felicia lived with two of her sisters while Ralph and Maxine lived with Felicia's mother. A child needs structure and predictability. He needs to be able to count on someone.

I remember when my son was about three years old; he would ask me to read him a story at night. His favorites were *The Little Engine That Could* and *Peter Rabbit.* After a few readings, these stories became rather boring to me. I used to try and turn two pages simultaneously (the old two-pages-at-a-time trick). I was rarely able to do this without getting caught. To my son's young mind if a piece of that story were missing, it was disastrous. It would put his world out of order. In a more dramatic way, for a child to be continuously moved from his family causes severe upset.

A child needs the presence of both parents. For a boy to break his mother bonding, he needs a father to bond with. Bonding involves spending time together, sharing feelings, warmth, touching and displaying desire to be with one another.

Max's dad was hardly ever around. When he was not working, he was drinking. He gave Max very little of his time. A very young child cannot understand that his dad is a sick alcoholic. Children are limited in logical ability. Their earliest way of thinking is through feelings (felt thought). Children are also egocentric. This doesn't mean they are selfish in the usual meaning of that word. They are not morally selfish.

Egocentric thinking means that a child will take everything personally. Even if a parent dies, a child can personalize it. A child might say something like, "If Mommy had really loved me, she would not have gone to God's house; she would have stayed with me."

We give time to those things that we love.

The impact of not having one's parents' time creates the feeling of worthlessness. The child is *worth less* than his parents' time, attention or direction. The young child's egocentricity always interprets events egocentrically. If Mom and Dad are not present, it's because of me. There must be something wrong with me or they would want to be with me.

Children are egocentric by nature (not by choice). Their egocentricity is like a temporary door and doorknob, in use until strong boundaries can be built. Strong boundaries result from the identification with parents who themselves have strong boundaries and who teach their children by modeling. Children have no experience; they need their parents' experience. By identifying with their parents, they have someone whom they can depend on outside themselves. As they internalize their parents, they form a dependable guide inside themselves. If their parents are not dependable, they will not develop this inner resource.

EMOTIONAL ABANDONMENT AND NARCISSISTIC DEPRIVATION

Children need mirroring and echoing. These come from their primary caregiver's eyes. Mirroring means that someone is there for them and reflects who they really are at any given moment of time. In the first three years of our life each of us needed to be admired and taken seriously. We needed to be accepted for the very one we are. Having these mirroring needs met results in what Alice Miller calls our basic narcissistic supplies.

These supplies result from good mirroring by a parent with good boundaries. When this is the case, as Miller states in *The Drama of the Gifted Child,* the following dynamics take place:

1. The child's aggressive impulses can be neutralized because they do not threaten the parent.
2. The child's striving for autonomy is not experienced as a threat to the parent.
3. The child is allowed to experience and express ordinary impulses, such as jealousy, rage, sexuality and defiance, because the parents have not disowned these feelings in themselves.
4. The child does not have to please the parent and can develop his own needs at his own developmental pace.
5. The child can depend on and use his parents because they are separate from him.
6. The parents' independence and good boundaries allow the child to separate self and object representation.
7. Because the child is allowed to display ambivalent feelings, he can learn to regard himself and the caregiver as "both good and bad," rather than splitting off certain parts as good and certain parts as bad.
8. The beginning of true object love is possible because the parents love the child as a separate object.

When parents are shame-based and needy, they are unable to take over the mirroring narcissistic function for the child. Furthermore, the fact that the parents are shame-based is a clear signal that *they never got their own narcissistic supplies.* Such parents are adult children who are still in search of a parent or an object who will be totally available to them. For such parents, the most appropriate objects of narcissistic gratification are their *own children.* Again Alice Miller writes:

A newborn baby is completely dependent on his parents and since their caring is essential for his existence, he does all he can to avoid losing them. From the very first day onward, he will muster all his resources to this end, like a small plant that turns toward the sun in order to survive.

What the shame-based mother was unable to find in her own mother she finds in her own children. The child is always at her disposal. A child cannot run away as her own mother did. A child can be used as an echo, is completely centered on her, will never desert her, can be totally controlled, and offers full admiration and absorbed attention.

Children have an amazing ability to perceive this need in the parent(s). The true self of the child seems to know it unconsciously. I'll expand on this in Chapter Thirteen. By taking on the role of supplying his shame-based parent's narcissistic gratification, the child secures love and a sense of being needed and not abandoned. *This process is a reversal of the order of nature. Now the child is taking care of the parents' needs, rather than the parents taking care of the child's needs. This* caregiver role is strangely paradoxical. In an attempt to secure parental love and avoid being abandoned, the child is in fact being abandoned. Since the child is there for the parent, there is no one to mirror the child's feelings and drives and nurture the child's needs. Any child growing up in such an environment has been wounded by this narcissistic deprivation. This phenomenon can happen in the best of families.

Alice Miller writes:

> There are large numbers of people who suffer from narcissistic disorders, who often had sensitive and caring parents from whom they received much encouragement; yet these people are suffering from severe depressions. They enter analysis in the belief, with which they grew up, that their childhood was happy and protected.

More often than not, these narcissistically deprived are talented, gifted, highly successful superachievers who have been praised and admired for their talents and achievements. Anyone looking at them on the outside would believe these people have it made. They appear strong and stable and full of self-assurance. This is not the case. Narcissistically deprived people do well in every undertaking and are admired for their gifts and talents, but they have a deep sense of emptiness and aloneness.

Once the drug of grandiosity is taken away, as soon as they are no longer the stars and superachievers, they are plagued by deep feelings of shame and guilt.

I have worked with many individuals of this type. I am one myself. It is difficult for anyone looking at our successes to know how shame-based we really are. As children we were loved for our achievements and our perfor-mance, rather than for ourselves. Our true and authentic selves were aban-doned. Fortunately the true self *never* goes away, and we can stop the drivenness to perform. I'll expand on reconnecting with our true selves in Part III.

In my own case it has taken me a lot of work to connect with my own true feelings—my anger, jealousy, loneliness or sadness. The good news is that I have been able to do it. Being disconnected from our feelings is the result of abandonment. No one was there to affirm our feelings through mirroring. A child can only experience his feelings when there is someone there who fully accepts them, names them and supports them.

Another consequence of this emotional abandonment is the loss of a sense of self. When used as another's narcissistic supplies, a person devel-ops in such a way as to reveal only what is expected of him and ultimately fuses with his own act or performance. He becomes a "human doing" with-out any real sense of his authentic self. According to Winnicotti, his true self remains in a "state of noncommunication." I described this earlier as no longer being in me. Such a person feels emptiness, homelessness and futil-ity. Our authentic self is not really lost. It has been repressed until a time when it is safe to come out.

THE FANTASY BOND

Perhaps the most troubling consequence of emotional abandonment is what Robert Firestone calls the "fantasy bond" and what Alice Miller calls "bond permanence." A child who has been denied the experience of con-necting with his own emotions is first consciously and then unconsciously (through the internal identification with the parent) dependent on his parents. Alice Miller writes:

He cannot rely on his own emotions, has not come to experience them through trial and error, has no sense of his own real needs and is alienated from himself to the highest degree.

Such a person cannot separate from his parents. He is fantasy bonded with them. He has an illusion (fantasy) of connection, i.e., he really thinks there is a love relationship between himself and his parents. Actually he is fused and enmeshed. This is an *entrapment* rather than a relationship. Later on this fantasy bond will be transferred to other relationships.

This fantasy-bonded person is still dependent on affirmation from his partner, his children, his job. He is especially dependent on his children. A fantasy-bonded person never has a *real connection* or a *real relationship* with anyone. There is no real, authentic self there for another to relate to. The real parents, who only accepted the child when he pleased them, remain as introjected voices. *The true self hides from these introjected voices just as the real child did.* The "loneliness of the parental home" is replaced by "isolation within the self."

Grandiosity is often the result of all this. The grandiose person is admired everywhere and cannot live without admiration. If his talents fail him, it is catastrophic. He must be perfect, otherwise depression is near. Often the most gifted among us are driven in precisely this manner. Many of the most gifted people suffer from severe depression. It cannot be otherwise because depression is about the lost and abandoned child within.

"One is free from depression," writes Alice Miller in The *Drama of the Gifted Child,* "when self-esteem is based on the authenticity of one's own feelings and not on the possession of certain qualities."

Emotional abandonment is most often multigenerational. The child of the narcissistically deprived parent becomes an adult with a narcissistically deprived child and will use his children as he was used for his narcissistic supplies. That child then becomes an adult child and the cycle is repeated.

Max's parents were narcissistically deprived. Jerome used fantasy bonds with alcohol and sex for his narcissistic supplies. Felicia used Ralph as her main narcissistic gratification. He became the family star, the moralistic, superachieving, righteous minister. Maxine and Max were both Lost Children. Felicia, although dutiful, was never really there to mirror and affirm their emotions. Max reenacted this same pattern on his children, using them for his narcissistic supplies. He would immediately run to them for nurturing and solace after his runaways. His daughters especially were a source of nurturing. Never once did I see any of his children express anger, hurt or resentment toward Max. They had never connected with their own feelings.

Max would become enraged when I spoke of his reenactment of his abandonment on his own children. His children minimized the impact of their lonely childhood. This is the delusional nature of deprived narcissism.

When emotionally abandoned people describe their childhoods, it is always without feeling. Alice Miller writes,

> They recount their earliest memories without any sympathy for the child they once were. Very often they show disdain and irony, even derision and cynicism. In general, there is a complete absence of real emotional understanding or serious appreciation of their own childhood vicissitudes and no conception of their true need—beyond the need for achievement. The internalization of the original drama has been so complete that the illusion of a good childhood can be maintained.

Max's children idolized and idealized him. They continued the delusion of their happy childhood. Max himself showed no real anger toward his parents. Only when he was drunk would the rage toward his father come out. He had no overt anger toward his mother.

ABANDONMENT THROUGH ABUSE

All forms of child abuse are abandonment. When parents abuse children, the abuse is about the parent's issues and not the child's. This is why it is abuse.

Abuse is abandonment because when children are abused, no one is there for them. What's happening is purportedly for the child's own good. But it isn't about the child at all; it's about the parent. Such transactions are crazy-making and induce shame. In each act of abuse the child is shamed. Young children, because of their egocentrism, make themselves responsible for the abuse.

The child says to himself, "My caretakers couldn't be crazy or emotionally ill; it must be me."

A child must maintain this idealization. Children's minds are magical, egocentric and nonlogical. They are completely dependent upon their parents for survival. The idealization ensures survival. *If my parents are sick and crazy, how could I survive? It must be me. I am crazy. There's something wrong with me, or they wouldn't treat me this way.*

The child doesn't have a chance. Alice Miller points out that the child "can't know what has happened to them." All abuse contributes to the internalization of shame. Some kinds of abuse are more intensely shaming than others.

SEXUAL ABUSE

Sexual abuse is the most shaming of all abuse. It takes less sexual abuse than any other form of abuse to induce shame. Sexual abuse is widespread. The estimates of the frequency of child abuse are staggering. Our awareness of this problem has grown tremendously over the past thirty years.

In the past our understanding was limited to a kind of "horror story" incest victim. Such stories involved physical, hands-on sexual abuse. Today we've greatly expanded our understanding of such abuse. In *Bradshaw On: The Family, I* present material on sexual abuse adapted from the work of Pia Mellody at The Meadows, a treatment center in Wickenberg, Arizona.

The following is from *Bradshaw On: The Family.*

Sexual abuse involves whole families. It can be divided as follows:

1. **Sexual Abuse.** This involves hands-on touching in a sexual way. The range of abusive behaviors that are sexual include sexualized hugging or kissing; any kind of sexual touching or fondling; oral and anal sex; masturbation of the victim or forcing the victim to masturbate the offender; sexual intercourse.

2. **Overt Sexual Abuse.** This involves voyeurism and exhibitionism. This can be outside or inside the home. Parents often sexually abuse children through voyeurism and exhibitionism. The criterion for in-home voyeurism or exhibitionism is whether the parent is being sexually stimulated. Sometimes parents may be so out of touch with their own sexuality that they are not aware of how sexual they are being.

The child almost always has a kind of icky feeling about it.

Overt incest can take place when a parent has repressed his or her sexuality and has faulty boundaries. Ralph and Max were both seduced by Felicia's unresolved sexuality. She asked them to help her undo her girdle and hook her bra. She often appeared in her panties and came into the bathroom to urinate when one of them was in the bath. They had no shower curtain, so while urinating, Mother could look at their genitals and they could see hers. These boundary violations took place during the boys' juvenile period—a time when both were too old and sexually overstimulated by their mother's behavior.

One client told me how her father would leer at her in her panties as she came out of the bathroom. Others speak of having no privacy in the house, much less the bathroom. I've had a dozen male clients whose mothers bathed their genital parts through eight or nine years old.

Children can feel sexual around parents. This is not sexual abuse unless the parent originated it and consciously stimulates it. It all depends upon the parents. Here I'm not talking about a parent having a passing sexual thought or feeling. It's about a parent using a child for his own conscious or unconscious sexual stimulation.

3. **Covert Sexual Abuse.**

   (a) **Verbal Abuse.** This involves inappropriate sexual talking: Dad or any significant male calling women "whores" or "cunts" or objectified sexual names; Mom or any significant female depreciating men in a sexual way. It also involves parents or caregivers having to know about every detail of their children's private sexual life, asking questions about a child's sexual physiology or questioning for minute details about dates. Covert sexual abuse also involves not receiving adequate sexual information.

   I've had several female clients who didn't know what was happening when they began menstruating. I've had three female clients who did not know their vaginas had openings until they were twenty years old!

   A covert kind of sexual abuse occurs when Dad or Mom talk about sex in front of the children when the age level of the children is inappropriate. It also occurs when Mom or Dad make sexual remarks about the children's bodies. I've worked with two male clients who were traumatized by their mother's jokes about the size of their penises, and female clients whose fathers and stepfathers teased them about the size of their breasts or buttocks.

(b) **Boundary Violation.** This involves children witnessing parents in sexual behavior. They may walk in on it because parents don't provide closed or locked doors. It also involves the children being allowed no privacy. They are walked in on in the bathroom. They are not taught to lock their doors or given permission to lock their doors. Parents need to model appropriate nudity, i.e., need to be clothed appropriately after a certain age. Children are sexually curious. Beginning at around age three or between ages three and six, children start noticing parents' bodies. They are often obsessed with nudity.

Mom and Dad need to be careful walking around nude with young children. If Mom is not being stimulated sexually, the nudity is not sexual misconduct. She simply is acting in a dysfunctional way. She is not setting sexual boundaries.

The use of enemas at an early age can also be abusive in a way that leads to sexual dysfunction. The enemas can be a body boundary violation.

4. **Emotional Sexual Abuse or Covert Incest.** Emotional sexual abuse results from cross-generational bonding. I've spoken of enmeshment as a way that children take on the covert needs of a family system. It is very common for one or both parents in a dysfunctional marriage to bond inappropriately with one of their children. The parents use the child to meet their emotional needs. This relationship can easily become sexualized and romanticized. If the parents have unresolved sexual issues, the daughter may become *Daddy's Little Princess,* or the son may become *Mom's Little Man.* In both cases the child is being abandoned. The parents are getting their needs met at the expense of the child's needs. The child needs a parent, not a spouse."

According to Pia Mellody, when "one parent has a relationship with the child that is more important than the relationship he or she has with the spouse, and that parent has unresolved sexual issues, a strong possibility exists that the child will be emotionally sexually abused."

Sometimes both parents emotionally bond with a child. The child tries to take care of both parents' feelings. I once worked with a female client whose father would get her in the middle of the night and put her in bed with him in the guest bedroom. He would do this mainly to punish his wife for sexually refusing him. The daughter has suffered greatly with confused sexual identity.

Cross-generational bonding can occur with a parent and a child of *the same sex*. A most common form of this in our culture is mother and daughter. Mother often has sexualized rage, i.e., she fears and hates men. She uses her daughter for her emotional needs and also contaminates her daughter's sexual feelings about men.

The issue is whether the parent is there for the development of his or her child's needs, rather than the child being there for the parent's needs. And while children have the capacity to be sexual in a way appropriate to their developmental level, *whenever an adult is being sexual with a child, sexual abuse is going on.*

OLDER SIBLINGS

Some sexual abuse may come from older siblings. Generally, sexual behavior by same-age children is not sexually abusive. The rule of thumb is that when a child is experiencing sexual "acting out" at the hands of a child three or four years older, and being introduced to sexual behaviors that are age inappropriate, it is usually sexually abusive.

For example, Jane is ten years old and Sally is seven. Jane and Sally engage in juvenile sex play (something quite common during the juvenile period). Jane wants Sally to use a dildo and have anal sex with her. This behavior sends up a red flag because it is far too sophisticated for a ten-year-old and suggests that Jane is reenacting something that has been done to her by an older person, which she is acting out on her young friend.

PHYSICAL ABUSE

Spare the rod and you spoil the child has been used forever as a biblical justification or injunction for corporal punishment. Physical violence against children (and women) is part of an ancient and pervasive tradition.

Generally speaking, physical violence is second only to sexual violence in terms of the toxic shame it creates. Furthermore, physical violence is highly addictive. I've already shown it to be a form of the character disordered syndrome of shame. Offenders are literally addicted to the power that physical violence gives them. Physical offenders like the fear they induce in others. Violent offenders are shame-based and can completely avoid their toxic shame by bullying and hurting others.

The profile of physically abusing parents includes the following: isolated, poor self-image, lack of sensitivity to others' feelings, usually physically abused themselves, deprived of basic mothering, have unmet needs for love and comfort, are emotionally retarded and in denial of problems and the impact of the problems, and feel there is no one to turn to for advice. Physically abusive parents have totally unrealistic expectations of children and expect the children to meet their needs for comfort and nurturing. When children fail to meet their needs, they interpret this as rejection and respond with anger and frustration, dealing with the children as if they were much older than they are.

There is no good data on the extent of physical abuse. The usual data covers those cases *that are reported.* It excludes those not treated by a physician, those cases treated by a physician but not identified as abuse and those cases identified as abuse but not reported. It's estimated there are two hundred unreported cases for every case reported.

The ownership of children by parents, and the belief that children are willful and need their wills broken, provide a rationale for spanking children. Jesus said nothing about spanking children. I have a compilation of several clinical studies in my new book on moral intelligence and the life of virtue. All these studies outline the real dangers and severe consequences that come from corporal punishment.

The victim of the physical violence is also bonded to the violence out of shame. In the beginning the victims bond out of sheer terror. But as the abuse continues, their self-worth is diminished. As the self-worth is diminished, the victims lose the ability to choose. They become like starving children looking for morsels and crumbs of love.

Because violence is irrational and impulsive, it is often random and unpredictable. The random quality of the violence sets up what Seligman calls "learned helplessness." Learned helplessness is a kind of mental confusion. The people can no longer think or plan. They become passively accepting of their abuse. I can't imagine a more soul-murdering destruction of human life.

Physical violence is common in family life because the tenets of the poisonous pedagogy promote and support corporal punishment. It's still endorsed as a way to teach children about life. Our common nursery rhyme about the old woman who lived in a shoe attests to the common acceptance of physical punishment.

Physical violence is the norm in many dysfunctional families. This includes actual physical spankings; having to get your own weapons of torture (belts, switches, etc.); being punched, slapped, slapped in the face, pulled on, yanked on, choked, shaken, kicked, pinched, tortured with tickling; being threatened with violence of abandonment; being threatened with jail or the police; witnessing violence done to a parent or sibling.

This last is a major issue in homes where wives are battered. A child experiencing their mother or siblings being battered is equivalent to the child being battered. A witness to violence is a victim of violence.

EMOTIONAL ABUSE

Some emotional abuse is nearly universal. I believe that everyone has been shamed to some degree by emotional abuse. The poisonous pedagogy is quite clear about the fact that emotions are weak. We are to be rational and logical and not allow ourselves to be marred by emotions. All emotions must be controlled, but anger and sexual feelings are especially to be repressed. I can't imagine that many people in modern American life were affirmed and nurtured in expressing their sexual and/or angry feelings.

EMOTIONAL SHAME BINDS

Our emotions are the core of our basic power. Two of the major functions they serve in our psychic life are:

1. *They monitor our basic needs,* telling us of a need, loss or satiation. Without our emotional energy, we would not be aware of our most fundamental needs.

2. They give us the fuel or energy to act. I like to hyphenate the word "e-motion." An e-motion is energy in motion. This energy moves us to get what we need. When our basic needs are being violated, our *anger* moves us to fight or run.

Our e-motions are the scenes that involve our affect system. All human development, according to Silvan Tompkins, is rooted in affect (feeling) dynamics because affects (feelings) are the primary innate biological motivator of human life.

Our anger is the energy that gives us strength. The Incredible Hulk becomes the huge, powerful hulk when he needs the energy and power to take care of others.

Our sadness is an energy we discharge in order to heal. As we discharge the energy over the losses relating to our basic needs, we can integrate the shock of those losses and adapt to reality. Sadness is painful. We try to avoid it. Discharging sadness releases the energy involved in our emotional pain. To hold it in is to freeze the pain within us. The therapeutic slogan is that grieving is the "healing feeling."

Fear releases an energy that warns us of danger to our basic needs. Fear is an energy leading to our discernment and wisdom.

Guilt is our morality shame and guards our conscience. It tells us we have transgressed our values. It moves us to take action and change.

Shame warns us not to try to be more or less than human. Shame signals our essential limitations. Shame limits our desire for pleasure and our interest and curiosity. We could not really be free without our shame. There is an anonymous saying, "Of all the masks of freedom, discipline (limits) is the hardest to understand." We cannot be truly free without having limits.

Joy is the exhilarating energy that emerges when all our needs are being met. We want to sing, run and jump with joy. The energy of joy signals that all is well.

Dissmell is the affect that monitors our drive for hunger. It was primarily developed as a survival mechanism. As we've become more complex, its use has extended interpersonally. Prejudice and rage against strangers (the ones who are not like us) have terrible consequences. Dissmell is a major sexuality factor.

Disgust follows the same pattern as dissmell. Originally a hunger drive auxiliary, it has been extended to interpersonal relations. Divorces are often dominated by disgust. Victims of abuse carry various degrees of anger and disgust. Rapists who kill operate on disgust, anger and sex fused together.

When our e-motions are not mirrored and named, we lose contact with one of our vital human powers. Parents who are out of touch with their own emotions cannot model those emotions for their children. They are out of touch and shut down. They are psychically numb. They are not even aware of what they are feeling. Their children have to unconsciously carry their feelings for them.

I cannot overemphasize the damage that occurs when our emotions are shame bound. Modern neuroscientists like Joseph Le Doux, Allen N. Shore and Diana Fosha have presented compelling evidence that our true sense of self is based on our authentic core feelings. Silvan Tompkins has shown that our feelings are the primary motivating source in our lives. Without acknowledging our core feelings, we lose our sense of self. Our false selves are based on our survival skills. Our false selves are like the script for a play. The script tells us what feelings we *should* have. We learn to accept the scripted feelings as authentic.

The denial of emotions is actually sanctified by our most sacred traditions of parenting rules. These rules especially shame children by denying emotions. Emotions are considered weak; I heard that throughout my childhood. "Emotions show weakness. Don't be so emotional."

Religion endorses the poisonous pedagogy. Anger is considered especially bad. Anger is one of the seven deadly sins. These sins send you to hell. In its most accurate teaching, the deadly sin is not really the emotion of anger, but the behaviors resulting from anger. Behaviors often linked to anger are screaming, cursing, hitting, publically criticizing or condemning someone and physical violence. These behaviors are certainly prohibitive. They are behaviors based on judgment, rather than emotions.

Many children are shamed for their anger. Children often see parents angry and rageful. The message is all too often that it's okay for parents to be angry, but it's not okay for children.

SEX-DRIVE SHAME BINDS

Perhaps no aspect of human activity has been as dysfunctionally shamed as our sexuality. Sexuality is the core of human selfhood. Our sex is not something we have or do; it is who we are. It's the first thing we notice about each other. Sexuality is a basic fact in all created things. If we shut off this drive, we would annihilate the human race in 120 years. Our sexual energy (libido) is our own unique incarnation of the life force itself. To have our sex drive shamed is to be shamed to the core.

All children have natural sexual curiosity. I can remember vividly when my next-door neighbor told me that the man's penis went into the woman's vagina. I was awestruck. It seemed unbelievable! Sexuality is somewhat awesome and confusing to a child. And children naturally explore their genitals, and at certain ages, engage in childhood sex play.

I have often outlined the following scenario to illustrate how our sexuality is shamed. One day little two-year-old Farquahr, while exploring his body, names his nose. He points to it and names it. Mom is exhilarated and calls Grandma to report Farquahr's brilliant achievement. Grandma comes over and asks Farquahr to perform his newfound ability, which he does with grandiose pride. On each occasion when he names his nose, he receives great praise. Later on he finds other parts of his body: ears, eyes, elbows, navel . . . and then one day, one Sunday with all the family in the living room (receiving the preacher), little Farquahr finds his penis! He's pretty excited. He thinks that if his nose impressed them, this will really impress them. So he wanders into the living room and proudly displays his penis!

Never has little Farquahr seen such action! Mom has him by the ear, and he's moving faster than he's ever moved before. Her face is contorted. She is visibly shaken and tells him in no uncertain terms never to show himself off again. He's told that what he did was bad! Children idealize their parents at their worst. The more out of control the parent, the more the child's security is threatened.

Variations of this scenario happen in the best of families. Parents who have had their own sexuality shamed cannot handle their children's natural sexuality. When their child explores his sexuality, parents react with disapproval or worse, disgust. Global comments such as "That's bad," "Don't ever touch yourself there," "Go get decent—put on your clothes," "Cover your privates" link sexuality to something bad, dirty and disgusting. This part of us must be disowned. The feeling of shame becomes linked to sexuality.

A child growing up in such a family (many of us) comes to believe and feel that sexuality is shameful.

Generally speaking, most of our vital, spontaneous, instinctual life gets shamed. Children are shamed for being too rambunctious, for wanting things and for laughing too loud. Much dysfunctional shame occurs at the dinner table. Children are forced to eat when they are not hungry. Sometimes children are forced to eat what they do not find appetizing.

Being exiled to the dinner table until the plate is cleaned is not unusual in modern family life. The public humiliation of sitting at the dinner table all alone, often with siblings jeering, is a painful kind of exposure.

I've had clients who eat standing up or on the run because of shameful scenes at the dinner table when they were children. When our instinctual life is shamed, the natural core of our life is bound up. It's like an acorn going through excruciating agony for becoming an oak, or a flower feeling ashamed for blossoming. What happens is that because our instincts are part of our natural endowment, they cannot be repressed. Once our instincts are shame-bound, they become like hungry dogs that must be watched.

SHAME—THE MASTER EMOTION

Shame has been called the master emotion because as it is internalized-all the other emotions are bound by shame. Emotionally shame-bound parents cannot allow their children to have emotions because the child's emotions triggers the parents' emotions. Repressed emotions often feel too big, like they would completely overwhelm us if we expressed them. There is also the fear of the shame that would be triggered if we expressed our emotions.

The shaming and binding of emotions were core parts of Max's internalized shame. Max had never been physically abused. But he was certainly sexually abused. As the third child, he carried his mother's and father's sexual issues. Both were unresolved incest victims. Jerome was a womanizer, although this was always a family secret. Max reported on several occasions that he felt his mother, Felicia, often acted seductively. Felicia certainly was emotionally abusing. She name-called, compared and yelled, and she did it with contempt and disgust. Most of all she continually made Max take care of her feelings. She criticized and scorned his feelings. According to Max she said things like "What are you angry about?" or "There's nothing to be afraid of," or "Stop that crying or I'll give you something to cry about." Max was profoundly sad. He could have cried for ages. I came to believe that his whole family system carried generations of unresolved grief. I could feel the sadness when I sat across from him.

ABANDONMENT THROUGH THE NEGLECT OF DEVELOPMENTAL DEPENDENCY NEEDS

As children, we had needs that depended on others for fulfillment. Children are dependent and needy. They need their parents for fifteen years. Their dependency needs can only be satisfied by a caregiver. Figure 3.5 outlines these needs. Children need someone to hold them and touch them. They need a face to mirror and affirm their feelings, needs and drives. Children need a structure with limits; they need predictability. They need a mutually trusting relationship; they need to know there is someone they can count on. Children need to have space and be different. They need security; they need to have enough nutritional food, clothing, shelter and adequate medical care. Children need their parents' time and attention. Children need direction in the form of problem-solving techniques and strategies.

NEED SHAME BINDS

When these needs are neglected, children are given the message that their needs are not important, and they lose a sense of their own personal value. They are not worth someone being there for them. They get the feeling they do not matter. As their needs are chronically rejected, children stop believing they have the right to depend on anyone. These dependency needs rely on the interpersonal bridge and the bond of mutuality for their fulfillment. The interpersonal bridge is broken when one is abandoned through neglect. Since we have no one to depend on, we come to believe that we have no right to depend on anyone. We feel shame when we feel needy. Since these needs are basic needs, i.e., needs we cannot be fully human without, we have to get them met in abortive ways.

FIGURE 3.5
Basic Dependency Needs

Adult Life

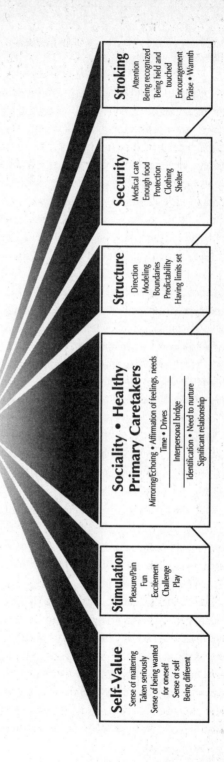

Self-Value
Sense of mattering
Taken seriously
Sense of being wanted for oneself
Sense of self
Being different

Stimulation
Pleasure/Pain
Fun
Excitement
Challenge
Play

Sociality • Healthy Primary Caretakers
Mirroring/Echoing • Affirmation of feelings, needs
Time • Drives
Interpersonal bridge
Identification • Need to nurture
Significant relationship

Structure
Direction
Modeling
Boundaries
Predictability
Having limits set

Security
Medical care
Enough food
Protection
Clothing
Shelter

Stroking
Attention
Being recognized
Being held and touched
Encouragement
Praise • Warmth

A neglected child may learn to get attention by getting into trouble or by annoying his parents. One will drink muddy water when he is dying of thirst. I know of children who get their touch and stimulation needs met by getting spanked. Much has been written about abortive adaptation. Suffice it to say, when one's basic dependency needs are not met at the proper time and in the proper sequence, the personality is arrested at those developmental stages. The child learns adaptive ways to get his needs met. Over the course of time, as one experiences need-deprivation, one loses awareness of these needs. Ultimately, one does not even know what one needs.

Being abandoned through the neglect of our developmental dependency needs is the major factor in becoming an adult child. We grow up; we look like adults. We walk and talk like adults, but beneath the surface is a little child who feels empty and needy, a child whose needs are insatiable because he has a child's needs in an adult body. This insatiable child is the core of all compulsive/addictive behavior.

In Max's case many of his needs were converted into sexual feelings. This is what accounted for his severe sexual addiction. It is often a major dynamic in sexual addiction. Once a person is abandoned, especially through abuse, he is made into an object.

Max was used by his brother to alter his brother's shame. He was physically abandoned by his father. He was used by the family system. To be used is to be made into an object. By being objectified, Max objectified himself.

Through his internalized shame, Max became an object of his own contempt, criticism, judgment and scorn. He was his own object of rejection. To objectify self and others is to lose personhood. Since Max could no longer experience himself as a whole person, he could no longer experience anyone else as a whole person.

Max spent hours hustling women. He was obsessed by women's breasts. He had no regard for women as people. He risked family and reputation to touch women's breasts in shopping malls or get glimpses of them through voyeuristic activities.

Another dynamic aspect of the sexual conversion of basic needs is the pleasure of sexual orgasm itself. When one is shamed through abandonment, the pain is deep and profound. One feels worthless; one feels painfully diminished and exposed. When one experiences sexual stimulation and climax, one has available an all-encompassing and power-ful pleasure. This pleasure can take the place of any other need. In a poignant passage, Kaufman sums up the process of converting all needs into sexuality. He writes:

> A young boy who learns never to need anything emotionally from his parents . . . is faced with a dilemma whenever he feels young, needy or otherwise insecure. If masturbating has been his principle source of good feeling . . . he may resort to masturbation in order to restore good feelings about self at times when he is experiencing needs quite unrelated to sexuality.

The ego defense of conversion transforms developmental needs into the need for something else. This could be food, money or excessive attention. In Max's case it was sex. Over the course of his childhood, his develop-mental needs became associated with his sex drive. This eventually resulted in the conversion of emotional needing into sexuality. Whenever Max felt insecure, anxious or needy, the inner event registered as sexual desire. Max turned continually to sex for the self-nurturing he was starving for but that addictive sex cannot provide.

ABANDONMENT THROUGH ENMESHMENT IN THE OVERT AND COVERT NEEDS OF THE FAMILY SYSTEM

I have already described the family as a social system—its components, rules, roles and its law of dynamic homeostasis. You have seen how a dys-functional family uses the members to maintain its balance. The more dys-functional the system, the more closed and rigid are the roles it assigns. In families that are chemically, sexually or violently dysfunctional, the needs of the system are overt. The system dispenses its roles for the members to play in order to keep balance.

All the rigid roles set up by family dysfunction are forms of abandon-ment. To be a family Hero, I had to be strong—never showing the scared, vulnerable part of myself. Heroes are not supposed to be scared. The roles are like scripts given out for a play. They prescribe what feelings you can or cannot have. After playing my Hero role for years, I no longer really knew who I was. In recovery I had to learn how to give up that role. To do so I had to learn to be vulnerable. I had to learn how to be a member of a group rather than the leader, to follow rather than lead. Because the roles maintain the balance of the system, they exist for the system. The children give up their own reality to take care of the family system—to keep it whole and balanced.

Each form of abandonment breaks the interpersonal bridge and the mutual-intimacy bond. A child is precious and incomparable. Unless treated with value and love, this sense of preciousness and incomparability diminishes. In toxic, internalized shame, it disappears completely.

INTERCONNECTION OF IMAGERY

Another way that internalization occurs is by internalizing images. These internal images can be of a shaming person, place or actual experience. They can also be word images, i.e., sound imprints. Hearing someone say certain words may trigger old experiences of shame. Individual shame experiences are fused together by means of language and imagery. Kaufman says, "Scenes of shame become interconnected and magnified." As the language, imagery and scenes associated with shame are fused together, the meaning of shame is transformed. "I feel shame" comes to mean "I am shameful, deficient in some vital way as a human being." Shame is no longer one feeling among many, but comes to constitute the core of oneself. Internalized shame creates a frozen state of being. Shame is no longer an emotional signal that comes and goes. It is a deep, abiding, all-pervasive sense of being defective as a person. This core of defectiveness forms the foundation around which other feelings about the self will be experienced. Gradually, over a period of time, this frozen feeling of belief recedes from consciousness. In this way shame becomes basic to one's sense of identity. One becomes a shame-based person.

INTERNAL SHAME SPIRALS

One experience of internalized shame is what Kaufman terms *the "internal shame spiral."* He describes it as follows:

A triggering event occurs. Perhaps it is trying to get close to some- one and feeling rebuffed. Or a critical remark by a friend . . . a per- son suddenly is enmeshed in shame, the eyes turn inward and the experience becomes totally internal, frequently with visual imagery present. The shame feelings flow in a circle, endlessly triggering each other. The precipitating event is relived internally over and over, causing the sense of shame to deepen, to absorb other neutral experi- ences . . . until finally the self is engulfed. In this way shame becomes paralyzing.

The spiral is one of the most devastating aspects of dysfunctional shame. Once in motion, it can cause the reliving of other shameful experiences and thereby solidifies shame further within the personality.

After shame is internalized, the fear of exposure is magnified intensely. Exposure now means having one's essential defectiveness as a human being seen. To be exposed now means to be seen as irreparably and unspeakably bad. One must find a way to defend against such exposure. As the defenses and strategies of transference are developed, internalized shame becomes less and less conscious.

Shame internalization has four major consequences. A shame-based identity is formed, the depth of shame is magnified and frozen, autonomous shame activation or functional autonomy results, and finally, internal shame spirals are made operative.

THE SCHOOL SYSTEM

Max went to private religious school through the eighth grade. He then went to a public high school. His school experience itself was fairly typical of most modern schools. Shaming has always been an integral part of the school system. Sitting in the corner with a dunce cap on is a common asso- ciation with school days. Even though most modern forms of education no longer use dunce caps, there are powerful sources of toxic shame still oper- ating in the school system. I taught in three high schools and four universi- ties. I found the educational system to be a major force in solidifying the internalization process of shame-based people.

John Bradshaw

PERFECTIONISM

Perfectionism is a family system rule and a core culprit in creating toxic shame. We see it also in both the religious and cultural systems. *Perfectionism denies healthy shame. It does so by assuming we can be perfect. Such an assumption denies our human finitude because it denies the fact that we are essentially limited.* Perfectionism denies that we will often make mistakes and that it's natural to make mistakes.

Perfectionism is involved whenever we take a norm or *standard* and absolutize it. Once absolutized, the norm becomes the measure of everything else. We compare and judge according to that *standard.*

In school we were compared to the perfect mark. As we failed to make that mark, we were graded on a descending scale, the lowest mark being an F. Think for a moment of the symbolism of the F as a mark. It is associated in mental imagery with the F word. When a child becomes a failure in school, it's not long before there is an association with being a failure as a person—a fuck-up. Children get this association very quickly in school. They also associate "bad" grades with being a bad or defective person. And most often the children who are failing are already shame-based when they come to school. In fact, their shame base often causes their school failure. As they fail in school, their internalized shame deepens. Toxic shame begets toxic shame.

Two of the most fallacious premises of the modern school system are that quantities of time are better than quality, and time is more important than the job to be done.

1. School semesters are longer and longer, as if longer quantities of time will produce more quality results. The opposite is the truth. All effective teachers must bide their time the last two months of school. By then we've taught everything that is humanly possible, and even if we had more time, most kids are at the overflow mark.

2. Schools and prisons are the only places where time is more important than the job to be done. If I set out for New York at the same time you do, and you arrive two hours later than me—you do not *fail New York!* But if we set out to learn algebra in September, and you learn it by June and I don't, I fail algebra.

Max exemplifies another route taken by shame-based children in school. Max followed the lead of his shame-based brother and sister. He became a superachiever in school. He was a straight-A student. Superachievement and perfectionism are two of the leading cover-ups for toxic shame. As paradoxical as it may seem, the straight-A student and the F student may both be driven by toxic shame.

I was a straight-A student. I was also the president of my class from the 7th grade on. In my senior year of high school, I was the editor of the school paper and number six academically. These were parts of my Hero role. How many high school principals would take a student who is senior class president, editor of the school paper and number six academically and tell him he needs help for his internalized shame problems? I was also a card-carrying alcoholic by my senior year in high school.

I started drinking at age fourteen, and I had several blackouts by my senior year. High achievement is often the result of being driven by toxic shame. Feeling flawed and defective on the inside, I had to prove I was okay by being exceptional on the outside. Everything I did was based on getting authenticated on the outside. My good feelings depended upon achievement.

I remember a shame-based client bragging to me that he was worth $1.2 million. This guy was obnoxious. He was brutally abusing his wife by flaunting affairs in front of her. His self-worth was his net worth. This was the only way he had to gauge it. Since he felt flawed on the inside, he had to have verification on the outside.

The school system promotes a shame-based measure of grading people's intelligence. It would be only half bad if such a system really did measure intelligence. I agree with John Holt that the true test of intelligence is not what you know or can regurgitate from memory on an exam. It's not what you know how to do, but "what you do when you don't know what to do." Harold Gardner has convincingly shown that we have eight or nine different kinds of intelligence. Unfortunately we only measure literacy and mathematical intelligence for our IQ.

Perfectionism also spawns destructive competition. Certainly there is a nurturing form of competitiveness. Such competition moves us to do better and expand and grow. But a perfectionistic system like the current school system encourages cheating and creates high levels of distress. Grades are often posted publicly for all eyes to see. And there is shaming exposure when one gets "bad" grades. Even the adjective "bad" lends itself to characterological shame. Each person is pitted against the next in a warfare of endeavor. The communal sense of joint venture and cooperation is lost.

RATIONALISM

Our schools display an enormous bias in educating the mind rather than the whole person. We place major emphasis on reasoning, logic and math, with almost no concern for emotions, intuition and creativity. Our students become memorizing mimics and dull conformists, rather than exciting and feeling creators.

Much work has emerged over the last few decades in studying the right hemisphere of the brain. This side of the brain is the source of "felt thought." Felt thought is the core of music and poetry. The right hemisphere is holistic and intuitive. It uses imagination rather than memory. Students who have a natural propensity for this side of the brain are penalized.

I know of brilliant students who were painfully shamed because of their intuitive and felt ways of knowing. Our rationalistic bias causes the shaming rejection of imagination and emotion. I remember once giving a teacher my "hunch" about a presented problem. I was told that guessing was not the mark of an educated mind. I was sent to the library to get the correct data. All in all our schools shame some of the most vibrant and creative aspects of the human psyche.

This is radically changing as the neuroscientists are showing us the primacy of affect and the emotional brain.

PEER GROUP SHAMING

I remember Arnold. He was a brilliant accountant. He had been viciously shamed in high school. His presenting problem was his criticalness of women. No woman was ever good enough. As his relationship with a woman would intensify, Arnold would start finding fault. He was a nitpicker of great expertise. The outcome of all this was that he was forty years old and fairly successful financially but painfully alone.

Arnold had had some shaming in early childhood from an authoritarian and military-type father. But this was tempered with enough love from his mother to save him from being terribly shame-based during early and middle child-hood. Later on, his family moved to a small town, and Arnold had to start the second semester of his sophomore year in a new high school. The town and the high school were cliquish and moneyed. Arnold was from a rather poor family. He rode the bus to a school where 95 percent of the kids had new cars. Arnold was scapegoated from the moment he set foot in the school. He was laughed at, made fun of and ridiculed by one group of girls. Some days he was hit with water bombs and sacks of horse shit as he waited for the bus. This treatment continued until the middle of his senior year. For two years Arnold suffered almost chronic shaming. This was an excruciating experience.

High school is the time of puberty. And puberty is a time of intense exposure and vulnerability. Whatever toxic shame a person carries from childhood will be tested in high school. Often teenage groups look for a scapegoat, someone everyone can dump and project their shame onto. This was Arnold's fate. He was viciously shamed by his female peer group. This accounted for his problem with women.

The peer group becomes like a new parent. Only this parent is much more rigid and has several sets of eyes to look you over. Physical appear-ance is crucial. Acne and poor sexual development can be excruciating. Conforming to the peer group dress standards is a must if one wants to avoid being shamed. All in all, it can be disastrous if one is not physically or financially endowed.

The elementary school years can also be a source of shame. Children can be terribly cruel. Any gay or lesbian child is especially vulnerable to ridicule. A child with developmental deficits, deformities or who is over-weight is also an easy target. Children will shame other children the way they've been shamed. And if a child is being shamed at home, he will want to pass the hot potato by shaming others. Children like to tease. And teas-ing is a major source of shaming. Teasing is often done by shame-based parents, who transfer their shame by teasing their children. Older siblings can deliver some of the cruelest teasing of all. I have been horrified listen-ing to clients' accounts of being teased by older siblings.

School was perhaps the only place in Max's life where he was not shamed. His toxic shame motivated him to be an achiever. He put himself through graduate school by working at night. He endured tremendous hardships in order to get his degree. It was a place in his life that he felt he accomplished something. Unfortunately, accomplishments do not reduce internalized shame. In fact, the more one achieves, the more one has to achieve. Toxic shame is about being; no amount of doing will ever change it.

THE RELIGIOUS SYSTEM

Max's religious upbringing was rigid and authoritarian. He was taught at any early age that he was born with the stain of sin on his soul and that he was a miserable sinner. He was also taught that God knew his innermost thoughts and was watching everything he did.

An early traumatic experience of shaming occurred when Max was nine years old. A young religious fanatic in his congregation caught Max touching himself in the church bathroom and made an awful scene. He dragged Max into the church and asked him to prostrate himself before the altar and beg God's forgiveness.

Many religious denominations teach the concept of man as wretched and stained with original sin. Original sin as taught by some religious bodies means you are bad from the moment you are born. The teaching of original sin accounts for a lot of the child-rearing practices that are geared toward breaking a child's unruly will and natural propensity toward evil.

GOD AS PUNITIVE

Max often told me he hoped God would forgive him for the evils he had done. And although he had a rather brilliant intellect, he still clung to some rather childish religious beliefs. God somehow kept score, and Max could never catch up. With original sin you're beat before you start.

I often ask myself how anyone could really believe in the fires of hell. Here was Max, whose life was a continuous torment and whose inner voices never stopped their incessant shame spirals, so what more could hell possibly be? Why would a just and loving God want to burn someone like Max for all eternity? Well, Max believed it, and that's what a therapist has to work with. His shame was greatly intensified by his belief that God knew all his inner thoughts and would punish him for his sins.

DENIAL OF SECONDARY CAUSALITY

One of the most insidious and toxically shaming distortions of many religions is the denial of secondary causality. What this means is that according to some church doctrines, the human will is inept. There is *nothing* man can do that is of any value. Of himself, man is a worm. Only when God works through him does man become restored to dignity. But it's never anything that man does of himself.

The theology here is abortive of any true doctrine of Judeo/Christianity. Most mainline interpretations see man as having true secondary causality. Thomas Aquinas, in the prologue to the second part of his *Summa Theologia,* writes, "After our treatise on God, we turn to man, who is God's Image, insofar as man, too, *like God, has the power over his works"* [italics mine].

This is a strong statement of human causality. Man's will is effective. In order to receive grace, man must be willing to accept the gift of faith. After acceptance, man's will plays a major role in the sanctification process.

The abortive interpretation sees man as totally flawed and defective. Of himself, he can only sin. Man is shame-based to the core.

DENIAL OF EMOTIONS

The religious system in general has not given human emotions much press. There are denominations and sects that are highly emotional. And from time to time charismatic renewal groups spontaneously arise to bring vitality and new vigor into the life of a church group. But in general, there's not a lot of permission to show emotions.

I see two basic types of religious structures—one I call the Apollonian and the other the Dionysian. Neither really permits a true and healthy expression of emotion.

The Apollonian type of religion is very rigid, stoic and severe. It can also be very intellectual. In either case, outpourings of emotions are not acceptable.

The Dionysian is the charismatic or cultic type of enthusiastic worship. These types of worship seem to favor free emotional expression, but, in reality, only certain types of emotions can be shown. There are emotional outbursts, but they have no true connection with feelings. The outburst type of religiosity is often a way to get the emotions over with. They are poured out, but the subject does not experience them for long. Honest emotions, especially anger, are not permitted anywhere. The same is true of sexual feelings. Religion has added its voice to sexual shame. Some interpretations of the Protestant Reformers actually imply that original sin was concupiscence or sexual desire. Some religious interpretations equate desire and sexuality with the result that any kind of strong desire is prohibited.

PERFECTIONISM—THE RELIGIOUS SCRIPT

Religion has been a major source of shaming through perfectionism. Moral *shoulds, oughts* and *musts* have been sanctioned by subjective interpretations of religious revelation. The Bible has been used to justify all sorts of blaming judgment. Religious perfectionism teaches a kind of behavioral righteousness. There is a religious script that contains the standards of holiness and righteous behavior. These standards dictate how to talk (there is a proper God voice), how to dress, walk and behave in almost every situation. Departure from this standard is deemed sinful.

What a perfectionistic system creates is a "how to get it right" behavioral script. In such a script one is taught how to act loving and righteous. It's actually more important to *act* loving and righteous than to *be* loving and righteous. The feeling of righteousness and acting sanctimoniously are wonderful ways to mood-alter toxic shame. They are often ways to interpersonally transfer one's shame to others.

WHEN GOD IS A DRUG—RELIGIOUS ADDICTION

Mood alteration is an ingredient of compulsive/addictive behavior. Addiction has been described as "a pathological relationship to any mood-altering experience that has life-damaging consequences." Toxic shame has been suggested as the core and fuel of all addiction. Religious addiction is rooted in toxic shame, which can be readily mood-altered through various religious behaviors. One can get feelings of righteousness through any form of worship. One can fast, pray, meditate, serve others, go through sacramental rituals, speak in tongues, be slain by the Holy Spirit, quote the Bible, read Bible passages, or say the name of Yahweh or Jesus. Any of these can be a mood-altering experience. If one is toxically shamed, such an experience can be immensely rewarding.

The disciples of any religious system can say we are good and others, those not like us, the sinners, are bad. This can be exhilarating to the souls of toxically shamed people.

Righteousness is also a form of *shameless behavior.* Since healthy shame says we can and will inevitably make mistakes (the Bible says the just man will fall seventy times seven), then righteousness becomes a kind of shameless behavior.

All in all the religious system has been a major source of toxic shame for many people.

THE CULTURAL SYSTEM

T. S. Eliot wrote, "This was a decent godless people. Their only monument the asphalt road and a thousand lost golf balls." In this quote from "The Rock," Eliot made a strong indictment on the hopelessness of modern man.

In *Bradshaw On: The Family,* society itself is seen as a sick family system built on the rules of the poisonous pedagogy. These rules deny emotions. This sets us up for the psychic numbing that leads to addiction. These rules of the poisionous pedagogy come from the time of kings. They are nondemocratic and based on a kind of master-slave inequality. They promote obsessive orderliness and obedience. They are rigid and deny vitality. Good children are defined as meek, considerate, unselfish and perfectly law-abiding. Such rules allow no place for vitality, spontaneity, inner freedom, inner independence and critical judgment. These rules cause parents, even well-intentioned ones, to abandon their children. Such abandonment creates the toxic shame I've been describing.

SOCIETY AS COMPULSIVE AND ADDICTED

Our society is highly addictive. We have sixty million sexual abuse victims. Possibly seventy-five million lives are seriously affected by alcoholism, with no telling how many more through other drugs. We have no idea of the actual impact on our economy of the billions of tax-free dollars that come from the illegal drug trade. Over fifteen million families are violent. Some 60 percent of women and 50 percent of men have eating disorders. We have no actual data on work addiction or sexual addictions. I saw a recent quotation that cited thirteen million gambling addicts. If toxic shame is the fuel of addiction, we have a massive problem of shame in our society.

Another indicator of the hopelessness that is rooted in and results from our shame is our feverish overactivism and compulsive lifestyle. Erich Fromm made an extensive diagnosis of this in his book *The Revolution of Hope.* He saw our overactivism as a sign of the restlessness and lack of inner peace that flows from our shame. We are human doings because we have no inner life. Our toxic shame won't let us go inward. It is too painful. It is too hopeless. As Sheldon Kopp says, "We can change what we are doing, but we can't change who we are." If I am flawed and defective as a human person, then there's something wrong with me. I am a mistake. I am hopeless.

THE SUCCESS MYTH

Someone once said, "Success is different at different stages of development—from not wetting your pants in infancy, to being well liked in childhood and adolescence, to getting laid in young adulthood, to making money and having prestige in later adulthood, to getting laid in middle age, to being well liked in old age, to not wetting your pants in senility." What's right about that description is the emphasis on making money, having prestige and being well liked.

Perhaps the greatest modern American literary tragedy is the play *The Death of a Salesman* by Arthur Miller. Miller was able to create a great Aristotelian tragic hero out of an ordinary, common man. Willy Loman is a symbol of the American success myth. He lives his life based on the belief that success is being well liked and making money. Willy dies lonely and destitute, taking his own life in order to get the insurance money that would prove he was successful. In his *Poetics* Aristotle states that the power of a great tragic hero results from the combination of his nobleness coupled with some tragic flaw. Willy is noble. He is willing to die for his faith. It is his faith that is the tragic flaw. He truly believes that if a man makes money and is well liked, he will be a success. This is what it means to make it.

The success myth also preaches a kind of rugged individuality. One is to make it on his own. One is to be self-made and to be one's own man. In this myth, money and its symbols become the measure of how well you make it. A man in his fifties with a low income has to feel the shaming pinch of this belief system. And as much as one might protest all this, money and the fame that goes with it still have enormous power in our lives.

RIGID SEX ROLES

The rigid sex roles still espoused by our society are measuring symbols of perfection. There are real men and real women. Before we were born, there was a blueprint of how to be a man and how to be a woman.

Real men are rugged individuals. They act rather than talk. They are silent and decisive. A real man never shows weakness, emotion or vulnerability. Real men win. They never give their opponent an advantage.

Real women are the helpmates of real men. They are the caregivers of the domestic scene. They are emotional, vulnerable and fragile. They are the peacemakers. In return they look for everlasting "romantic love." They look for a prince who will reward them for all they have given up, the reward being that they will be taken care of for the rest of their lives.

Many believe these roles are a thing of the past. But I suggest that you watch the way parents take care of little boys and little girls. Notice the way we dress the sexes, and above all notice children's toys. Child's play is the precursor of the adult world of work. Children's toys are still highly sexist. Watch the way a liberated mother and father handle their daughter, and then watch the way they handle their son. They won't even touch them the same way.

Our sex role scripts are rigid and divisive. They are also shaming in that they are caricatures of maleness and femaleness. They are overidentifications with parts of us, but fail to allow for completion and wholeness. Each of us is the offspring of a male and a female. Each of us has both male and female hormones. Each sex is determined by the majority of hormones it possesses. And each sex needs to integrate its contrasexual opposite side in order to be complete and whole. The rigid sex roles set standards that disallow wholeness and completion. Such standards shame our contrasexual opposite parts. A man is shamed for seeking to embrace his vulnerability. A woman is designated a bitch for becoming assertive and actualizing her maleness.

THE MYTH OF THE "PERFECT 10"

Our culture presents a physical perfectionistic system that is cruelly shaming to the physically unendowed. The perfect woman or man is a "10."

The perfect 10 has very definite attributes that enhance the sexual shaming that occurs in our society. The perfect 10 woman has perfectly round breasts with matching hips and buttocks. The perfect 10 man has a muscular, tanned and proportionately perfect body. His penis is eight inches plus.

These physical ideals have caused untold suffering and shame to an incredible number of people. I have file after file of men and women who have suffered intense shame over the size of their genitals or breasts. Small to flat-chested women with histories of high school pain and isolation have peopled my counseling office over the last twenty years. Males worried about the size of their penises are commonplace in counseling annals. Sex is either secretive or banal. As banal, bantering about genital and breast sizes is common on the talk shows and in the comic routines of club comedians.

Max was obsessed with the idea that his penis was too small. He also thought himself very unattractive because of a slight scar resulting from being hit in the mouth with a baseball. Max also had acne as an adolescent. All of this physical data added greatly to his pain and shame. And all of this was in spite of the medical data, which Max knew, that the average male genital is five to six inches erect and the absolute fact that women found Max enormously attractive.

Comparing ourselves to the perfect 10 mythical standard is a major source of sexual shame in our society.

DENIAL OF EMOTIONS

Our culture does not handle emotions well. We like folks to be happy and fine. We learn rituals of acting happy and fine at an early age. I can remember many times telling people "I'm fine," when I felt like the world was caving in on me. I often think of Senator Edmund Muskie, who cried on the campaign trail when running for president. From that moment on he was history. We don't want a president who has emotions. We would rather have one who can act! Emotions are certainly not acceptable in the workplace. True expression of emotions that are not "positive" are met with disdain.

THE MYTH OF THE GOOD OL' BOY AND THE NICE GAL

The good ol' boy and the nice gal are a kind of social conformity myth. They create a real paradox when put together with the "rugged individual" part of the success myth. How can I be a rugged individual, be my own man and conform at the same time? Conforming means "don't make waves" or "don't rock the boat." Be a nice gal or a good ol' boy. This means we have to pretend a lot. From *Bradshaw On: The Family*:

We are taught to be nice and polite. We are taught that these behaviors (most often lies) are better than telling the truth. Our churches, schools and politics are rampant with teaching dishonesty (saying things we don't mean and pretending to feel ways we don't feel). We smile when we feel sad, laugh nervously when dealing with grief, laugh at jokes we don't think are funny, tell people things to be polite that we surely don't mean.

Playing roles and acting are forms of lying. If people act like they really feel and it rocks the boat, they are ostracized. We promote pretense and lying as a cultural way of life. Living this way causes an inner split. It teaches us to hide and cover up our toxic shame. This sends us deeper into isolation and loneliness.

4

The Hiding Places
Of Toxic Shame

Where are you, Adam?

According to the book of Genesis, Adam went into hiding after the fall. By trying to be more than human, Adam felt less than human. Before the fall, Adam was not ashamed; after the fall he was. Toxic shame is true agony. It is a pain felt from the inside, in the core of our being. It is excruciatingly painful.

FELT SENSE OF TOXIC SHAME

Toxic shame results from the unexpected exposure of vulnerable aspects of a child's self. This exposure takes place before the child has any ego boundaries to protect herself. Early shaming events happen in a context where the child has no ability to choose. The felt experience of shame is being exposed and seen when one is not ready to be seen. Toxic shame is often manifested in dreams of being naked in inappropriate places or in not being prepared, as in suddenly having to write your final exam without having studied for it.

The unexpected quality of a shaming event creates a lack of self-trust in a child. As toxic shame develops, the child stops trusting his own eyes, judgment, feelings and desires. These faculties form our basic human power. The distrust of our basic faculties results in the feeling of powerlessness. As vulnerable aspects of the self are shamed, they are disowned and separated from our felt sense of self. This self-separation process results in a split self. We are beside ourselves. We become an object to ourselves: When I become an object, I am no longer in me. I am absent from my own experience. What I feel is emptiness and exposure. I have no boundaries and therefore no protection. I must run and hide. But I feel like there is no place to hide since I am totally exposed. They are after me, and they are going to take me by surprise. The hunter is always approaching. There is never a moment when I can relax. I must be constantly guarded lest I'm ever unguarded. I am alone in the most complete way.

The agony of this chronic stage of being cannot be endured for long. At the deepest level, toxic shame triggers our basic automatic defensive cover-ups. Freud called these automatic cover-ups our primary ego defenses. Once these defenses are in place they function automatically and unconsciously, sending our true and authentic selves into hiding. We develop a false identity out of this basic core. We become master impersonators. We avoid our core agony and pain and over a period of years, we avoid our avoidance.

Figure 4.1 gives you a visual picture of the various layers of protection that we use to create our defenses against the core agony of shame. Each layer is progressively less conscious. The deepest layers—our ego defenses, family system roles and scripts—are automatic and unconscious. Each characteristic element of our shields of secrecy seems to have a life of its own.

PRIMARY EGO DEFENSES

Freud was the first to clearly define an automatic process for self-preservation that is activated in the face of severe threat. He calls this process the primary ego defense system. In my book *Creating Love,* I call these ego defenses autohypnotic trances. Understanding ego defenses as trance states has been very helpful to many readers. All of us need to use these defenses from time to time. They were intended by nature to be situational rather than chronic.

A child's ego is undifferentiated at birth. Each child needs to develop boundaries and ego strengths. Children need their ego defenses more than adults. They need them until they can develop good boundaries. To develop

FIGURE 4.1
Layers of Defense Against
the Agony of Internalized Shame

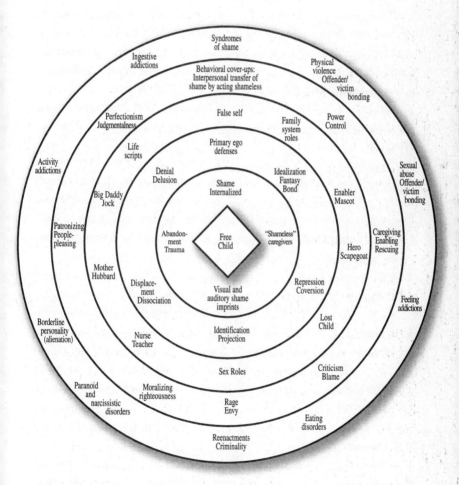

strong ego boundaries, children need parents with strong boundaries. No shame-based parent has these. Toxic shame greatly damages our boundaries. Without strong boundaries for protection, a child cannot thrive. Having damaged boundaries is like living in a house without locks on the doors.

Along with their egocentricism, nature provides children with primary ego defenses to take the place of boundaries. Each ego defense allows the child to survive situations that are actually intolerable.

DENIAL AND FANTASY BONDING

Perhaps the most elementary ego defense is denial. In the face of threat, people deny what is going on, or they deny the hurt of what is going on or the impact on their lives of what is going on.

Robert Firestone has elaborated on Freud's notion of denial. He describes the most fundamental ego defense as the fantasy bond. The fantasy bond is an illusion of connectedness that the child creates in relation to the primary caregiver, who is shaming her.

Paradoxically, the more a child is violated, the more she creates the fantasy bond. Bonding to abuse is one of the most perplexing aspects of shame inducement. Abuse is usually unpredictable, a sort of random shock. Abuse lowers one's self-value and induces shame. As one loses more and more self-respect, one's world of choices and alternatives is diminished.

Children must have secure attachment bonds. When they do not have such a bond, they create it. The fantasy bond (really bondage) is the illusion that someone is there for them, someone who loves and protects them. The fantasy bond is like a mirage in the desert. Once set up, the denying fantasy bond functions automatically and unconsciously. Years later, when reality is no longer life-threatening, the fantasy bond remains. This explains why abandoned (abused) children are described as having a *compulsion* to protect their parents.

NUMBING OUT

Any intolerable event is signaled by strong emotions. Emotions are a form of energy in motion. They signal us of a loss, a threat or a satiation.

Sadness is about losing something we cherish. Anger and fear are signal of actual or impending threats to our well-being. Joy signals that we are fulfilled and satisfied. Whenever a child is shamed through some form of abandonment, feelings of anger, hurt and sadness arise. Since shame-based parents are shame bound in all their emotions, they cannot tolerate their children's emotions. Therefore, they shame their children's emotions. When their emotions are shamed, children numb out, so they don't feel their emotions. It is not clear exactly how the mechanism of numbing out works. It certainly has to do with tensing muscles, changing breathing patterns and fantasizing abandonment. Once an emotion is toxically shame bound, one feels numb. The emotional avoidance is sealed by *learning to avoid the avoidance.*

DISSOCIATION

Dissociation is the ego defense that accompanies the most violent forms of shaming—sexual and physical violence. The trauma is so great and the fear so terrifying that one needs instant relief. Dissociation is a form of instant numbing. It involves denial and regression but includes strong elements of distracting imagination.

An incest victim simply goes away during the experience of violation—like a long daydream. The same is true of physical violence. The pain and humiliating shame are unbearable—the victim leaves her body.

This is the reason these forms of victimization are so difficult to treat. The memories are screened while the feelings remain. The victim often feels crazy, like she is living in unreality. The victim often has a split (sometimes multiple) personality. Because the connection between the violence and the response to violence has been severed, the victim thinks the craziness and shame are about her, rather than about what has happened to her.

Dissociation is not limited to sexual and physical violation. Emotional battering, severe trauma and chronic distress are also precipitating factors in dissociation. Dissociation can last a lifetime.

DISPLACEMENT

Displacement is closely connected to dissociation.

A client of mine, whose alcoholic father used to come into her room and violate her shortly after the bars closed, frequently woke up about 3:00 A.M. and saw a shadowy figure in her room. She also had a recurring nightmare of a black monster who poked her and punched her with his black thumb. When she came for therapy she made no mention of being an incest victim. She had a history of being sexually used by considerably older men.

She was only twenty-six at the time she began her therapy. On her second visit, she began shame-faced sobbing, describing how her father forced her to engage in fellatio. She reconstructed a two-and-a-half year trauma beginning at about age four-and-a-half. She was her dad's favorite. He threatened her with severe punishment if she told anyone. He also gave her the only warmth and attention she experienced in the family. She also discovered that her father had sexually violated her two younger sisters. It took her a long time to fully connect her emotions with the events. Once she did, her shadowy displacement and her black-thumbed monster disappeared from her dreams.

DEPERSONALIZATION

Closely related to displacement is depersonalization.

Depersonalization is a behavioral manifestation of being violated. It happens most often in the context of a significant other, with whom the individual no longer perceives the reality of her own subjective self. She experiences herself as an object. This results in the loss of awareness of inner experience. As violation continues, the individual no longer perceives the reality of her self or her environment.

IDENTIFICATION

When victimization takes place the victim often identifies with the persecutor. By so doing the victim no longer feels the helplessness and the shame of humiliation of the victimization. Persecuting offenders were often previously victims who identified with their offenders. In identifying they no longer have to feel the shame.

CONVERSION

I spoke of affect and need conversion when I described how Max compensated for his abusive and neglectful abandonment by converting most of his feelings and needs into sexual thoughts, feelings and behaviors. There are other ways that conversion defends us against toxic shame.

FEELING RACKETS

I've already explained how in the process of internalizing shame, vital parts of our human reality are disowned. The split-off parts of our internal experiences (our feelings, needs and drives) clamor for expression. They are like our hungry dogs locked in the basement. We must find some means to quiet them. One way is through feeling conversion. In feeling conversion, we convert what is forbidden or shameful into another more acceptable or tolerable feeling.

We have already seen this with the feelings of sexuality. Other feelings can be used to replace our shame-bound feelings. Anger is often blocked from conscious awareness and converted into more tolerable or family-authorized feelings, such as hurt or guilt. The person feeling anger no longer feels it; he feels the acceptable feeling.

Three-year-old Herkamer is furious because his mother promised to take him to Baskin-Robbins and is now backing out. Herkamer storms and stomps, telling his mom (as three-year-olds are wont to do) that he hates her. Mom is a shame-based codependent. She is terrified of anger, her own and anyone else's. Herkamer's anger triggers her own anger toward her own parents. Since this anger is bound in guilt and shame, she stops herself from feeling her shame by guilting and shaming Herkamer.

She tells him how hurt she feels when he is angry at her. She begins to cry, since she learned to convert her anger into sadness as a little girl. Crying when feeling angry is a common female *feeling racket*.

A scene from Mom's childhood went as follows: Her dad was angry because she wouldn't stop playing in her room and get to sleep. When he expressed his anger, she started sobbing. Dad felt bad and picked her up and started stroking her. He gave her a glass of cold juice and rocked her to sleep. As a little girl Herkamer's mom learned that sadness is acceptable and gives her power. Anger did not work in her family. When Herkamer tells her he hates her, she cries, telling him that maybe someday she won't be home when he wants her.

Poor Herkamer is devastated. His abandonment, terror and separation anxiety are triggered. He rushes to his mom, feeling terrible guilt. His awareness of his anger is completely lost. His anger has been converted into guilt.

Sometimes parents react with anger to their children's expression of anger, fear or sadness. When this happens the child's feelings are either bound in shame or are converted into fear or terror.

My own feeling of anger was dominated by fear much of my life. When I felt anger, it was immediately converted into fear to the point of terror. Even when I could express the anger, my lips would quiver, my voice would crack and my body would tremble. Eric Berne, the founder of Transactional Analysis (TA), called this feeling "conversion process." I'm describing a "racket formation." *A racket is a family-authorized feeling used to replace an unacceptable and shameful feeling.*

SOMATIC CONVERSION

A third form of conversion is the conversion of needs and feelings into some form of bodily or somatic expression. Needs and feelings can be changed into bodily sickness.

When one is sick, one is usually cared for. When one is sick, one can feel as bad as one really feels. This conversion dynamic is especially prevalent in family systems where sickness is given attention and rewarded.

I was asthmatic as a child. Frequently when I wanted to miss a day of school, I would induce an asthma attack. I learned early on that sickness got a lot of sympathy in my family system. Getting attention with sickness is a very common phenomenon. When people want to miss work, they call in sick. Sickness works!

Conversion of feelings into sickness is the basis of psychosomatic illness. In Max's family there were several generations of hypochondriasis. His maternal great-grandmother was bedridden off and on for years. His maternal grandmother was literally bedridden for forty-five years, and his mom, Felicia, continually struggled with ulcers, colitis and arthritis. Max himself obsessed on illness a lot.

My own belief is that families don't convert feelings and needs to actual physical illness unless there are predisposing genetically based factors, such as a genetic history of asthma, arthritis or particular organ weakness. When parental modeling and high rewards for somatic illness are added to a genetic predisposition, the conversion of feelings and needs into bodily or somatic expression is a real possibility.

PROJECTION

Projection is one of the most primitive defense mechanisms. Its most dramatic forms of manifestation are psychotic delusions and hallucinations. Once we are shamed-based, projection is inevitable. Once we've disowned our feelings, wishes, needs and drives, they clamor for expression. They are vital parts of ourselves.

One way to handle them is to attribute them to others. If my own anger is disowned, I may project it onto you. I may ask you why you are angry.

A female client of mine hated other women. She was especially vehement about very sexy women. My client was the supervisor of a group of hard-nosed, redneck, front-line superintendents in a chemical plant. Her father was a macho chauvinist who shamed his wife at home and in public. As a young girl growing up, my client had been a tomboy. She had identified with her father. She was his fishing and hunting buddy. At ten she could "shoot a gun as well as any man," her dad would brag. This woman completely rejected and disowned her femininity and her sexuality. She would project her own internal shaming onto other women, verbally disdaining them for their sexuality and femininity.

Projection is used when repression fails. It is a major source of conflict and hostility in human relationships. Projection is the basis for children considering their parents omnipotent. Children are one with the world. Christopher Morley's poem "To a Child" describes children as:

Born comrade of bird, beast and tree
And unselfconscious as the bee . . .
Elate explorer of each sense
Without dismay, without pretense . . .

This animism and omnipotence are parts of children's egocentricity.

They easily project this onto their parents. Parents are gods—they are omnipotent.

Such projected omnipotence is another way to understand the potential for shame in the parent-child mutual bond. Gods are perfect. If an abusing transaction takes place in the parental relationship, it can't be the parent's problem (God is perfect); it must be the child's.

SECONDARY EGO DEFENSES

Freud described other, secondary, ego defenses. These take over when the primary process defenses seem to fail. This is especially true of repression.

For example, a shameful feeling may begin to surface. It is frightening, so the person mobilizes a secondary line of defense. Secondary defenses that are often used when primary ones fail are: inhibition, reactive formation, undoing, isolation of affect and turning against self.

1. **Inhibition.** A reclusive client of mine was paralyzed and unable to move whenever he went to a club and tried to dance. He remembered an incident about dancing when he was twelve years old. His mother was a periodic alcoholic. One night she came home partially drunk. She playfully put on some music and invited her son to dance with her, which he did. He was awkward, and she was shaming to him. During one part of the dancing, my client had an erection. His mother noticed it and teased him about it. He was shamed to the core. His later inability to dance was an example of the ego defense of inhibition. By inhibiting the muscles he used to dance, he safeguarded himself against the possible experiencing of shame.

2. **Reactive Formation.** Reactive formation is used to ensure that a repressed, disturbing feeling that would trigger shame is kept out of conscious awareness. Reactive formation is used when repression seems to be weakening. The trait of kindness is often developed to counteract an impulse of cruelty. To be cruel would induce shame. The exact opposite of cruelty is kindness. Kindness ensures that one will not be cruel and therefore can avoid feeling shame. A reactive formation always has some of the characteristics of the very impulse

whose expression it is designed to prevent. Commenting on this, White and Gilliland write in *Elements of Psychopathology*:

> The trait of kindness . . . will have a rigid and inappropriate quality to it. It will be imposed on others under all circumstances, whether or not warranted. . . . it will have a coercive and thinly sadistic quality. The person who exhibits such reactive kindness is a person who *kills with kindness.*

3. **Undoing.** Undoing is a magical behavior aimed at canceling out a feeling, thought or behavior that one fears will cause shame or has actually caused shame.

   One student I counseled spent an excessive amount of time in elaborate study rituals. He was brilliant, but failing in college because of these rituals. He would spend hours before he started to study lining up his books, pens, pencils, note pad, etc., until he achieved a certain complicated pattern. Each item had to be positioned so as not touch any other item. This was most important in relation to his rather large collection of books.

   During the time of counseling with him I noticed a general pattern of touch avoidance. He had been severely shamed as a little boy for touching and showing off his penis when the minister came to call. On a subsequent occasion he was caught masturbating by his mother and spanked abusively for it. He was subsequently told he would go blind if he ever truly masturbated. (So was I, but during my adolescence I was willing to risk it.)

   My client's elaborate nontouching ritual was a magical way of undoing his wish to touch his penis and masturbate.

4. **Isolation of Affect.** Isolation of affect is a way to convert a shame-engendering feeling or impulse into a thought. By so doing the person can disown any responsibility for the feeling or impulse.

   I once read a case of an incest victim who was obsessed with the thought of "fucking Jesus." She was a perfectly proper Christian lady. She was also quite intelligent and realized the absurdity of the idea.

   She had been incested for four years by an uncle who was the only paternal figure she had had in her life. He had come into her life when she was six years old. Her mother worked and left her with a maid who was rigidly religious and judgmental. This maid emotionally battered the child. My client once expressed angry disbelief about the maid's religious teaching and was deeply shamed for it. She had also felt rage at her uncle. Yet she had deeply loved him as a child. He was the only one who showed her affection and gave her gifts. None of these conflicts had been worked out: her rage, her guilt and shame, her love for her uncle's paternal care. Since she had not worked all this out, it came together in a recurring thought of "fucking Jesus." The thought just occurred *without any feeling.* The thought distracted her from her painful and shamefully confusing feelings.

This is a rather dramatic example of confused feelings being converted in a thought pattern. *Any mental preoccupation can distract one from one's feelings.*

5. **Turning Against Self.** Turning against self is an ego defense whereby a person deflects hostile aggression from another person and directs it onto self. This defense is extremely common among people who have been abandoned through severe abuse. Because a child so desperately needs his parents for survival, he will turn his aggressive rage about his abuse into abuse of himself. The extreme form of this is suicide. In such cases (the French call it self-murder), the person so identifies with the offender that he is killing the offender by killing himself.

Common but less intense examples include nail biting, head banging, accident proneness and self-mutilation. In later life people may injure themselves socially or financially. In all cases the rage at the offender is so fearful and shameful it is turned against self.

The power and strength of ego defenses lies in the fact that they are automatic and unconscious. They were the best decisions available to you at the time. And they kept you sane. They literally saved your life. The very defenses that were once life-giving later on become the preservers of our toxic shame.

THE FALSE SELF

I spoke earlier about the rupture of the self as the deepest cut of internalized shame. Once internalized, we no longer have the feeling of shame—we are it. Because we experience ourselves as flawed and defective, we cannot look at ourselves without pain. Therefore we must create a false self. The false self is the second layer of defense erected to alleviate the felt sense of toxic shame.

All major schools of therapy speak about this false self. The Jungians call it the "persona" (the mask). The TA people call it the "adapted child."

Bob Subby speaks of the "public self," which he contrasts with the "private self." He uses an excellent drawing to illustrate the point. Figure 4.2 is an adaptation of Bob's drawing. The tiny little figure that gets smaller and smaller is the shame-based authentic self. The larger figure is the false or public self.

I divide the false self into three categories:

1. The cultural false self
2. Life scripts
3. The family system roles

The Cultural False Self

In a previous section I outlined our cultural sex roles, pointing out how these roles set up a perfectionistic system of measurement. Since each of us is utterly unique and unrepeatable, there is no way to compare us or measure us. In this way our rigid sex roles are shaming.

It's important to see the dynamics of how sex roles come into being. Sociologists describe the process with the phrase "the social construction of reality." As we understand this social construction process, it is easier to see how we can readily identify with these roles and make them our false selves.

FIGURE 4.2
Shame Internalization
Adaptation of Robert Subby's Private Self/Public Self

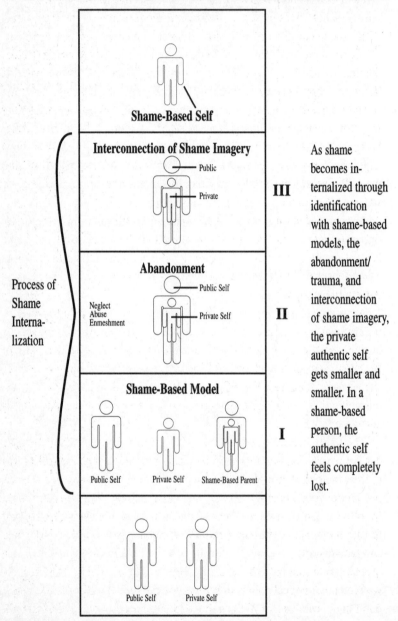

Process of Shame Internalization

Shame-Based Self

Interconnection of Shame Imagery
Public
Private
III

Abandonment
Public Self
Neglect Abuse Enmeshment
Private Self
II

Shame-Based Model
Public Self Private Self Shame-Based Parent
I

Public Self Private Self

As shame becomes internalized through identification with shame-based models, the abandonment/trauma, and interconnection of shame imagery, the private authentic self gets smaller and smaller. In a shame-based person, the authentic self feels completely lost.

Chart adapted from Robert Subby's *Lost in the Shuffle: The Co-dependent Reality*

THE SOCIAL CONSTRUCTION OF REALITY

Each of us is born into a social order that has already arrived at a "consensus reality." This phrase is used by sociologists to describe the product of our social construction of reality. Human beings are creatures of habit.

As we humans act in repetitious ways, necessitated by circumstances relating to survival, these repetitions become habitual. These habitual behaviors soon become socially acceptable ways of behaving. They are socially agreed upon. After a while these socially agreed upon habitual ways of behaving become what sociologist's term "legitimized." After being legitimized for a while, they become unconscious. The unconscious legitimizations gradually evolve into *laws of reality*. We no longer question them. We accept them: they are predictable. They ensure our security. If someone tries to change them, we get very upset.

In fact, they are not reality at all. As cultural anthropologists have continuously pointed out, other cultures often do things quite differently. The laws of reality that emerged from our legitimized habituations are actually a "consensus reality." The consensus reality is what we've all agreed on as constituting reality.

A prominent part of every culture's consensus reality is its notion of what a man is, what a woman is, and what a marriage and family are. At birth it was already decided how you and I must be and behave in order to be a real man or a real woman. These stereotyped roles are perfect for shame-based identities. When I play the role of a real man, I receive generous cultural rewards. These stereotyped roles often shame the parts of our authentic self that do not correspond to the role ideal.

I certainly believe in some biological grounding in the sexes. But our current sex roles go far beyond biological grounding. They are caricatures of their biological ground. As I pointed out before, they also deny the obvious androgynous polarity in every man and woman. Each of us resulted from the union of male and female. Each of us embodies both male and female hormones. A healthy person is a balance between so-called male and female traits.

These roles not only shame us but they become our refuge of hiding. As we pretend to be real men and women, we can hide the fact that we really don't know who we are. We can mood-alter by playing our role to the hilt.

In the mood alteration of being a real man or woman, we can avoid our painful shame.

LIFE SCRIPTS

Eric Berne, the founder and original creator of transactional analysis, developed the notion of life scripts. He observed the fact that a part of the population lives very tragic lives. Their lives are tragic because they seem to have no choice. They are like actors playing their roles according to a script. Berne felt that the majority of the population acted out banal or melodramatic lives. The melodramatic scripts were described by Thoreau when he said that the mass of humanity live lives of quiet desperation. Berne felt that very few people live truly authentic lives.

Life scripts are like the scripts for a movie or a play. They describe a certain type of character. They proscribe what he is to feel and not feel and how he is to behave in life. Tragic scripts usually end in killing someone or oneself, or living out one's life in a form of chronic suicide, or being considered crazy.

Claude Steiner, the TA therapist, speaks of three basic tragic scripts: the *no mind* (crazy) script, *no love* (kill someone or yourself) script, and the *no feel* (addictions) script. These tragic scripts are set up through the shaming of our basic powers: to know, love and feel.

The formation of scripts is complicated. The core mechanism of the process occurs by means of choices resulting from injunctions and attributions, script modeling, and life experiences.

INJUNCTIONS

Injunctions come from the shame-based child in the parent. Injunctions are usually nonverbal. They take the form of "don't be" messages: don't be a girl; don't be a boy; don't be important or successful. All toxic scripts have the injunction "Don't be you." An injunction shames the authentic self and causes self-rupture.

ATTRIBUTIONS

Attributions are more conscious and usually come from verbal emotional abuse. Messages like "How can you be so dumb or stupid?" or "What do you use for brains?" sets one up for the no mind script. Messages like "You really love your brother, don't you?" or "That's not my little boy who is acting hateful," sets one up to never know what his own feelings of love are. Messages like "I know you're not really angry," or "There's nothing to cry about," discount one's feelings and cause confusion.

Attributes can come directly, as when Mom is talking to her friend and says of your brother, "He's my well-behaved child," and of you, "She's my little hellion." Other types of parental attribution messages are:

- You're always going to have trouble with your studies, weight, anger, etc.
- You're never going to amount to anything.
- You've always been selfish. God help the person you marry.
- Every man in this family has been a lawyer.
- No woman in our family has ever been divorced.

Script messages tell us the way we are or what role we are supposed to play in life. They shame who we authentically are and create self-rupture.

MODELS

I've already covered parental models as part of the dynamics of shame internalization. Script models are not limited to parents. They could come from fairy tales, movies, TV, or other actual cultural or family models. Women who had unavailable, abusive fathers might magically identify with *Beauty and the Beast* and act out that fairy tale over and over by marrying beastly men.

Women are often given the magical belief that if they wait long enough, their prince will come. Magic plays a part in many shame-based people's lives. Hiding behind fantasies of "someday," "if only," and "when," a person may live out his life waiting for a fairy godmother or godfather. The fantasy bond sets people up for magical transferences to other fantasy bonds.

LIFE EXPERIENCES

A person's experiences help shape the script. What is happening in the family is a major factor in script formation. If Mom's an alcoholic, a child may take on a helper or rescuing role. As the child experiences attention and praise for this role, it becomes a strong element in sealing the script as a rescuer. Another child might get lots of attention for being sickly. This may contribute to a script that embodies lifelong sickness. Children growing up in a shame-based, dysfunctional family may learn to experience anxiety and distress as a way of life. Later they may feel uncomfortable if things are going too well.

FAMILY SYSTEM ROLES

All families have roles. The father and mother play their roles of modeling what it is to be a man or woman, father or mother. Parents also model how to be intimate, have boundaries, cope with problems, fight fair, problem-solve, etc. The role of children is to be curious and to be learners. Members of a healthy family have flexible roles. Mom may be the heroine because she baked a special cake. Daughter may take over that role when she volunteers to do the dishes. Son becomes the hero when he notices smoke coming out the stove and prevents a fire. Dad's the hero when he takes the family on a vacation.

I have already described the dysfunctional family system roles in some detail. Ask yourself, "How did I function in my family? What role did I play to keep the family together?"

In our Center for Recovering Families in Houston we have discovered a large number of family system roles in addition to the roles I've discussed. Some other roles are Parent's Parent, Dad or Mom's Buddy, Family Counselor, Dad's Star, Mom's Star, Perfect One, Saint, Mom or Dad's Enabler, Rascal, Cute One, Athlete, Family Peacemaker, Family Referee, Family Sacrifice, Religious One, Winner, Loser, Martyr, Super Mom, Super Spouse, Clown, Super Dad, Chief Enabler, Genius, Mom or Dad's Scapegoat.

We suggest that people really work at getting a feeling for the role(s) they played by putting a name on it. You may find that you played several roles. Each role has a felt sense, and the felt sense of the role will stay with you even if you give it up. You may have been the baby. You were cute and quickly became the family Mascot. Two years later your little brother came along and knocked you out of a job. You will retain the felt sense of being a Mascot. What is important to underscore is that when we play roles, we put aside our true and authentic selves. *The role is a false self.* In dysfunctional family systems the roles are necessitated by the needs of the family system in its attempt to balance itself in the wake of the primary stressor. The primary distress may be Dad's alcoholism, Mom's pill addiction or eating disorder, Dad's violence, incest, Mom's religious addiction, etc. Each role is a way to handle the family distress and shame. Each role is a way for each member to feel like he has some control. As one plays the role more and more rigidity sets in. As one becomes more and more unconscious of one's true self, one's self-rupture increases. The shame that promotes the role is intensified by the role. What a paradox! The roles are necessitated by the family system's shame as ways to overcome the shame, and they in fact freeze and enhance the shame. The old French proverb applies here: The more you try to change, the more it stays the same.

The most important thing to say about the roles is that they don't work. My being a Hero has done absolutely nothing to change my shame-based family system. Max's playing his Scapegoat and Lost Child role did nothing to change his family system's dysfunction.

The power of these roles for a shame-based person is their rigidity and predictability. Staying in the role gives one a sense of identity and control. Even the Scapegoat can be somebody. This is why roles are so hard to give up, especially the Hero, Caregiver, Superachiever or Star type of roles. They are mood altering. One feels good being a caregiver. How could I be flawed and defective when I'm taking care of all these people?

I can remember saying this to myself when I had a counseling load of fifty people a week. What I couldn't grasp is that there is no way to change your being by your doing. The shame-based core cries out, "You're flawed and defective! There's something wrong with you!" All the doing in the world won't change that.

The dysfunctional family system roles are ways we lose our reality. Over a period of time the fact that we are playing a role becomes unconscious. We believe we are the *persona* that the role calls for. We believe the role-designated feelings are our feelings. *The role literally becomes addictive.*

THE CHARACTEROLOGICAL STYLES
OF SHAMELESSNESS

A third layer of protection against the felt sense of toxic shame is acting "shameless." This is a common pattern for shame-based parents, teachers, preachers of righteousness and politicians. Acting shameless embodies several behaviors that alter the feeling of shame and interpersonally transfer one's toxic shame to another person. The transactional theorists call this passing the "hot potato."

These characterological styles of shamelessness include perfectionism, striving for power and control, rage, arrogance, criticism and blame, judgmentalness and moralizing, contempt, patronization, caregiving and helping, envy, people-pleasing and being nice. Each behavior focuses on another person and takes the heat off oneself.

PERFECTIONISM

Perfectionism flows from the core of toxic shame. A perfectionist has no sense of healthy shame; he has no internal sense of limits. Perfectionists never know how much is good enough.

Perfectionism is learned when one is valued only for doing. When parental acceptance and love are dependent upon performance, perfectionism is created. The performance is always related to what is outside the self. The child is taught to strive onward. There is never a place to rest and have inner joy and satisfaction.

Perfectionism always creates a superhuman measure by which one is compared. And no matter how hard one tries, or how well one does, one never measures up. Not measuring up is translated into a comparison of good versus bad, better versus worse. Good and bad lead to moralizing and judgmentalism. Perfectionism leads to comparison making. Kaufman writes: "When perfectionism is paramount, the comparison of self with others inevitably ends in the self feeling the lesser for the comparison."

Comparison making is one of the major ways that one continues to shame oneself internally. One continues to do to oneself on the inside what was done on the outside. Judgment and comparison making lead to a destructive kind of competitiveness. Competition aims at outdoing others, rather than simply being the best one can be. Competing to be better than others is mood altering and becomes addictive.

STRIVING FOR POWER AND CONTROL

Striving for power is a way to control others. Power is a form of control. Control is the grandiose will disorder I've already discussed. Those who must control everything fear being vulnerable. Why? Because to be vulnerable opens one up to being shamed.

All my life I used up my energies by always having to be guarded. This was a mighty waste of time and energy. The fear was that I would be exposed. And when exposed, all would see that I was flawed and defective as a person—an imposter.

Control is a way to ensure that no one can ever shame us again. It involves controlling our own thoughts, expressions, feelings and actions. And it involves attempting to control other people's thoughts, feelings and actions. Control is the ultimate villain in destroying intimacy. We cannot share freely unless we are equal. When one person controls another, equality is ruptured.

We need to control because our toxic shame drives us outside ourselves. We objectify ourselves and experience ourselves as lacking and defective. Therefore, we must move out of our own house.

The striving for power flows from the need to control. Achieving power is a direct attempt to compensate for the sense of being defective. When one has power over others, one becomes less vulnerable to being shamed. Power seeking often becomes a total dedication and life task. In its most neurotic form it is an out-and-out addiction. Individuals spend all their energies planning, scheming, gaming and jockeying for position in order to climb the ladder of success. Power is inherent in certain roles or positions. Such roles are often sought as jobs to cover up shame.

"If I can just gut it out and be a doctor," one client told me, "then no one can ever look down on me again."

Parents, teachers, doctors, lawyers, preachers, rabbis and politicians are roles that carry inherent power.

Those in the power game always attempt to maximize power in relation to others. They often strive for inherent power jobs and secure their position by finding people who are less secure and weaker to work for them. To share power is precisely what such people are unable to do.

For the power addict, power is the way to insulate against any further shaming. One can, through having power over others, reverse the role of early childhood.

The power strategy often includes using power to actively seek revenge. Shame-based parents do to their children what their own parents did to them. They reenact their own victimization on their own children—this time as offender. Investigation of the parent's own childhood reveals that they were also abandoned and abused, often in exactly the same way.

RAGE

Rage is probably the most naturally occurring cover-up for shame. It comes close to being an actual primary ego defense. It would be, except for the fact that not all children rage. Some children will express rage when they are shamed; others will suppress it and sometimes turn it against themselves.

When rage is used as a defense, it becomes a characterological style. Rage protects in two ways: either by keeping others away or by transferring the shame to others. People who have held their rage in often become bitter and sarcastic. They are not pleasant to be around.

Although the rage, expressed as hostility or bitterness, was originally intended to protect the self against further experiences of shame, it becomes internalized. Rage becomes a state of being, rather than a feeling among many other feelings.

Internalized rage foments a deep bitterness within the self. Bitterness destroys the self with its myopic vision and its quest for negativity. Rage often intensifies into hatred. If the person with internalized rage also acquires power, then it can result in violence, revenge, vindictiveness and criminality.

ARROGANCE OR PRIDE

Arrogance or pride is defined as offensively exaggerating one's own importance. The proud, arrogant person alters her mood by means of her exaggeration. The victims of arrogance are those who are unequal in power, knowledge or experience. The victim feels inadequate around the know-it-all, be-all, proudly arrogant person. He believes he is inadequate because of his lack of knowledge, experience or power. Anyone who is on the arrogant person's same level simply sees her as arrogant.

Arrogance is a way for a person to cover up shame. After years of arrogance, the arrogant person is so out of touch, she truly doesn't know who she is. *This is one of the great tragedies of shame cover-ups: not only does the person hide from others, she also hides from herself.*

CRITICISM AND BLAME

Criticism and blame are perhaps the most common ways that shame is interpersonally transferred. If I feel put down and humiliated, I can reduce this feeling by criticizing and blaming someone else. As I go into detail about how another has failed, I get out of my shameful feeling (mood-alter).

Criticism and blame are defense strategies against toxic shame. They are effective mood alterers and become addictive over long periods of continued use. Children subject to criticism and blame are shamed to the core. Children have no way to decode their parents' defensive behavior. Mom yelling, "You never think of anyone but yourself," is interpreted as "I am bad." Mom may be ashamed over the state of her life, marriage and house. Instead of saying, "I feel sad and frustrated over the state of things right now," she says, "You never think of anyone but yourself." While criticizing and blaming, Mom is relieved from her toxic shame, but is acting shameless. When parents act shameless, their children have to take on their parents' toxic shame.

JUDGMENTALISM AND MORALIZING

Judgmentalism and moralizing are offshoots of perfectionism. Moralizing and judgmentalism are ways to win a victory over the spiritual competition. Condemning others as bad or sinful is a way to feel righteous. Such a feeling is a powerful mood alteration and can become highly addictive.

When one is using perfectionism, moralizing and judgment to mood-alter one's own shame, one is acting shameless. The children who are the victims of perfectionism, judgment and moralizing have to carry their shameless caregiver's shame. This is not only emotionally abusive and soul murdering, *it is spiritually abusive,* since only God is perfect. God alone is shameless. *To act shameless is to play God.* Children of shameless parents are given a distorted foundation for experiencing God.

CONTEMPT (DISGUST)

In contempt, one is intensely conscious of another person who is experienced as disgusting. In contempt, the self of the other is completely rejected. Parents, teachers and moralizing preachers often act shameless in behaving contemptuously toward children, students and disciples. When a major caregiver or teacher contempts another person under her tutelage, that person experiences himself as offensive and feels rejected in no uncertain terms.

The child learns to condemn self in introjecting the caregiver's voice and in identifying with the condemning caregiver. The child lacks any means of protection. Identification allows the child to feel protected. The child condemns others as he has been condemned.

PATRONIZING

To patronize is to support, protect or champion someone who is unequal in benefits, knowledge or power, but who has not asked for your support, protection or championing. Being patronizing leaves the other person feeling shame. The interpersonal transfer of shame through patronization is very subtle. On the surface you seem to be helping the other person through support and encouragement, yet in reality the helping doesn't really help.

Patronizing is a cover-up for shame and usually hides contempt and passive-aggressive anger.

CAREGIVING AND HELPING

Strange as it seems, taking care of and helping another person often intensifies her shame. Caregiver is a common family system role. The caregiver actually doesn't help the other person. Helpers are always helping themselves.

A person who feels flawed and defective feels powerless and helpless. Such a person can alter her feelings of defectiveness by helping and taking care of others. When she is caregiving others, she feels good about herself. So the goal of the caregiver is the caregiving, not the good of the person being cared for. The caregiving is an activity that distracts one from one's feelings of inadequacy. Distraction is a way to mood-alter.

Caregiving and helping as defensive strategies against toxic shame lead to enabling or rescuing. A caregiving spouse of an alcoholic actually enables the alcoholic's disease, thereby increasing his toxic shame. Parents often enable or rescue their children, doing for them what they could do for themselves. The children wind up feeling inadequate and defective. Rescuing or enabling is robbery. It robs the other person of a sense of achievement and power, thereby increasing toxic shame.

PEOPLE-PLEASING AND BEING NICE

People-pleasing nice guys and sweethearts also act shameless and pass their shame on to others. In their book *Creative Aggression,* doctors George Bach and Herb Goldberg outline in detail the neurotic behavior of being a nice people-pleaser.

In many ways being "nice" is the official cultural cover-up for toxic shame. The nice guy is as American as motherhood and apple pie. The nice person hides behind a defensive facade of being a friendly, well-liked person.

The goal of the nice person is his own image, not the other person. Being nice is primarily a way of manipulating people and situations. By doing so, he avoids any real emotional contact and intimacy. By avoiding intimacy, he can ensure that no one will see him as he truly is: shame-based, flawed and defective.

Bach and Goldberg sum up the price of being nice. It is self destructive and indirectly shaming to others because it is hostile. The nice guy:

1. Tends to create an atmosphere wherein no one can give any honest feedback. This blocks his emotional growth.
2. Stifles the growth of others, since he never gives any honest feedback. This deprives others of a real person to assert against. Others feel guilt and shame for feeling angry at the nice guy. The other turns his aggression against himself, generating shame.
3. Nice behavior is unreal; it puts severe limitations on any relationship.

ENVY

Perhaps Richard Sheridan was right when he observed, "There is no passion so strongly rooted in the human heart as envy." Dante named envy as one of the deadly sins. One classical writer wrote, "Envy is the pain of mind that successful men cause their neighbors."

The most common definition of envy is "discomfort at the excellence or good fortune of another." Such discomfort is frequently accompanied by some verbal expression of belittlement. However, the expressions of envy can rage from out-and-out disparagement to subtle innuendo. The latter is what makes envy so mysterious.

Because of this talent for disguise, envy takes forms that are impossible to recognize. An envious person may conceal his envy both from others and himself.

I can remember hearing a public speaker who I have been compared to. I was truly impressed by the power and energy of his delivery and message. Later, when recounting this to others, I heard myself say, "I really liked his power and energy . . . although I must admit I was surprised at how often he had to read from his notes." If you had asked me to take an oath pertaining to whether I was envious or not, I would have vowed that I was not envious and passed the oath.

But in fact, I was envious, and my nit-picking detail was a way to take back all the positive things I said. My envy made me oblivious to the content as I focused on details like his reading from notes. Later, when I got honest about this speaker, I thought that his manner was too dramatic and egocentric. What I disliked was his self-assertion. This is a common focus when envy comes in the form of disparagement or belittlement. Almost always when envy is disparaging, it is a projection of our own self-assertion.

I have had many people come up to me after giving a lecture and say, "That was a great lecture, but didn't you get your main ideas from such and such a place?" Such praise is really an assertion of the other person's knowledge. Such self-assertion is also an attempt at provoking envy in the envied one. But the envious deny self-assertion just as they deny envy.

Besides self-assertion, envy may disguise itself in admiration or greed. Apropos of admiration, I can remember feeling disgusted with myself as I grandiosely praised a person I actually envied. Upon analysis, I found myself saying almost the exact opposite of what I felt. This is envy's ultimate disguise, to pass itself off as its exact opposite.

As Leslie Farber has beautifully said:

> True admiration, which, because it is free of conscious will, always has the option of silence. Envy's limitation of admiration clamors for public acknowledgment. The more stinging the envy, the more ardently must the envious one dramatize himself as an admirer whose passion . . . shames the more reticent responses of others.

The most childish form of envy is greed. When I envy someone, I begrudge her some thing or some qualities she possesses: wisdom, courage, charisma, etc. The envier magically believes that if he had that quality, he would be okay. Envy in the form of greed is exploited by modern advertising, which offers the posthypnotic suggestion that we are what we possess.

Ultimately self-assertion, admiration and greed are the disguises envy uses to cover up the core issue, which is toxic shame. The apprehension of another's superiority forces a critical evaluation of self. To be toxically shame-based is to feel the excruciating depression of self. Another's excellence exacerbates the pain of the ruptured self. In order to avoid the pain of split self, the envy takes the form of self-assertive disparagement. Admiration, in the form of indiscriminating praise, can be more shaming to another than criticism.

As Farber says:

> It may arouse his own envy toward the exalted image *we* impose
> on him and, in his awareness of the immense disparity between it and
> his own image of himself, remind him even more sharply of his
> limitations.

Envy as admiration and self-assertive belittlement of another's self-
assertion are ways that toxic shame is interpersonally transferred. Envy as
greed is based on the shame-induced belief that I can only be okay by
means of something outside of myself.

COMPULSIVE/ADDICTIVE BEHAVIORS

In *Bradshaw On: The Family,* I presented a range of compulsive/addic-
tive behaviors that suggested there are a lot more addicts than most people
realize. We so often limit this area by overfocusing on alcohol and drug
abuse. Pia Mellody has defined addiction as "any process used to avoid or
take away intolerable reality." Because it takes away intolerable pain, it
becomes our highest priority. It does so much for us that it takes time and
energy from the other aspects of our lives. It thus has life-damaging
consequences.

To be shame-based is to be in intolerable pain. Physical pain is horrible,
but there are moments of relief. There is hope of being cured. The inner
rupture of shame and the "mourning" for your authentic self is chronic. It
never goes away. There's no hope for a cure because you *are* defective. This
is the way you are. You have no relationship with yourself or with anyone
else. You are totally alone. You are in solitary confinement and chronic
grief.

You need relief from this intolerable pain. You need something outside
of you to take away your terrible feelings about yourself. You need something or someone to take away your inhuman loneliness. You need a mood-
altering experience.

There are myriad ways to mood-alter. Any way of mood-altering pain is
potentially addictive. If it takes away your gnawing discomfort, it will be
your highest priority and your most important relationship. Whichever way

you choose to mood-alter will be the relationship that takes precedence over all else in your life. Just as with excruciating physical pain, you will do anything to stop it.

Ever had a throbbing toothache? You can't think of anything or anyone else. You become "tooth centered." If the doctor gives you a prescription for medicine to take away the pain, it will take precedence over spouse, work and family. Whatever mood-alters our chronic pain will take precedence over everything else. This mood-altering relationship will have to be chronic since the pain is chronic. The chronicity will become life-damaging and pathological. You will do anything to keep mood-altered. If someone tries to take this relationship away from you, you will perform mental gyrations to prove how much you need it. You will deny it's causing you any harmful consequences. You will believe it is good for you in spite of the fact that it is life-damaging (delusion).

In this way the mood alterers we use to take away our toxic shame become our addictions. If you're shame-based, you're going to be an addict—no way around it. Addictions form the outer layer of our defenses against toxic shame.

As Fossum and Mason have said, "One of the most clearly identifiable aspects of shame is addictive behavior."

The addiction hides the shame and enhances it, and the shame fuels the addiction. Furthermore, addiction is most often a family disease. We saw that clearly in Max's genogram.

Again Fossum and Mason write, "Addiction is the central organizing principle of the family system—maintaining the system as well as the shame. When we address addiction in families, we open the door to the families' shame."

INGESTIVE ADDICTIONS

Some mood-altering phenomena are more inherently addictive than others. This is why chemicals and food have been the focus of compulsive/addictive behavior.

ALCOHOL AND OTHER DRUGS

Some chemicals have inherently addictive properties. A drug like alcohol, which affects the electrical activity of the limbic system (the portion of the brain controlling emotional response), has powerful addictive qualities. Alcohol is also a behavioral stimulant since it lowers inhibition. Alcohol is a mind-altering chemical and seriously affects body chemistry and nutrition over long periods of usage. Clear and progressive stages of addiction have been observed and are now unanimously accepted by researchers in the field.

There is some discussion now of two types of alcoholism. One type seems to be the result of a natural genetic weakness and predisposition to alcohol intolerance. Another type seems to be acquired over long periods of chronic use. What all agree on is that children of alcoholics have from five to nine times greater chance of becoming alcoholic than children from non-alcoholic families.

In my own case, my paternal grandmother and my father both seem to have been genetic alcoholics. My dad was in trouble from his first drink. I also believe I'm a genetic alcoholic, i.e., I was in trouble from the first drink. I had my first alcoholic blackout at age fifteen. Blackouts are a form of brain amnesia. The memories associated with experiences are erased after a certain threshold of tolerance is reached. Blackouts are a powerful warning about genetic alcoholism.

The genetic data would seem to refute the position that toxic shame is the core of addiction. While I would never want to say there has never been a case of purely genetic alcoholism, I would honestly have to say I've never seen one. I've been an active part of the recovery community for thirty-nine years. I've counseled some five hundred alcoholics and run the Palmer Drug Abuse Program in Los Angeles for four years, having been a consultant to that program for ten years prior to that. In all those years I've never seen anyone who did not have abandonment issues and internalized shame along with their physical addiction. My guess is that the same is true for other depressant drugs, like tranquilizers and sleeping pills, likewise for stimulants, hallucinogens, nicotine and caffeine.

I agree with Fossum and Mason that addiction is much more than one single identifiable "disease." I prefer to use the term "addictiveness" to describe the problem. I've seen thousands of addicts who stop one addiction and start a new one. The key recovery issue centers on the grief work. I'll discuss the work in Chapter Seven.

Along with my own chemical predisposition to alcoholism (and my other chemical addictions) I was also damaged by toxic shame. To recover, I had to put the cork in the bottle, but I also had to do the work I'll describe in Parts II and III of this book.

EATING DISORDERS

Eating disorders or food addictions are likewise a combination of genetic factors and distorted emotional coping. Food addictions are clear syndromes of toxic shame. Clinicians usually divide eating disorders into four categories: obesity, anorexia nervosa, bulimia and what is referred to as the fat/thin disorder.

OBESITY

Figures on obesity range up to thirty-four million, with 60 percent of women and 50 percent of men being overweight. Fossum and Mason define obesity as being fifteen pounds overweight. Generally, strong defensive rationalizations are used to "excuse" obese behavior and deny its life-damaging consequences. These include glandular disorders, heredity, aging, childbearing, lifestyles, necessary social eating and, one I've often heard, having big bones. There is no doubt there is some genetic predisposition for obesity. No one seems to know exactly what portion of the problem is genetic. However, to date, six fat genes have been discovered. My discussion will be limited to the emotional components of the problem.

Jane Middelton-Moz, a brilliant clinician in the Seattle area, in *Children of Trauma: Rediscovering the Discarded Self,* tells of watching the origins of a possible eating addiction while sitting in an airport. A mother and father were having a verbal fight. Their eighteen-month-old child was lying on a seat next to them. They were paying no attention to the child. Each time the child made any noise, the mother thrust a juice bottle in her mouth. A person sat down next to the child and startled her. She began to cry in alarm. The mother looked in her purse and found another bottle filled with milk and thrust it into the child's mouth. The mom and dad were both more than twenty pounds overweight.

This child is going to see overeating modeled for her. She is also learning to repress emotional expression and stuff her feelings with food.

As least one part of the dynamics of obesity is the result of a self-indulging and abusing pattern of survival learned in a dysfunctional family. Obese people have been shame-bound in either their angry or sad feelings. They feel empty and lonely and eat to be full and filled (fulfilled). Anger manifests in the gut (a tight gut), and eating and being full take away the feeling of anger by deluding people into believing that their tight gut is about being full, rather than about anger that needs to be expressed. Obese people often act jolly and happy to cover up their fear of the potential shame if they expressed deep sorrow or anger.

For the most part, diets are the greatest hoax ever perpetrated on a suffering group of people. Ninety-five percent of the people who diet gain the weight back within five years. Diets underscore one of the most paradoxical aspects of toxic shame. In dieting and losing weight, one has the sense of controlling and fixing the problem. As you saw earlier, control is one of the major strategies of covering up shame. All the layers of cover-up are attempts to control the outside so the inside will not be exposed.

One of the landmarks in naming the demon I'm calling toxic shame is the outline of the control-release dynamics by Fossum and Mason in their book *Facing Shame.*

Figure 4.3 is an adaptation of their work. Control and release are natural polarities in human activity. You had to learn to hold on and let go as a child learning muscle balance. Later on you learned more sophisticated balance, as in dancing (some of us, that is). In dancing you let go within a learned structure. At first you learned the individual dance steps. They were awkward and you did them with conscious control. Soon you forgot the instructions and just danced. The steps were now unconscious. The control and release fused together in an unconscious two-step or waltz.

When healthy shame is internalized, it becomes toxic and destroys all balance and boundaries. You become grandiose: either the best, or the "best-worst." With toxic shame, you are either more than human (superachieving) or less than human (underachieving). You are either extraordinary or you are a worm. It's all or nothing. You either have total control (compulsivity), or you have no control (addiction). They are interconnected and set each other up.

Fossum and Mason write:

> When shame underlies the control and release it seems to intensify both sides of the tension. . . . Shame makes the control dynamic more rigidly demanding and unforgiving and the release more dynamic and self-destructive. The more intensely one controls, the more one requires the balance of release and the more abusingly or self destructively one releases, the more intensely one requires control.

Diets follow this control and release cycle. An addiction is an addiction. The word means to give oneself up (from Latin *addicere*). To be addicted is to surrender oneself to something obsessively. The answer for addicts is not trying to control the addiction. The answer is to be aware of powerlessness and unmanageability and surrender. *Surrender means facing up to the fact that one can't control it. That's why it is an addiction.*

FAT/THIN DISORDER

Many eating addictions are not visible. In the fat/thin disorder one obsesses on food constantly. The mental obsession is the mood alteration. It is really a mental distraction. By being in your mind and constantly thinking about eating or not eating, you can distract yourself from your feelings.

I've personally groped with this disorder for years. I go through cycles of exercise; good nutritional, nonsugar diets, and then (usually after months of control) I eat a donut or a piece of carrot cake. Usually I do this while traveling. It is then that my loneliness and vulnerability are most exposed. I usually reward myself for all the hard work I've done.

Once I eat the sweets, the release phase starts. I start obsessing on what I've done. I've blown it now. I might as well eat some more. I'll binge just for today and start my control tomorrow. Ah! But tomorrow never comes! The sugar craves sugar. The mental obsessing keeps me thinking about sweets, and I'm off and running into the release cycle.

This cycle usually lasts until I start developing breasts! Then I know it's time to diet, exercise and give up sugar. Here, as in all compulsive/addictive behavior, there is no balance. It's all or nothing.

ANOREXIA NERVOSA

The number of fasting, self-starving women is growing steadily in our culture. Anorexia is certainly one of the most paradoxical and life-threatening of all the eating disorders. It is most common in affluent families with daughters ages thirteen to twenty-five. It is almost epidemic in some affluent private schools.

Anorexics most often come from families that are dominated by perfectionism. Affluent families are often focused on self-image actualizing. Respectability and the upper class have a very special look and image to keep up. The following patterns predominate: perfectionism; nonexpression of feelings (no talk rule); a controlling, often tyrannical and rigid father; an obsessive mother, completely out of touch with her sadness and anger; a pseudointimate marriage with great pretense at looking good; great fear of being out of control in the whole family system; and enmeshment and cross-generational alliances. These factors appear in various combinations.

The anorexic person takes control of the family with her starving and weight loss. She is a metaphor for what's wrong with the family. She is rigidly controlled, denies all feelings, and is superachieving and encrusted in a wall of pretense. She becomes the family system Service Bearer and Scapegoat. Mom and Dad become more intimate as their fears for her life intensify.

The addiction usually begins with feeding/fasting cycles and a strong craving for sweets. It is often accompanied by excessive exercise and depression. The use of laxatives and forced vomiting usually accompany starvation as the disease progresses. There is intense mood alteration and altered states of consciousness accompanying the stages of starvation.

Anorexics dramatically underscore the *refusal to be human* that lies at the heart of toxic shame. This includes a disdain for, and denial of, their bodies. Such disdain extends to renouncing their instinctual and emotional life. Anorexics renounce their sexuality by literally refusing to develop the signs of womanhood (menstruation and breast development). They renounce their emotions by refusing to eat. For anorexics food seems to equal feelings. Since all their feelings are shame-bound, refusing to eat is a way to avoid feeling toxic shame.

There is also enmeshment and boundary confusion between the daughter and mother. The daughter is often carrying the mother's repressed anger

FIGURE 4.3
The Shame-Bound Control-Release Triggers

Total Control
- Dieting
- Anorexia
- Hoarding
- Depressive
- Stoic
- Teetotaler
- Sexual anorexia

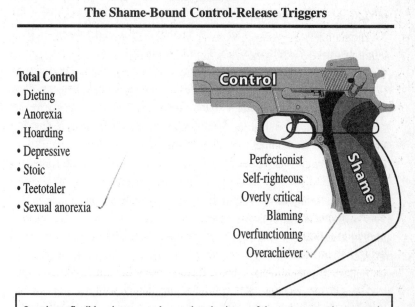

Perfectionist
Self-righteous
Overly critical
Blaming
Overfunctioning
Overachiever

Imagine a flexible wire wrapped around each trigger of the two guns and connected so that when one trigger is fired, the other trigger is pulled. Control triggers release and vice versa.

Slob
No-good sinner
Self-critical
Self-blaming
Underfunctioning
Underachiever

Release (Out of Control)
- Overeating
- Bulimia
- Compulsive spending
- Manic
- Hysterical
- Alcoholic
- Sexual compulsivity

*Toxic shame underlies both
control and release cycles.*

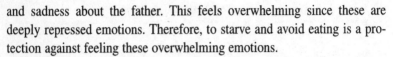

and sadness about the father. This feels overwhelming since these are deeply repressed emotions. Therefore, to starve and avoid eating is a protection against feeling these overwhelming emotions.

Anorexia is complicated and I certainly don't believe the foregoing does it clinical justice. My wish is that you see this addictive disorder as rooted in the mood alteration of family shame. Believing that you can live while refusing the nourishment of food is the ultimate rejection of one's humanity. It is an attempt at being more than human.

BULIMIA

Anorexics often solve their starving problem through the binge-purge cycle of bulimia. Bulimia can also be developed without any preceding anorexic condition. It is not limited to females, since many males become bulimic out of their addiction to physical fitness. In order to keep their youthful bodies, many male "fitness addicts" begin vomiting.

Kaufman definitely sees bulimia and bulimarexia, as well as anorexia, as shame-based syndromes. He sees toxic shame in both the binging and the purging cycle. Following Tomkins, he sees binging on food as a substitute for interpersonal needs, which are shame-bound:

> When one feels empty inside, hungry to feel a part of someone, desperate to be held close, craving to be wanted and admired but these have become taboo through shame, one turns instead to food.

Food can never satisfy the longing, and as the longing turns into shame, then one eats more to anesthetize the shame. The meta-shame, the shame about eating in secret and binging, is a displacement of affect, a transforming of the shame about self into the shame about food. The same dynamic takes place in obesity.

In bulimia the binging cycle intensifies the shame, which then triggers the purge cycle, which adds self-disgust and self-contempt. Vomiting is a disgust reaction. A disgusting emotional situation often elicits the feeling of nausea. We say, "That makes me sick to my stomach," or "I can't stomach that," or "That's hard to swallow." Vomiting may consciously be a behavior to keep the weight down, but unconsciously bulimics resort to vomiting as a way to cleanse themselves of the shameful amount of food they just devoured. By vomiting one literally bathes in shame.

Tomkins describes bulimic vomiting as affect magnification. Magnifying something will bring it to its peak intensity, which allows it to discharge. The vomiting intensifies the humiliation and self-disgust. This brings the toxic shame to a peak, and there is an exploding effect wherein one feels cleansed and purified.

Kaufman writes, "By magnifying feelings of humiliation in intensity and duration, they are finally spent, their fire burned out."

Many shame-based people seem to be in touch with their feelings because they express intense emotions. But as Cermak has pointed out, the emotional outbursts are a way to get over the feelings. It's a masochistic strategy of reduction through intensification. Magnification can also go in the opposite direction. Feelings can be intensified to the point of explosion, or they can be diminished to the point of numbness.

FEELING ADDICTIONS

There are other ways to mood-alter without using chemicals or food. I have already described feeling rackets, whereby one undesirable feeling is replaced by a family-authorized feeling. Any emotion can be addictive. The most common addiction to an emotion is that form of intensified anger we call rage.

Rage is the only emotion that can't be controlled by shame. Actually, the intensified anger we call rage is anger that is "carried" or that has been shamed. Anger, like sexuality, is a preserving emotional energy. Anger is the *self*-preserving feeling. Our anger is energy by which we protect ourselves. Our anger is our strength. Once our identity has become shame-based, we use our anger in an abortive way. When our shame is hooked, the shamed anger becomes rage, tries to protect us and does its job. Rage frightens those around us.

RAGE ADDICTION

When we are raging, we feel unified within—no longer split. We feel powerful. Everyone cowers in our presence. We no longer feel inadequate and defective. As long as we can get away with it, our rage becomes our mood-alterer of choice. We become rage addicts.

In the early days of my marriage I was a rageaholic. In my toxic shame, I had no boundaries. My primary mood alteration was being a nice guy caregiver Daddy. I let my children run all over my boundaries. I gave up my needs for their needs, with the exception of my need to appear as the wonderful and good-guy Dad. Finally, something would happen, the last straw. Then I'd start raging, yelling and screaming at my wife or children.

As I write this it astounds me that I didn't see this behavior as abusive and dysfunctional. It was the only way I knew to protect my boundaries, my shame-based inner core. My raging began to stop when my wife and children stood up to me. This is not always a stopper. Be careful of it if the offender is also physically violent. But it stopped me. I've been working on rage for twenty years now. I can assure you it can be changed.

I've seen families demolished by rage. In one family I worked with the mother was a rageaholic. She tyrannized her family and used her rage to manipulate and get her own way. The father had allied with his oldest daughter in a Surrogate Spouse relationship. The father had unresolved sexual issues and romanced his oldest daughter, giving her icky kisses and telling her he wished she was his wife. The daughter, victimized by this emotional incest, had never had a healthy sexual relationship. She was twenty-nine years old and still living with her father.

ADDICTION TO SADNESS, FEAR, EXCITEMENT, RELIGIOUS RIGHTEOUSNESS AND JOY

Any emotion can be addictive. Most of us can think of a person who is addicted to melancholy or to anxiety and fear. I frequently encounter what I call "joy" addicts. They wear a frozen smile on their faces. They are never angry. They laugh at inappropriate times and only speak about happy and joyful things.

The feeling of righteousness is the core mood alteration among religious addicts. Religious addiction is a massive problem in our society. It may be the most pernicious of all addictions because it's so hard for a person to break his delusion and denial. How can anything be wrong with loving God and giving your life for good works and service to mankind?

As I write, I think of the daughter of a minister I counseled. She was shame-based to the core. She thought of herself as the Whore of Babylon. She had been abandoned by her shame-based, self-righteous minister father. He was so busy saving souls and being Mr. Wonderful that he had no time for her. I remember being at a conference years later and seeing this man and his obese wife. He was still pompous and passive-aggressive. Such men are dangerous. They hide their shame with patronizing self-righteousness, and they transfer it to their children and disciples.

If you're anger phobic, i.e., terrified of your own anger, then you can be sad all the time. Your sadness will mood-alter your rage.

If you come from the kind of dysfunctional family where you never knew what to expect, you may have come to believe that life is one unexpected excitement after another. You may have learned to constantly seek out new and unexpected things in order to create excitement (addiction to excitement).

ADDICTION TO SHAME

Shame-based people are always addicted to their toxic shame. It is the source and wellspring of all their thoughts and behavior. Everything is organized around preventing exposure. You can't ever give up your mask and defenses against exposure. Toxic shame is like a herd of charging rhinos or a school of hungry, man-eating sharks. You cannot let your guard down for one second.

ADDICTION TO GUILT

You can also be addicted to toxic guilt. Toxic guilt says you have no right to be unique, to be the very one you are. To stay in toxic guilt forces you into constantly taking self-inventory. *Life is a problem to be solved, rather than a mystery to be lived.* Toxic guilt keeps you endlessly working on yourself and analyzing every event and transaction. There is never a time for rest because there is always more you need to do. Guilt puts you in your head a lot. Guilt is also a way to feel powerful when you are really powerless. "I've made my mother mad," or "I'm responsible for her sickness," are statements rooted in the grandiosity of toxic shame.

THOUGHT ADDICTIONS

Thoughts and mental activity are also potentially addictive. Thought processes are part of every addiction. Mental obsession, or going over and over something, is a part of the addictive cycle. It is also addictive in itself. I mentioned earlier the ego defense called "isolation of affect." By focusing on a recurring thought you can avoid painful feelings. You can also avoid feelings by ruminating, turning thoughts over and over in your head. You can be addicted to abstract thinking.

One of my degrees is in philosophy. I spent years of my life studying the great philosophers. In itself this is not harmful. For me, the reading and teaching of philosophy was a way out of my feelings. When I was reading the *Summa Theologia* of Thomas Aquinas or Emmanuel Kant's *Critique of Pure Reason* or Wittgenstein's treatise on logical positivism, I could completely mood-alter my toxic shame.

Intellectualizing is often a way to avoid internal states that are shame-bound. One's very way of intellectualizing can be addictive. Generalizing and universalizing keep one in categories so broad and abstract that there's no contact with concrete, specific, sensory-based reality. Abstract generalizing is a marvelous way to mood-alter.

DETAILING

Detailing is another thought process that mood-alters. Many obsessive/compulsive types use this form of mental activity.

An example comes to mind from my client file. I once had a person whose presenting problem was that people found her boring. I asked her to tell me about it. What follows is an adapted version of her report. She said:

Well, when I started to come to this appointment, I wanted to wear my blue silk dress. But I forgot that I sent it to the cleaners. I'm very disappointed with our cleaners. They used to do such good work and have such good prices. They've actually ruined two of my son Bobby's good jackets. Although it's hard to get Bobby to take care of his clothes. He's just like his dad. They like to be comfortable, and both of them are sloppy. I don't mind that as long as they pick up in the kitchen. That is my one bugaboo, keeping the kitchen clean. 'Cause I spend so much time there. This morning my husband left the top off the yellow corn meal. He likes stone-ground corn meal, but Bobby likes that old Weingarten corn meal . . . you know you used to get . . .

If I haven't lost you yet, I will if I go on. After fifteen minutes, I was starting to doze off. I was bored! I stopped her and gently began to point out her obsession for detail. She was a detail addict.

I learned in the course of our time together that her father was absolutely crazy. He had kept her home at gunpoint until she was thirty-two years old. She had grown up in west Texas in a small town where her dad was the sheriff. He could get away with anything. He was violent and verbally abusive. His classic line to her was, "Women should keep their mouths closed and their legs open."

My client was a victim of physical, emotional and sexual violence. When she got away from him, she never stopped talking. But her talking and detailing was a way to avoid her excruciating shame and loneliness.

Mental obsessing is a common element in all codependent relationships. Obsessing on one's alcoholic spouse or lover or children or parents is a way to stay in your head and out of your feelings. Relationships can be tremendously addictive. People go from one bad relationship to another or stay in one that is destructive and life-damaging. The feeling and experience of love is a powerful mood-alterer and can be an addiction.

ACTIVITY ADDICTIONS

Another form of mood alteration is through behavior or activity. I've already described the ritual and magical behavior that constitutes the ego defense of undoing. Certain obsessive/compulsive ritualized behaviors have the goal of taking one away from one's fears of certain shameful desires, feelings or impulses.

The more common forms of activities that mood-alter are working, buying, hoarding, sexing, reading, gambling, exercising, watching sports, watching TV, and having and taking care of pets. No one of these activities is an addiction if it has no life-damaging consequences. But all of these activities can be full-fledged and life-damaging addictions. Each is a way to get so involved in an activity that one is mood-altered by doing the activity.

Work addiction is a serious addiction. The work addict, who spends thousands of hours at work, can avoid painful feelings of loneliness and depression. I know of an experimental retreat that was conducted with ten CEOs of large companies. These people were asked to avoid anything during a four-day weekend that would take them out of their feelings. They were not to read, drink, smoke, watch TV, talk about business, use the telephone, exercise, etc. By the third afternoon, this troop of dynamic, high-rolling super-achievers was depressed. They were in touch with their emptiness and loneliness. In many cases their children were in serious trouble with drugs or the law. Their children were often carrying their loneliness and pain.

The same dynamic is true for the other activity addictions. They are all ways to cover up the loneliness and pain nestled in the underbelly of toxic shame. The toxic shame is the villain, the black hole sucking up their life, driving them to more and more accomplishments.

WILL ADDICTION

The human will loses its cooperative relationship with the intellect because of the contamination resulting from the shame-bound emotions.

The intellectual operations of perception, judgment and reasoning are crucial to the will in its choice-making duties. Perception, judgment and reasoning allow the will to see the available alternatives when making choices. It is clear there is cognitive input from the nondominant hemisphere of the brain. It is the seat of emotional regulation. The orbitofrontal lobe of this part of the brain is a *wellspring of intelligence.* This intelligence has been referred to as "felt thought" and is involved in music and poetry. It is also clear to neuroscientists that the major component in good choosing is affect. When our affects are bound in shame, we lose connections with our emotional intelligence.

As one's emotional energy is frozen and shame-bound, the dominant (analytic) part of the brain is seriously biased and impaired. The will loses its power to envision alternatives; the will loses its eyes, as it were. Without eyes the will is blind. It no longer has resource data from which to make choices. Without resource data, the will has no content outside of itself. With only itself as content, *the will can only will itself.* This affects *a pathological relationship to one's own will.* Such a relationship is mood altering.

In moments of self-willed impulsiveness, one no longer feels split or self-ruptured. In those moments one feels self-connected, powerful and whole. As Leslie Farber points out, "The will becomes a self." This willing simply for the sake of willing leads to life-damaging willfulness. To be willful is to be full of will. This willfulness leads to self-centeredness, control madness, dramatic extremes and to willing what cannot be willed (unreality). Willfulness has no boundaries.

Such willfulness is the core of all addictions. All addicts are ultimately addicted to their own wills. In AA this is expressed as "I want what I want when I want it." It is also referred to as "self-will run riot."

Addiction to one's own will is the way that toxic shame causes spiritual bankruptcy. This is why spiritual healing is necessary when it comes to healing the syndromes of toxic shame.

One may wonder after an exposition like this whether everyone isn't an addict. Stanton Peele called addiction "mankind's great unifying experience." But if everyone is an addictive/compulsive and everything is addictive, then the word addiction loses all meaning. My answer is that we have to understand the toxic shame that fuels the addictive/compulsive behavior. Not everyone uses substances, feelings, thought processes and activities addictively, because not everyone is shame-based. However, when I look at our culture, schools, religions and our family systems, my belief is that large numbers do carry toxic shame. Who knows the percentage, and what does it really matter? What we know is that addiction is the number one problem in our country.

The statistics I gave earlier on the extent of addiction do seem fairly accurate. If we had these statistics for polio or smallpox, we would call it an epidemic. The Black Plague was Mickey Mouse compared to our addiction stats.

REENACTMENTS

Another way toxic shame is covered up is through a paradoxical phenomenon called reenactment, or "acting out" or "acting in." Examples of such behavior are: repeatedly entering into destructive and shaming relationships that repeat early abusive trauma; some criminal behavior; doing to your children what was done to you as a child; and doing to yourself what was done to you.

In order to grasp these types of behavior, it's important to review the nature of human emotions. E-motions are energy in motion. They are the energy that moves us—our human fuel. Our emotions are also like the red light oil gauge on our car signaling us about a need, a loss or a satiation. Our anger is our strength; our fear is our discernment; our sadness is our healing feeling; our guilt is our conscience former; our shame signals our essential limitation and is the source of our spirituality.

When our emotions are shamed, they are repressed. Repression involves tensing muscles and shallow breathing. One set of muscles is mobilized to block the energy of the emotion we're ashamed to feel. Sadness is commonly converted into a false smile (reactive formation).

I have often smiled when I felt sad. Once the energy is blocked, we no longer feel it. However, it is still a form of energy. It is dynamic. I already gave you the example of how repressed anger intensifies. Our anger explodes because it cannot be repressed anymore. In reenactment, the emotional energy is "acted out" or "acted in." The behavior that set up the shaming event is repeated with surrogates who reenact the original shaming scene, or a person shames himself in the way he was originally shamed. This can occur through destructive self-talk, or it can happen when a person cuts himself or drives himself mercilessly, refusing to take breaks, get proper rest or take legitimate vacations.

"Cutters" form a signifigant part of our population (an estimated three million as of 2005). They inflict wounds on themselves in various ways with various objects. They try to punish themselves for their carried toxic shame and guilt (immortality shame).

REENACTING VICTIMIZATION

Incest victims often continue to reenact their earlier sexual violation in one relationship after another. In being violated such a person is used and then abandoned. The abuse is often translated into the message that sex is the only way they are desirable or worthwhile: "I have to be sexy and sexual or else I'm nothing."

Leander was thirty years old. She had already established herself as a businesswoman. She had her own ad agency. Her husband wanted her to quit her job to have children. He was verbally shaming to her and threatening to destroy her business. She hated her husband, who demanded oral sex four times a week. Leander was having an affair. When I talked to her husband, I determined quickly that he was an offender. He talked about her like she was an object. He told me he didn't care what she did as long as she took care of his sexual needs four times a week and gave him a baby.

Leander's affair was with a well-known womanizer. Over the course of the therapy, she had the baby, gave up her career and had several more affairs. She finally divorced her husband and continued to have one affair after another. Each time she chose a high-rolling, wealthy male with a history of womanizing (a Level I sex addict). Each time she was showered with gifts, used sexually and abandoned. And each time she was reenacting the sexual abuse she had experienced from her alcoholic father.

From age five until age ten she had frequently performed fellatio on her father. She was his favorite; he showered her with gifts. He gave her the only love she got in her childhood. Leander was extremely seductive. She wore clothes that made a man immediately look at her sexually. She came to see that her seduction was a way to act out her shame. It was a way to gain control over the situation she had previously been powerless in. It was a way to work out her unresolved grief.

In every single case when the man left her, she could have the feelings she was forbidden to have in the original situation. She would cry; she would be angry and rage. Each reenactment was an abortive attempt to act out the feelings she had dissociated from. In her normal dissociated state, she was out of touch with these feelings. She often felt like she was crazy. In acting out the feelings, she felt less crazy.

This repetition compulsion, this urge to repeat, is referred to by Alice

Miller as the "logic of absurdity." It happens in less cruel ways to many people.

I know a man who grew up with an emotionally unavailable mother. He was married four times, all to emotionally unavailable women. The best-selling book, *Women Who Love Too Much* by Robin Norwood, describes variation after variation of this reenactment.

CRIMINAL BEHAVIOR

In Alice Miller's work on criminality, she presents the case of Jurgen Bartsch, who was a child murderer. He murdered four boys between 1962 and 1966. With some minor deviations his modus operandi was the same. After he enticed a boy into a former air-raid shelter not far from his home, he beat the child into submission, tied him up with butcher's string, manipulated his genitals while he masturbated, killed the child by strangulation or by blows, cut open the body, emptied out the stomach and buried the remains. Bartsch testified that he would achieve sexual climax while he was cutting up the corpses.

The details of this account are truly nauseating. One feels outrage and horror. Surely such a person has criminal genes or some pathological sexual drive and perversion. However, as Alice Miller outlines the details of Jurgen's childhood, one cannot easily dismiss her thesis that there is a direct relationship between Jurgen's criminality and his early childhood. She writes, "Every crime contains a concealed story that can be deciphered from the way the misdeed is enacted and from its specific details."

The specific details are beyond the scope of my purpose here. Bartsch was an orphan who was adopted after his parents made a careful search to find the right child. Jurgen would spend hours, ritually looking for the right boy to murder. Jurgen was beaten as a baby. On many occasions he was found black and blue and bruised. He was beaten by his mother in the same room that his father, who was a butcher, was cutting up carcasses. Later, as the beatings continued, he was locked in an old underground cellar. This went on for six years. He was forbidden to play with any other children. He was sexually abused by his mother. She bathed him until he was twelve years old, manipulating his genitals. At the age of eight he was seduced by his thirteen-year old cousin, and later, at thirteen, by his teacher. His crimes bore the imprint of each detail of his life. He "acted out" his pent-up hatred on the little boys, who all wore lederhosen (just as Jurgen had done as a child). He cut them up with a butcher knife as he had seen his father do while Jurgen was being whipped, beaten and abused by his mother. She would often give him wet kisses on the mouth after she had beaten him. Jurgen also kissed his victims.

Jurgen was a victim who became an offender. He awakens our outrage and horror. "But," as Alice Miller writes, "the horror should be directed at the first murder, [the abuse] which was committed in secret and went unpunished."

When a child is being violated, his normal reaction is to cry out in anger and pain. The anger is forbidden because it would bring more punishment. The expression of pain is also forbidden. The child represses these feelings, identifies with the aggressor and represses the memory of the trauma. Later, disconnected from the original cause and the original feelings of anger, helplessness, confusion and pain, he acts out these powerful feelings against others in criminal behavior, or against himself in drug addiction, prostitution, psychic disorders and suicide.

Again Alice Miller writes, "Someone who was not allowed to be aware of what was being done has no way of telling about it except to repeat it."

In a lesser way many parents who have not worked through their own childhood trauma will reenact it on their own children.

A slogan we use in our Center for Recovering Families is "You either pass it back or you pass it on."

From this section, you can see the extent and life-damaging power of internalized shame. Its power lies in its darkness and secrecy. By exposing this demon, we can begin to set up educational programs and therapeutic approaches to prevent shame from being internalized in families.

We can find creative ways our society, schools and religions can counteract the dynamics of shame-based identity formation. Such a search is crucial. It moves us in the direction of actually finding a way to prevent addiction, violence and crime.

PART II

The Solution—
The Recovery and
Uncovery Process

A Parable: The Prisoner in the Dark Cave

There once was a man who was sentenced to die. He was blindfolded and put in a pitch black cave. The cave was one hundred yards by one hundred yards. He was told there was a way out of the cave, and if he could find it, he was a free man.

After a rock was secured at the entrance to the cave, the prisoner was allowed to take his blindfold off and roam freely in the darkness. He was to be fed only bread and water for the first thirty days and nothing thereafter. The bread and water were lowered from a small hole in the roof at the south end of the cave. The ceiling was about eighteen feet high. The opening was about one foot in diameter. The prisoner could see a faint light up above, but no light came into the cave.

As the prisoner roamed and crawled around the cave, he bumped into rocks. Some were rather large. He thought that if he could build a mound of rocks and dirt that was high enough, he could reach the opening and enlarge it enough to crawl through and escape. Since he was five feet, nine inches and his reach was another two feet, the mound had to be at least ten feet high.

So the prisoner spent his waking hours picking up rocks and digging up dirt. At the end of two weeks, he had built a mound of about six feet. He thought that if he could duplicate that in the next two weeks, he could make it before his food ran out. But as he had already used most of the rocks in the cave, he had to dig harder and harder. He had to do the digging with his bare hands. After a month had passed, the mound was nine and one-half feet high and he could almost reach the opening if he jumped. He was almost exhausted and extremely weak.

One day, just as he thought he could touch the opening, he fell. He was simply too weak to get up, and in two days he died. His captors came to get his body. They rolled away the huge rock that covered the entrance. As the light flooded into the cave, it illuminated an opening in the wall of the cave about three feet in circumference.

It was the opening to a tunnel that led to the other side of the mountain.

This was the passage to freedom the prisoner had been told about. It was in the south wall, directly under the opening in the ceiling. All the prisoner would have had to do was crawl about two hundred feet and he would have found freedom. He had so completely focused on the light that it never occurred to him to look for freedom in the darkness. Liberation was there all the time, right next to the mound he was building, but it was in the darkness.

Introduction: The Externalization Process

To heal our toxic shame we must come out of hiding. As long as our shame is hidden, there is nothing we can do about it. In order to change our toxic shame we must embrace it. There is an old therapeutic adage that states, "The only way out is through."

Embracing our shame involves pain. Pain is what we try to avoid. In fact, most of our neurotic behavior is due to the avoidance of legitimate pain. We try to find an easier way. This is perfectly reasonable.

In the case of shame, the more we avoid it, the worse it gets. We cannot change our "internalized" shame until we "externalize" it. Doing the shame reduction work is simple but difficult. It mainly involves what I call methods of externalization. Externalization methods include:

1. *Coming out of hiding by social contact, which means honestly sharing our feelings with significant others.*
2. *Seeing ourselves mirrored and echoed in the eyes of at least one non-shaming person. Reestablishing an "interpersonal bridge."*
3. *Working a Twelve Step program.*
4. *Doing shame-reduction work by "legitimizing" our abandonment trauma. We do this by writing and talking about it (debriefing). Writing especially helps to externalize past shaming experiences. We can then externalize our feelings about the abandonment. We can express them, grieve them, clarify them and connect with them.*
5. *Externalizing our lost Inner Child. We do this by making conscious contact with the vulnerable child part of ourselves.*
6. *Learning to recognize various split-off parts of ourselves. As we*

make these parts conscious *(externalize them)*, we can embrace and integrate them.

7. *Making new decisions to accept all parts of ourselves with uncondi-tional positive regard. Learning to say, "I love myself for . . ." Learning to externalize our needs and wants by becoming more self-assertive.*

8. *Externalizing unconscious memories from the past, which form col-lages of shame scenes, and learning how to heal them.*

9. *Externalizing the voices in our heads. These voices keep our shame spirals in operation. Doing exercises to stop our shaming voices and learning to replace them with new, nurturing and positive voices.*

10. *Learning to be aware of certain interpersonal situations most likely to trigger shame spirals.*

11. *Learning how to deal with critical and shaming people by practic-ing assertive techniques and creating an externalization shame anchor.*

12. *Learning how to handle our mistakes and having the courage to be imperfect.*

13. *Finally, learning through prayer and meditation to create an inner place of silence wherein we are centered and grounded in a person-ally valued Higher Power.*

14. *Discovering our life's purpose and spiritual destiny.*

All of these externalization methods have been adapted from the major schools of therapy. Most therapies attempt to make that which is covert and unconscious into something overt and conscious.

These techniques can only be mastered by practice. You must do them, then reinforce them by doing them again. They will work if you will work.

5

Coming Out
of Hiding and Isolation

One man is no man.

—Ancient proverb

*Shame-based clients require the kind of
security-giving relationship
that has been lacking in their lives.*

—Gershan Kaufman

The excruciating loneliness fostered by toxic shame is dehumanizing. As a person isolates more and more, he loses the benefit of human feedback. He loses the mirroring eyes of others. Erik Erikson has demonstrated clearly that identity formation is always a social process. He defines identity as "an inner sense of sameness and continuity which is matched by the mirroring eyes of at least one significant other." It was the contaminated mirroring by our significant relationships that fostered our toxic shame.

In order to be healed we must come out of isolation and hiding. This means finding a person, or ideally a group of significant others, whom we are willing to trust. This is tough for shame-based people.

I remember frantically looking for a hypnotist when I was told I needed to go to a Twelve Step program. It terrified me to think of being exposed to the scrutiny of other people.

Shame becomes toxic because of premature exposure. We are exposed either unexpectedly or before we are ready to be exposed. We feel helpless and powerless. No wonder then that we fear the scrutinizing eyes of others. However, the only way out of toxic shame is to embrace the shame—we *must* come out of hiding.

153

FINDING A SOCIAL NETWORK

The best way to come out of hiding is to find a nonshaming intimate person or social network. The operative word here is "intimate." We have to get on a core, gut level because shame is core, gut level stuff. Toxic shame masks our deepest secrets about ourselves; it embodies our belief that we are essentially defective. We feel so awful, we dare not look at it ourselves, much less tell anyone. The only way we can find out we were wrong about ourselves is to risk exposing ourselves to someone else's scrutiny. When we trust someone else and experience their love and acceptance, we begin to change our beliefs about ourselves. We learn that we are not bad; we learn that we are lovable and acceptable.

True love heals and affects spiritual growth. If we do not grow because of someone else's love, it's generally because it is a counterfeit form of love. True love is unconditional positive regard. Unconditional positive regard allows us to be whole and accept all the parts of ourselves. To be whole we must reunite all the shamed and split-off aspects of ourselves.

Virginia Satir speaks of the five freedoms that accrue when one is loved unconditionally. These freedoms involve our basic powers. These are the power to perceive, the power to love (choose and want), the power to emote, the power to think and express, and the power to envision or imagine.

When we are whole and fully self-accepting, we have the freedom to see and hear what we see and hear, rather than what we should or should not see and hear; the freedom to think and express what we think, rather than what we should or should not think or express; the freedom to feel what we feel, rather than what we should or should not feel; the freedom to love (choose and want) what we want, rather than what we should or should not love (choose and want); the freedom to imagine what we imagine, rather than what we should or should not imagine. When we are loved unconditionally, i.e., accepted just as we are, we can then accept ourselves just as we are.

Self-acceptance overcomes the self-rupture of toxic shame. Self-acceptance is the way to gain our personal power. When we accept ourselves, we are unified; all our energy is centered and flows outward.

Since it was personal relationships that set up our toxic shame, we need personal relationships to heal our shame. This is crucial. *We must risk reaching out and looking for nonshaming relationships if we are to heal our shame. There is no other way.* Once we are in dialogue and community, we will have further repair work to do. But we can't even begin that work until affiliative relationships are established.

Twelve Step groups have had far and away the greatest success in healing shame-based people. Remember that toxic shame is the root of all addiction. Twelve Step groups literally were born out of the courage of two people risking coming out of hiding. One alcoholic person (Bill W.) turned to another alcoholic person (Dr. Bob) and they told each other how bad they really felt about themselves. I agree with Scott Peck in seeing the founding of AA as one of the most important events of the past century. Twelve Step programs are always worked in the context of a group. The group comes first.

Because we are essentially social, we cannot live happily and fulfilled without a social context. Another way to say this is that humans need to love and be loved. We have needs, and we need to be needed. These are basic needs. We cannot be fully human unless these needs are met.

To heal our shame, we have to risk joining a group. We have to be willing to expose our essential selves. AA teaches alcoholics to introduce themselves at meetings with "My name is X. I am an alcoholic." Identification of the core problem is essential to recovery. It verbally states one's acceptance of powerlessness and unmanageability. It is indicative that one has embraced one's shame by surrendering.

You do not need to go to AA as the only way to heal your shame. Finding a nonshaming clergyperson or therapist and establishing a secure attachment with them can be the beginning of healing. If you are an addict, you have to stop using whatever drug you're addicted to or stop acting out with food, sex, gambling, work or whatever the activity addiction is. Your addiction has been your false secure base—your primary relationship. You have to give up your false idol if you want to rejoin the human race. Healing your toxic shame demands that you surrender to your powerlessness over it.

This surrendering is the core of the spiritual paradox that tells us we can only win by losing. This is hard for any hard-driving American. As with most spiritual laws, it is paradoxical. To find one's life, one must lose one's life. This is a literal truism for shame-based people. We must give up our delusional false selves and ego defenses to find the vital and precious core

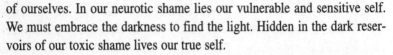

of ourselves. In our neurotic shame lies our vulnerable and sensitive self. We must embrace the darkness to find the light. Hidden in the dark reservoirs of our toxic shame lives our true self.

Watching an ocean roaring onto a pure white-sand beach at high noon on a sunny day is an exhilerating experience. We can look out on the horizon and be enthralled. Yet if this were all there was, we would miss out on something spectacular. We would miss seeing a heaven filled with twinkling lights on a starry night. Because to see the stars we need darkness.

The parable at the beginning of this section is an adaptation of a story told in therapeutic circles. The story is typical of human endeavor. We always look for our solutions in the obvious places. It never occurs to us there is a way out in the *darkness*. This is the only way with toxic shame.

GUIDELINES FOR SELECTING A GROUP

There are certainly intimate groups other than Twelve Step groups. One might find such a group in one's church or synagogue. Many have found nonshaming intimacy in psychotherapy groups or with individual therapists. Several things are crucial to look for:

• The group must be nonjudgmental and nonshaming. As you risk being in a group, be aware that you can leave it if you feel unduly exposed or shamed.

• The group should be democratic and noncontrolling. Each person can be real in such a group. Each person can be different. This is what no shame-based person has ever experienced.

• The leader of the group needs to model healthy shame. This means he or she will not act "shameless" (controlling, perfectionistic, rigid). The leader will be a person who is walking the walk as he talks the talk. The leader will be like a guide who has gone ahead of the group and can tell them what's in the next valley.

• Many of us were shamed in our preverbal life by not being touched and held. Before language, the interpersonal bridge is built through touch and holding. Infants who are not touched and interacted with die of a kind of stroke deprivation called "mirasmus." Marcel Geber, who went on a United Nations commission to study protein deficiency in

Ugandan children, found their infants and toddlers to be the most advanced children in the world. It seems that the infants were continually held by the Ugandan mothers. Their bodies were in continuous contact and movement.

- Most shame-based people need a group that touches and hugs in a respectful way. What this means is that no one just comes up and hugs you. Boundaries need to be respected. If it's too threatening to be physical, you can abstain without any explanation. You will be taught to ask if you want a hug, and you will be asked before someone hugs you.

- Finally the group must allow for the full expression of all emotions. This is the most crucial dynamic of the group process. One must be able to express feelings openly and freely. Shame is the master emotion because it binds all the other emotions. Freely expressing our feelings is like thawing out. As shame binds all our feelings, we become psychologically numb. Getting in touch with our feelings is difficult at first. You may feel overwhelmed at times. You may also feel confused. Sometimes we feel worse before we feel better. The important thing is to feel. Our feelings are who we are at any given moment. When we are numb to our emotions, we lose contact with who we are.

Go slowly in learning to identify and express emotions. This is what we never learned because of the "no talk" rules and poor modeling in our dysfunctional families. Emotions will feel strange and scary at first. We will fear being overwhelmed by our emotions. Some people will have to do more intense work with their emotions. *In the beginning, just to be feeling our emotions is shame-reducing.* Sharing emotions with another is to be vulnerable. It is to externalize and come out of hiding.

Robert Firestone, in his book *The Fantasy Bond*, states that we are not functioning in a fully human fashion until we have true friendship and are living in community. The opposite is to live our life in a fantasy bonded illusion of connectedness. All addictions and enmeshed relationships are fantasy bonds, creating a life of inner withdrawal and self-indulging gratification. Such a life is inhuman. Only in the life of dialogue and community can we truly live and grow.

6

Twelve Steps for
Transforming Toxic Shame
into Healthy Shame

*Perhaps the fastest-growing spiritual movement
in the world today is the Twelve Step Program.*

—Keith Miller
Sin: Overcoming the Ultimate Addiction

I owe my life to participation in a Twelve Step program. Therefore, it is impossible for me to be unbiased concerning its ability to heal the shame that binds you. No one argues with the fact that Twelve Step programs have a proven record for dealing with addictions. I will describe my understanding of how the steps work to heal toxic shame. Since toxic shame is the fuel of addiction, I think it will be apparent why Twelve Step programs do so well with toxic shame.

Step One states, "We admitted we were powerless over (whatever the addiction) and our lives had become unmanageable." This step acknowledges the most powerful aspect of any shame syndrome—its functional autonomy.

An old adage about alcohol illustrates this:

Man takes a drink.
Drink takes a drink.
Drink takes a man.

Alcohol has its own inherent chemical properties of addiction. Toxic shame is an internalized state which, once internalized, functions the same way as a chemical. The second sentence of Step One underscores the functional autonomy of compulsive/addictive disorders. In my own compulsivity support group, we often speak of toxic shame as an entity in itself with its own power.

In the face of it, we are powerless. All recovering persons come to a turning point in their lives precipitated by the pain of their addiction.

Pain made me aware of my powerlessness and unmanageability. The only way out of the pain was to come out of hiding—I had to surrender. I had to embrace my shame and pain. In my own case the pain had become so agonizing that I was ready to go to any length. Embracing my pain led me to expose my pain, sorrow, loneliness and shame. This is what I had feared doing for so long. As I confessed how bad I really felt, I saw acceptance and love in the mirroring eyes of others. As they accepted me, I began to feel like I mattered. I began to accept myself. *The interpersonal bridge was being repaired.*

Step Two asks us to reach out to something greater than ourselves. It states, "We came to believe that a power greater than ourselves could restore us to sanity."

I've spoken earlier of the Genesis account of the fall. Genesis suggests that four relationships were broken by Adam's toxic shame: the relationship with God, the relationship with self, the relationship with brother and neighbor (Cain kills Abel), and the relationship with the world (nature). The Twelve Steps restore those relationships. Step Two starts by accepting something greater than ourselves. Step Three says, "We made a decision to turn our will and our lives over to the care of God as we understand God." While there is conscious mention of God as the Higher Power, it is left to each person to decide how he or she understands God.

I remember a guy who made an oak tree his Higher Power. I remember him running into a meeting one day and saying, "They just cut down my Higher Power!" Twelve Step groups do not impose any notion of God onto their members.

The restoration of a bond of mutuality with God has enormous power to heal toxic shame. Toxic shame is a disorder of the will. As disabled, the will becomes grandiose. As shame-based people get entrenched in their cover-ups, they become more shameless. They hide their mistakes with per-fectionism, control, blame, criticism, contempt, etc. To be shameless is to play God. This grandiose God-playing is a spiritual disaster. It is spiritual bankruptcy. Steps Two and Three reconnect the essential bond of dependence in man with a Higher Power.

Shame-based people also do not believe *they have the right to depend on anyone.* This is a consequence of the violated dependency needs that were ruptured through the abandonment trauma. To turn one's will and life over to God is to restore a right relationship of dependence. To go to meetings and trust other people is to risk depending again.

Healthy shame is the permission to be human. To be human is to be essentially limited. It is to be finite, needy and prone to mistakes. Healthy shame lets us know that we are not God and that we truly need help.

The first three steps restore the proper relationship between ourselves and the source of life. Admitting powerlessness and unmanageability, having faith that a greater power can restore us to sanity, and making a decision to give up control and submit our will to the care of God as we understand God restores us to our healthy shame and grounds us in our fundamental humanness. The shamelessness, grandiose control madness and God-playing are given up.

With Steps One through Three we rejoin the human race; we accept our need for community and the essential limitations of our human reality. Scott Peck once defined emotional illness as avoiding reality at any cost, and mental health as accepting reality at any cost. Steps One through Three restore us to reality.

Step Four states, "We made a searching and fearless moral inventory of ourselves."

In this step we begin restoring our relationships with ourselves and our neighbors (the second and third broken relationships suggested in the biblical story of the fall). Our shame defenses kept us from showing ourselves to anyone else. More tragically, these defenses kept us from looking at ourselves. As I've suggested, to be shame-based is not to be in one's self. It is to make oneself an object of alienation.

By restoring a relationship of trust with God as we understand God, and by sharing honestly and vulnerably with our group, we come to have a relationship with ourselves. Being mirrored by the loving and honest eyes of others allows us to accept ourselves. The process of self-reunion takes place slowly and gradually.

I didn't write a Step Four inventory for two years after entering a Twelve Step program. This is not right or wrong. The taking of the steps is an individual process.

Most Twelve Step programs strongly advise that new members get a sponsor. A sponsor is a person who has some quality emotional health and is working a healthy program. A sponsor serves as a model and offers firm guidance in helping one work one's own program.

In my own case, writing my inventory needed to wait while I struggled with the first three steps. My intellectual cover-ups were very strong. I had been a professor and had degrees in psychology, philosophy and theology.

I had taught all these subjects at the university level. I struggled with the simplicity of the Twelve Step program. Part of my facade was the act of being a sensitive intellectual who saw the awesome complexity of human suffering and pain. I drank because I bore so much awareness of human suffering. As I suggested elsewhere, this was all hogwash. It was a subtle way to maintain my delusion and denial.

One of the significant lessons in my life was given me by Abraham Low, the founder of Recovery, Inc. He said that "intellectualizing about our problems is complex but easy, while doing something about them is simple but difficult." Shame-based intellectuals love to analyze.

When I did write out my Step Four, I found that much of my wrongdoing resulted from my drinking and fear. I came to see that the core of all my problems was my sense of inadequacy. At that time I didn't understand shame. Toxic shame was the inner core of all my wrongdoing.

I realized in taking my inventory that my core problem was moral rather than immoral. In fact, my first attempts at inventory were long lists of immoral behavior. What my sponsor helped me see was that I was involved in continuous moral failure. In my grandiosity I was either superhuman (exceptional) or inhuman (wormlike). I was never first human. I tried to be more than human (shameless). I wound up less than human (shame-full).

To be moral one must have a fully functioning will, the choice-making faculty. Moral acts require judgment, reason, being in touch with our feelings and ability to choose. I think shame-based people are premoral because of their disabled wills. It's hard to attribute full human power to a false self.

This does not mean that real wrongs have not been done to others by shame-based people. They certainly were in my case. In this step I took responsibility for the wrongs I had done, but I got in touch with the core problem. Some years later I took this step again in the light of my understanding of toxic shame. Then I clearly saw that 95 percent of the shame I bore was a result of abandonment issues and "carried shame." Once I could see this, I was willing to do something about it. For a shame-based person to see that most of the shame he bears is "carried shame" is hope-giving. Remember, internalized shame feels hopeless and irremediable. If we are essentially a mistake, flawed and defective, then there's nothing we can do about it.

Step Four helps one focus on one's wrongdoings in such a way as to open the *possibility of remedy*. In Step Four one begins a process of transforming toxic shame into healthy shame, which is the foundation for healthy guilt.

Steps Five, Six and Seven state: "We admitted to God, to ourselves and to another human being the exact nature of our wrongs" (Step Five), "We were entirely ready to have God remove all these defects of character" (Step Six), "We humbly asked God to remove our shortcomings" (Step Seven). I group these together because each is a part of the process of surrendering our controlling and grandiose wills. Each is a step of owning responsibility for our lives and giving up control. Each is an act of hope.

In Step Five, we come out of hiding. We talk about our shame. We tell God and another human being about our shame (the exact nature of our wrongs). In my opinion, this step not only helps one focus on one's wrongs as mistakes and sometimes awful acts, but helps one see that these acts flowed from character defects that were used as defenses for shame. By telling another human being, we embrace the pain of our shame and expose ourselves to the eyes of another. We let another see how bad we have really felt about ourselves. There is no pretense or cover-up.

Step Six is an act of faith and hope. We feel good enough about ourselves to believe that God will remove these defects of character. At least we are willing to ask and believe that we have the right to depend on someone or something greater than ourselves. Grandiose control and God-playing are over. We need God's help. We need help, and we know it, and we ask for it. The presumption in asking for the removal of these defects is the belief that we are worthy of their being removed.

In Step Seven we humbly ask God to remove our shortcomings. To humbly ask is to be restored to our healthy shame. We know we have failed. We are human, and we've made mistakes (like all humans). But we also believe we can be helped. We can change and grow. We can learn from our pain and misfortune.

With this step I was restored to my healthy shame. Out of this healthy shame, I felt my guilt. Guilt is the morality shame that forms our conscience. To be shameless is to have no conscience. Our conscience tells us that we have failed. We have transgressed our own values. Guilt moves us to change. *A guilty person fears punishment and wants to make amends. A shame-based person wants to be punished.* As I connected with my moral shame, my guilt and my conscience, I was moved to make amends.

Steps Five, Six and Seven restore us to ourselves. We accept ourselves enough to be willing to talk about our wrongs. We have enough hope about ourselves that we can ask our Higher Power for help. We are ready to be responsible, to remedy our wrongs, to move on and grow.

Steps Eight and Nine are the remedial steps. They state: "We made a list of all the persons we had harmed, and became willing to make amends to them" (Step Eight), "We made direct amends to such people wherever possible, except when to do so would injure them or others" (Step Nine).

In Steps Eight and Nine, we turn to the third broken relationship outlined in the biblical story of the fall, our relationship with other people. Perhaps the greatest wound a shame-based person carries is the inability to be intimate in a relationship. This inability flows directly out of the fundamental dishonesty at the core of toxic shame. To be a false self, always hiding and filled with secrets, precludes any possibility of honesty in relationships. As I've suggested elsewhere, shame-based people always seek out relationships with shame-based people. Hockey players don't usually hang out with professional bridge players. They don't know each other's rules. We tend to find those who play by the same rules.

Secretiveness, dishonesty and game-playing were certainly the substance of my relational history.

During my drunken episodes, I raged and became violent. I destroyed property and violated people's boundaries and their rights. Being moved to remedy our wrongs is the purpose of moral shame as guilt. Guilt is the "conscience former," and it moves us to repair our damages, to move on and to grow.

Steps Ten, Eleven and Twelve are the steps that help us maintain these restored relationships. Step Ten says, "We continued to take personal inventory and when we were wrong, promptly admitted it." Step Eleven says, "We sought through prayer and meditation to improve our conscious contact with God, as we understand God, praying only for knowledge of God's will for us and the power to carry that out." Step Twelve says, "Having had a spiritual awakening as a result of these steps, we tried to carry this message to others and to practice these principles in all our affairs."

Step Ten is the maintenance step for our relationship with ourselves. It keeps us in touch with our healthy shame, the emotion that tells us we can and will make mistakes. By continually being in touch with our fundamental humanness and our essential limitations, we can accept ourselves. To acknowledge our mistakes is to embrace and express our vulnerability and our finitude. Such a consciousness keeps tabs on our tendency to become grandiose and shameless.

Step Eleven continues and deepens our bond of mutuality with God. It promotes a relationship of conscious contact. This is a true relationship. We've come full circle, starting from the broken and abandoning source relationships that set us up to internalize our shame and ending with a friendship with God as we understand God.

Step Twelve announces that a spiritual awakening is the goal and product of the Twelve Steps. It underscores the fact that toxic shame and all its cover-ups end in spiritual bankruptcy. Toxic shame is soul murder. Because of it we become other-ated human doings, without an inner life and without inner peace. Shame-based people long for true inner serenity and peace.

The spiritual life is an inner life. It cannot be attained on the outside. The spiritual life is its own reward and seeks nothing beyond itself. Once we achieve inner peace and conscious contact, we want to overflow.

Step Twelve moves us to carry the message to our brothers and sisters who are still hidden behind the masks of toxic shame. This step calls us to practice the spiritual principles of rigorous honesty and service toward others in all our affairs. It asks us to put our bodies where our mouths are, to practice what we preach, and to walk the walk as we talk the talk. It asks us to attract others by modeling a life of self-disciplined love and respect. As we model our restored relationships with God, self, our neighbors and the world, we can show others there is a way out. There is hope.

7

Liberating Your Wounded Inner Child and Redoing Toxic Shame Scenes

Probably I, too, would have remained trapped
by this compulsion to protect the parents . . . had I not come
in contact with the Child Within Me, who appeared late
in my life, wanting to tell me her secret . . .
now I was standing at an open door . . . filled
with an adult's fear of the darkness. . . . But I could
not close the door and leave the child alone
until my death. . . . I made a decision that
was to change my life profoundly . . . to put my trust
in this nearly autistic being who had survived
the isolation of decades.

—Alice Miller
Pictures of Childhood

Bradshaw On: The Family describes three distinct phases of my own shame reduction and externalization process. Figure 7.1 gives you a visual picture of these phases.

The first phase is the recovery phase. Through the group's support and mirroring love, I recovered my own sense of worth. I risked coming out of hiding and showing my shame-based self. As I saw myself reflected in the nonshaming eyes of others, I felt good about myself. I reconnected with myself. I was no longer completely alone and beside myself. The group and significant others restored my sense of having an interpersonal bond.

The recovery process is a first-order change. What that means is that I changed one kind of behavior for another kind of behavior within a given way of behaving. I quit drinking and isolating. I shared my experiences,

FIGURE 7.1
Bliss Non-Attachment

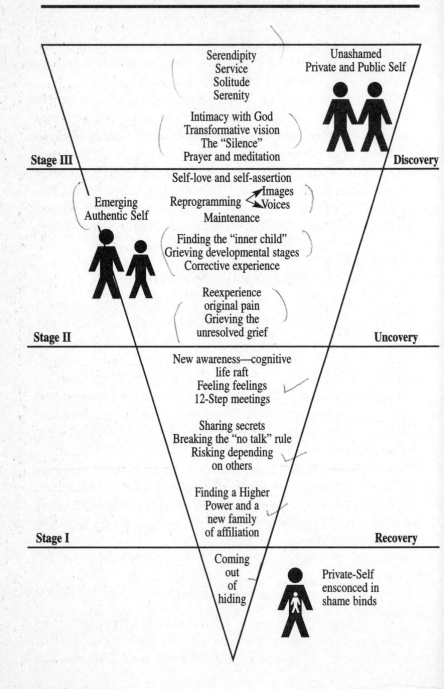

Serendipity
Service
Solitude
Serenity

Unashamed
Private and Public Self

Intimacy with God
Transformative vision
The "Silence"
Prayer and meditation

Stage III   **Discovery**

Self-love and self-assertion

Emerging
Authentic Self

Reprogramming ⟨Images / Voices
Maintenance

Finding the "inner child"
Grieving developmental stages
Corrective experience

Reexperience
original pain
Grieving the
unresolved grief

Stage II   **Uncovery**

New awareness—cognitive
life raft
Feeling feelings
12-Step meetings

Sharing secrets
Breaking the "no talk" rule
Risking depending
on others

Finding a Higher
Power and a
new family
of affiliation

Stage I   **Recovery**

Coming
out
of
hiding

Private-Self
ensconced in
shame binds

strength and hope. I started talking and sharing my feelings. I started feeling my feelings again. I shifted my dependency to the new family I had discovered. There was still a dependent and shame-based child in me who turned the new group into my parents' safeguarding security.

My shame was reduced but still active. This was evidenced by the fact that I was still compulsive and having trouble with intimacy. I chose women who I felt needed me, confusing love with pity. I set up rescuing-type relationships in which others became dependent on me and saw me as all powerful. I started working twelve-hour days, including Saturday. I smoked more and started eating lots of sugar. Indeed, I had stopped a life-threatening disease called alcoholism, I had reduced my shame, I felt better about myself, but I was still compulsive and driven. I was not yet free.

SECOND ORDER CHANGE

In order to reduce the core of my shame and stop being compulsive, I needed a *second order change*. I needed to grieve the pain of my abandonment. This is the pathway to second order change. It involves going back and resolving the unresolved issues in my family of origin. In order to get free I had to do my family-of-origin work. I still needed to grow up and truly leave home.

Fritz Perls once said, "The goal of life is to move from environmental support to self-support." The goal of life is to achieve undependence. Undependence is grounded in a healthy sense of shame. We are responsible for our own lives.

The philosopher Gurieff is said to have suggested that, "Until we resolve our source relationships, we are never really in another relationship." Leaving home means breaking our source relationships. And since we carry much of our shame as a result of those relationships, leaving home is a powerful way of reducing shame.

LEAVING HOME

What does leaving home involve? How do we do it? Leaving home is the second phase of the journey to wholeness. I call it the Uncovery Phase. It involves making contact with the hurt and lonely Inner Child who was abandoned long ago. This child is a metaphor for that part of us that houses our blocked emotional energy. This energy is especially blocked when we have experienced severe abuse. In order to reconnect with the wounded and hurt child, we have to go back and reexperience the emotions that were blocked.

For many of us, the only way to cure our compulsivity is to go back and reexperience the emotions. The blocked emotions must be reexperienced as they first occurred. The unmet and unresolved dependency needs must be reeducated with new lessons and corrective experiences.

Our lost childhood must be grieved. Our compulsivities are the result of old blocked feelings (our unresolved grief) being acted out over and over again. We either work these feelings out by reexperiencing them or we act them out in our compulsivities. We can also act them in as depression or suicide, or project them onto others as interpersonal strategies for transferring shame.

We must leave home and become our own person in order to cure our compulsivities. Even though I was in recovery, I had never left home. I had never uncovered the sources and set-up for my toxic shame. I had never done the "original pain" feeling work. I had never dealt with my family of origin.

ORIGINAL PAIN FEELING WORK

Any shame-based person has been in a family of trauma. Children of trauma experience too much stimulus within a short period of time to be able to adequately master that stimulus. All forms of abandonment trauma stimulate grief emotions in children and then simultaneously block their release.

I watched a man and his young daughter in the airport recently. I was getting a haircut and he was sitting two chairs down. He constantly scolded the child, and at one point angrily told her that she was a lot of trouble, just like her mother. I assumed he was separated or divorced. As he walked out, he slapped her a couple of times. It was really painful to watch. As the child cried, he slapped her again. Then he dragged her into the ice cream parlor and bought her ice cream to shut her up. This child is learning at a very early age that she's not wanted, that it's all her fault, that she's not a person, that her feelings don't count and that she's responsible for other people's feelings. At her age, she will have a hard time finding an ally who can sit down with her and validate her sadness and allow her to grieve.

Trauma is bound to happen somewhere along the way in any normal childhood. In a healthy, respectful family a child's feelings are validated.

As Alice Miller has repeatedly written, "It is not the trauma we suffer in childhood that makes us emotionally ill, but the inability to express the trauma."

When a child is abandoned through neglect, abuse or enmeshment, there is outrage over the hurt and pain. Children need their pain validated. They need to be shown how to discharge their feelings. They need time to do the discharge work and they need support. An abandoned child would not necessarily become shame-based if there was a nourishing ally who could validate his pain and give him time to resolve it by doing his grief work.

I think of a healthy family I know in which the father was severely injured in a home accident. The six-year-old son was playing outside when he heard an explosion. He was shocked to find his father in the basement, bleeding and apparently crippled. The father directed him to call an ambulance. A neighbor kept him until his mother returned from work. The boy was in a state of shock. The mother took him to a child play-therapist. He was afraid to go into the basement of the house. He was angry with his mother for not being home, and, his father for going away (being taken to the hospital).

Over the next months the boy worked his feelings out in the context of symbolic play. His mom and dad were both happy that he was able to express his anger toward them. (Shame-based parents would have guilted him for expressing anger.) They gave him support as he worked through his fears of going into the basement where the new heater was. They shared their own feelings with the child.

VALIDATION

In order for grief to be resolved, several factors must be present. The first factor is validation. Our childhood abandonment trauma must be validated

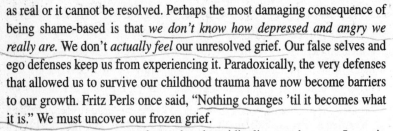

as real or it cannot be resolved. Perhaps the most damaging consequence of being shame-based is that *we don't know how depressed and angry we really are*. We don't *actually feel* our unresolved grief. Our false selves and ego defenses keep us from experiencing it. Paradoxically, the very defenses that allowed us to survive our childhood trauma have now become barriers to our growth. Fritz Perls once said, "Nothing changes 'til it becomes what it is." We must uncover our frozen grief.

I remember my paternal grandmother ridiculing me because I was in hysterics over my dad going out to get drunk. He had just had a fight with my mom and left the house in anger, vowing to get drunk. I began to cry and was soon out of control. I was ridiculed and shamed by this grandmother. I was told that I was a "big sissy" and ordered to get hold of myself. I've never forgotten this experience. Years later I still carried the unresolved grief.

SUPPORT

The greatest tragedy in all of this is that we know grief can naturally be healed if we have support. Jane Middelton-Moz has said, "One of the things we know about grief resolution is that grief is one of the only problems in the world that will heal itself with support." (For a clear and concise discussion of unresolved grief read *After the Tears* by Jane Middelton-Moz and Lorie Dwinell.)

The reason people go into delayed grief is that there's nobody there to validate and support them. You cannot grieve alone. Millions of us adult children tried it. We went to sleep crying into our pillows or locked ourselves in the bathroom.

Delayed grief is the core of what is called post-traumatic stress disorder. As soldiers come back from the war, they have common symptoms of unreality: panic, being numbed-out psychically, easily startled, feeling depersonalized, needing to control, having nightmares and sleeping disorders. These same symptoms are common for children from dysfunctional families. They are the symptoms of unresolved grief.

"GRIEF WORK"

After validation and support, one needs to experience the feelings that were not allowed. This must be done in a safe, nonshaming context. The feelings involved in "grief work" are anger, remorse, hurt, depression, sadness and loneliness. Grief resolution is a kind of "psychic work" that has to be done. It varies in duration, depending upon the intensity of the trauma. One needs enough time to finish this work.

Since this book was first published, I have written a book and done a PBS series entitled *Homecoming: Reclaiming and Championing Your Inner Child.* This book was number one on the *New York Times* bestseller list for over a year and is now in thirty-one languages. I do an Inner Child Workshop based on this book that has been attended worldwide by over 350,000 people. I use the model family system that I presented in Part I as a way for people to see how they lost their authentic selves and got stuck in a false self.

In the workshop, I outline the developmental dependency needs of each of us that must get met in order to develop a healthy foundation for our authentic sense of self. In *Homecoming,* and in the workshop, I offer indices of suspicion that help a person understand whether their needs were met at each of the developmental stages of early childhood. When a person realizes she was abandoned at a developmental stage in her childhood, she begins to feel the loss that she had to repress because of the family's "silence rule." I have professional therapists at the workshop who provide an envelope of safety so that participants can allow themselves to feel the feelings they have avoided.

At the end of the workshop, I make it clear that grief work is a process that may take a substantial amount of time to finish. I encourage the participants to continue their work with a qualified therapist. Some people need residential treatment. I once developed a residential treatment program at Ingleside Hospital that specialized in original pain and inner child work that was highly successful for many years. I had to terminate the program because of the refusal of many managed care insurance carriers to support emotional illness treatments. Medication was used sparingly in our program; our goal was to get people in touch with their feelings. Yet a number of insurance carriers would not pay for long-term care unless we used medication.

Long before I founded the John Bradshaw Center at Ingleside Hospital, I referred my clients and workshop participants needing intensive long-term care (two weeks to one month) to the Meadows Treatment Center in Wickenburg, Arizona. As early as 1979, when I was developing my inner child work, I realized the Meadows was meeting success with its intensive feeling work. I have since become a fellow at the Meadows, which offers a wide range of emotional and addictive disorders and can treat the entire family. The program is fashioned by Pia Mellody, whom I quoted earlier. The Meadows also offers a four-and-a-half-day intensive called Survivors. It is an excellent program for the helping and healing of toxic shame and family of origin issues. I obviously recommend it without reservation.

There are many other methods for doing original pain work. It must be done if the grief is to be resolved and the reenactments and compulsive lifestyle stopped.

CORRECTIVE EXPERIENCE

The unresolved grief work is a reexperiencing process, liberating and integrating your lost Inner Child.

Since the neglect of our developmental dependency needs was a major source of toxic shame, it is important to understand what we needed to achieve in each of our early developmental dependency stages. Each developmental stage was unique, with its own special needs and dynamics. In infancy we needed a mirroring of unconditional love. We needed to hear words (nonverbal to an infant) like "I'm so glad you're here. Welcome to the world. Welcome to our family and home. I'm so glad you're a boy or girl. I want to be near you, to hold you and love you. Your needs are okay with me. I'll give you all the time you need to get your needs met." These affirmations are adapted from Pam Levin's book *Cycles of Power.* In infancy we needed a secure attachment figure who created an empathic mutuality. We needed our healthy narcissistic supplies, i.e., to be loved for who we were.

I like to set up small groups (six to eight people) and let one person sit in the center of the group. The person in the center directs the rest of the group as to how close he wants them to be. Some people want to be cradled and held. Some want only light touching. Some who were stroke-deprived don't feel safe enough for such closeness. Each person sets his own boundary.

After the group is set, we play lullaby music, and each person in the group communicates a verbal affirmation while touching, stroking or just sitting near the subject.

Those who have been neglected will start sobbing when they hear the words they needed to hear, but did not hear. If a person was a Lost Child, he will often sob intensely. These words touch the "hole in his soul."

After the affirmation the group discusses their experience. I always try to have a mixed group so a person hears male and female voices. Often a person will report that he especially loved hearing the male voice or the female voice, whichever he never heard as a child. Sometimes, if a person has been abused by a parent, he will not trust the voice that corresponds to that parent's sex. The group sharing, hearing the affirmations, being touched and supported, offers a corrective experience.

I also suggest other ways people might get their infancy needs met as those needs are recycled in new experiences. They usually need a friend who will give them physical support (lots of touching) and who will feed them (take them out to eat). They need lots of skin satisfaction. They may need a nice warm bath or to be wrapped up in a blanket. They may want to try a body massage.

We go on to toddler needs, repeating the group process. Since the toddler needs to separate, we let the person sit near but separate from everyone. I usually do an age-regression type meditation, in which I ask the one in the middle to experience herself as a toddler. I give affirmations like, "It's okay to wander and explore. It's okay to leave me and separate. I won't leave you. It's okay to test your limits. It's okay to be angry, to have a tantrum, to say no. It's okay for you to do it and to do it your way. I'll be here. You don't have to hurry. I'll give you all the time you need. It's okay to practice holding on and letting go. I won't leave you."

After each person has heard these affirmations several times the group shares again. Frequently people express deep emotions as they share. Often they remember an episode of abandonment that was long forgotten. Some get into more unresolved grief work.

We go through all the developmental stages through adolescence. Adolescence is important because many people went through painful abandonment and shaming incidents during adolescence. Remember Arnold?

I usually ask each person to write a letter to his parent(s) telling them the things he needed but didn't get.

Wayne Kritsberg has them write the letter with the nondominant hand. I sometimes follow his lead. Writing with the nondominant hand helps create the feeling of being a child. Great emotion is discharged as the person reads his letter to the group. After the letter is read, I ask the group to give the person affirmations that correspond to the unmet needs he described in his letter to his parents.

Toward the close of the workshop I have each participant encounter her Lost Child. I cannot describe the power of this exercise. I have put it on several of my cassette tapes. There's no way to convey its power through the written word. I'll outline the meditation. You can put it on a tape recorder and listen to it. I recommend using Daniel Kobialka's "Going Home" as background music.

MEDITATION: EMBRACING YOUR LOST INNER CHILD

Sit in an upright position. Relax and focus on your breathing. Spend a few minutes becoming mindful of breathing. Be aware of the air as you breathe it in and as you breathe it out. Notice the difference in the air as it comes in and as it goes out. Focus on that difference for one minute. Now imagine that you're walking down a long flight of stairs. Walk down slowly as I count down from ten. Ten . . . (ten seconds) nine . . . (ten seconds) eight . . . (ten seconds), etc. When you reach the bottom of the stairs, turn left and walk down a long corridor with doors on your right and doors on your left. Each door has a colored symbol on it . . . (one minute). As you look toward the end of the corridor there is a force field of light. . . . Walk through it and go back through time to a street where you lived before you were seven years old. Walk down that street to the house you lived in. Look at the house. Notice the roof, the color of the house and the windows and doors. . . . See a small child come out the front door. . . . How is the child dressed? What color are the child's shoes? Walk over to the child. . . . Tell him that you are from his future. . . . Tell him that you know better than anyone what he has been through . . .

his suffering, his abandonment . . . his shame. . . . Tell him that of all the people he will ever know, you are the only one he will never lose. Now ask him if he is willing to go home with you. . . . If not, tell him you will visit him tomorrow. If he is willing to go with you, take him by the hand and start walking away. . . . As you walk away see your mom and dad come out on the porch. Wave good-bye to them. Look over your shoulder as you continue walking away and see them getting smaller and smaller until they are completely gone. . . . Turn the corner and see your Higher Power and your most cherished friends waiting for you. Embrace all your friends and allow your Higher Power to come into your heart. . . . Now walk away and promise your child you will meet him for five minutes each day. Pick an exact time. Commit to that time. Hold your child in your hand and let him shrink to the size of your hand. Place him in your heart. . . . Now walk to some beautiful outdoor place. . . . Stand in the middle of that place and reflect on the experience you just had. . . . Get a sense of communion within yourself, with your Higher Power and with all things. . . . Now look up in the sky; see the purple-white clouds form the number five. . . . See the five become a four . . . and be aware of your feet and legs. . . . See the four become a three . . . Feel the life in your stomach and in your arms. See the three become a two; feel the life in your hands, your face, your whole body. Know that you are about to be fully awake—able to do all things with your fully awake mind—see the two become a one and be fully awake, remembering this experience.

I encourage you to get an early photo of yourself, preferably a photo of yourself before you were seven years old. I suggest you put it in your wallet or purse. Put the picture on your desk so you can be reminded of this child who lives in you.

Much data supports that the child lives within us in a fully developed state. This child is the most vital and spontaneous part of us and needs to be integrated into our lives.

NEOTENY

In his book *Growing Young,* the distinguished anthropologist Ashley Montagu presents an evolutionary theory to complement Charles Darwin's. It

FIGURE 7.1
Represented Reality

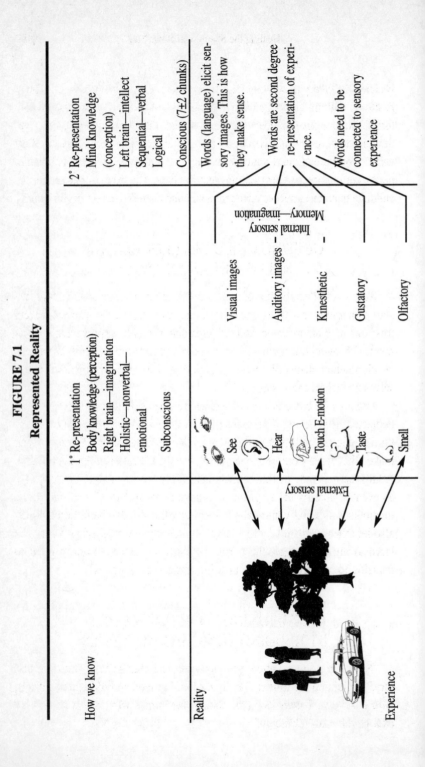

is called the theory of neotony. This theory is difficult to describe briefly, but it has to do with the prolonged early childhood and juvenile period that characterizes human development. Montagu argues that the human species was designed to develop "in ways that emphasize rather than minimize the childlike traits." The human child naturally loves, is nonjudgmental, friendly, spontaneous, curious, open to new learning, etc. We cannot recover our innocence, our childlike qualities, until we have reclaimed and championed our Inner Child.

GETTING CHILD DEVELOPMENTAL
NEEDS MET AS AN ADULT

We recycle developmental needs all through our lives. Each time we start something new we trigger our infancy needs. After we are secure and trust our new environment, our toddler part wants to explore and experiment. Our own children trigger our needs as they go through their various developmental stages. We have an opportunity as an adult to care for ourselves at each of these stages.

As adults we can create a context where we can get our needs met. I was neglected in fathering. I've asssembled a group of men who serve as supporting friends and give me feedback. I've learned that as an adult I can make what I get from others serve my needs. Children never get enough. Adults learn as they mature to make what they get be enough. So I can take an event of sharing in my group and make fathering out of it. If one of the members is especially nurturing to me, I can allow that to be fathering. I can also let other events in my life serve as fathering and mothering. I can also learn as an adult to get the things I specifically need. I can be good to myself and treat myself with nurturing respect and kindness.

CHAMPIONING YOUR INNER CHILD
BY REDOING TOXIC SHAME SCENES

"Now I'm going to show you how you can change your personal history," exclaimed the trainer David Gordon. I gulped and thought to myself, *Wait a minute. I know we can change the future with new choices, but change the past? Come on!*

David Gordon was my primary trainer in what is an exciting new model of change called Neuro-Linguistic Programming (NLP). Changing your personal history was one technique that I learned then and have used and adapted over the last six years. Of all the techniques in this book, I consider this to be one of the most powerful for healing the shame that binds you. You can rework many of the shame scenes that your Inner Child found especially painful.

What follows is my adaptation of the NLP technique. I call this process "giving back the hot potato." It works best with a memory involving a caregiver (parent, minister, teacher, priest) who shamed you by using one of the interpersonal strategies for transferring felt shame.

THE NATURE OF ANCHORS

The technique itself is based on a phenomena of human programming that the NLP people call "anchoring." An anchor is like the "on" button of a stereo that plays an old recorded memory. An anchor triggers the sounds, sights (images), feelings, and even tastes and smells of an old recorded memory. Words themselves are anchors. Words are triggers that stimulate the images and feelings of old memories.

In fact, if you look at Figure 7.1 you can see that the reality we experience can only be represented as we talk about it. What I mean is that we can never convey our lived experience exactly as it happened. When we talk about it, we talk about the way we interpreted the experience by means of our two representational systems—our sensory perceptual and intellectual ways of knowing.

Sensory perception is our first and most immediate way of knowing. Our intellectual knowing is always two degrees removed from reality. The philosopher Gottfried von Leibniz taught us that concepts (intellectual knowledge) are always based on precepts (sensory knowledge). Every thought we think carries sensory data with it. Every thought we think was first perceived, seen, heard, touched, tasted, smelled. Concepts trigger sensory images—either visual images, auditory self-talk or feelings (kinesthetic) responses.

When we talk about toxic shame, many memories are unconsciously elicited. These shame memories are often enmeshed in collages of imagery. When shame has become internalized, these images are often triggered and send the shame-based person into shame spirals. These spirals seem to operate independently of us. They seem to have a life of their own.

Shame spirals are also triggered by internal self-talk. Such inner talk is based on old beliefs we have about ourselves and the world. These beliefs were fostered by our shame-based caregivers. Auditory shame spirals result from introjected parental voices that were originally the actual voices of our shaming caregivers. They play like recordings in our head. The transactional analysis therapists estimate there are twenty-five thousand hours of these recordings.

Giving back the hot potato is a way to change old imagery through the use of kinesthetic anchors (touch anchors). It is a form of reexperiencing the past with corrective resources. It is also a way of giving back what Pia Mellody calls the induced or carried shame.

When a caregiver acts "shameless" by raging, condemning, criticizing or being judgmental, we take on the shame they are avoiding. While they avoid their shame, we have to carry it. In actual fact it is our shame, i.e., we actually experience being shamed by their acting in a shameless manner. We accepted their judgment as being about us, when it was really about them. It is in this sense that we carry their shame.

In order to understand this technique, let me quote from Leslie Bandler, one of the early pioneers and creators of NLP:

> A basic premise of my work is that people have all the resources they need to make the changes they want and need to make. . . . The resources I am speaking of . . . lie in each of our personal histories.

Each and every experience we have ever had can serve as an asset. Most every one has had the experience of being confident or daring or assertive or relaxed at some time. The therapist's task is to make those resources available in the contexts in which they are needed. Bandler, Grindler, Delozier and I have developed a method called "anchoring" which does just that.

Leslie goes on to explain that just as certain stimuli, like an old song, can bring back past experiences, we can learn to deliberately associate a memory with a specific experience. We can do this by accessing the memory and touching our thumb and finger together while we are reexperiencing that memory. Once the association has taken place, the touch of thumb to finger will then trigger the experience. We can then retrigger the experience at will.

Language works the same way. I remember sitting in a meeting with a friend some ten years ago. I looked over and saw that he was crying. I asked him what was the matter and he said, "Fluffy died." Fluffy was his dog. When I heard this, I thought it was weird for a grown man to be crying over the death of a dumb animal. The word "dog" had no first degree representation associated with it for me. I had no experience of owning a dog. As a child I was afraid of dogs. I had been a paper boy! Dogs were our natural enemy. It didn't make sense to me for someone to cry over a dog, because I had no sensory memories of warmth with a dog.

Some eight years ago I bought my son a little Shetland sheepdog. We called him Cully. When I come into the house and Cully sees me, he jumps two feet off the ground and tinkles on himself (I never had a friend do that). No matter when or how many times I come in, Cully goes crazy because he's so glad to see me. I have become very attached to Cully. I now have the sensory experience to know why someone would cry if he lost his dog. It makes sense to me now: If someone told me his dog died, the word "dog" would immediately trigger my experience with Cully. So words are anchors that trigger past sensory experience. Again, as Leslie Bandler writes:

> If I ask you to remember a time when you felt truly satisfied with yourself, my words send you on a search through your past experiences. . . . you know how you can become angry again by remembering a past argument or frightened again by remembering a terrifying movie or incident. Thus by bringing up a memory (an internally generated experience) we reexperience many of the same feelings which occurred when that memory was formed.

In my version of the NLP technique, I would have you select a past shame memory and anchor it. This is done by simply closing your eyes and letting your memory take you back to a time when Mom or Dad or a teacher or preacher was laying his or her shame on you.

One of my clients remembered being shamed in the second grade. He was at a Catholic parochial school, and the priest who was in charge of the church handed out the children's report cards. It was this priest's custom to throw the cards on the ground if a child got a D or an F. My client was an undiagnosed dyslexic and having a terrible time learning to read. He got an F in reading and the good priest threw his card on the ground. My client was ashamed and humiliated and somehow couldn't pick the card up. (He was a fingernail biter). Everyone laughed as this child suffered an excruciating moment of being shamed. This memory, as with most dissociated painful memories, was easy to anchor. He anchored it with the thumb and finger of his left hand.

I then asked him what resource(s) he now had that, if he had had them then, would have helped him handle that experience better. He thought for a moment. Then he said firmly, "I'm articulate now, and I've learned to be assertive."

I said, "Close your eyes, and think of a time when you were being articulate. The memory can come from any time in your life. You are speaking firmly and clearly, saying exactly what you want to say."

As my client searched for that past experience, I saw his face begin to change. His jaw loosened and he looked more confident. I asked him to touch his right thumb to a finger on his right hand. I had him hold the touch for thirty seconds as he reexperienced being articulate. Then I had him take a deep breath and relax. I suggested that he think of a pleasant memory from the past in order to separate the experience of being verbally expressive from the next anchor we were going to make—the assertiveness anchor.

After a moment I said, "Now think of a time when you were actually being assertive." I took some time to let him get fully into the details of the memory. I asked him, "Who was there? What did they have on? How were you dressed?" When he was reexperiencing being assertive, I had him touch his right thumb to the same right finger and make the assertive anchor in exactly the same way he did for the anchor associating verbal expression. I had him hold it for thirty seconds, and then I asked him to take a deep breath and go back to the pleasant memory he had accessed earlier. Up to this point we had:

1. Made a shame anchor (X) of the second grade report card scene with the touch of his left thumb to one of his left fingers.
2. Made a resource anchor (Y) with the touch of his right thumb to one of his right fingers. This anchor embodied two strengths my client now had that he did not have in the second grade: verbal expressiveness and assertiveness.

Now we were ready for the redoing of the old memory. It may help you understand this process if you think about a premise used in cybernetics. That premise states that the brain and central nervous system cannot tell the difference between real and imagined experience if the imagined experience is vivid enough and in detail.

Most people can achieve sexual arousal by using their *imagination*. This means there is full kinesthetic response without another real person being there. Paranoid personalities live in a threatened and hypervigilant universe by virtue of fantasies and hallucinations that they themselves create. Normal people often create terrible stress and anxiety by worrying about the future—something that hasn't even happened yet. These are all ways behavior is programmed by simply using one's imagination.

In step three of the process I asked my client to take the inner child back into the shame scene with the new resources of verbal expressiveness and assertiveness. This is accomplished by touching the two anchors X and Y simultaneously. I tell my client not to change anyone else's behavior in the scene. He is to focus only on his own responses to the report card incident. He is free to respond any way he wants to with his assertiveness and verbal expression. I encourage him to really tell the priest what he feels. I may even suggest things like "How awful for you to bully and humiliate a child like me. I'm doing the best I can. You're a poor model of the love of God," etc.

It's best when the words come spontaneously. They can be actually said out loud or subvocally. What I look for is good energy in expressing the anger about the shame.

Finally, I ask the person to give his shameless caregiver back the shame he has been carrying for him for years. I like to symbolize it as a black, *soggy* bag. The symbolic giving back is important. Once the experience feels better internally, I ask the person to take a deep breath, relax and open his eyes.

WELL-FORMED ANCHORS

This work can be done without anyone else. And each scene can be done several times. I've personally worked on more than one hundred shame memories. Some scenes I've done ten times. The key to this work is making good resource anchors. The shame anchors are usually easy because of the high voltage of the pain. Achieving well-formed resource anchors will require time, practice and patience. The conditions for well-formed anchors are:

1. **Pure Access State.** This means that the best anchor is the one with the highest energy voltage—when you're feeling the feeling most intensely.
2. **Well-Timed Application.** We need to set the anchor (thumb and finger) when the energy is at or near its apex.
3. **Can Be Duplicated.** We can check as to whether we've made a good anchor by testing it. When we touch our thumb and finger, the past experience is triggered. If we've made a good anchor, it will have high voltage.

The last point is a crucial one. Always check your resource anchor at least once before doing the corrective experience to be sure you have a good anchor.

A couple of things excite me about this method. The first is that the *person using it uses his own actual resources.* This is crucial for shame-based codependents who have poor awareness of their own inner strengths and believe they must be helped from the outside. Using a person's own strengths and resources is what good therapy is all about. The power is in the one we're trying to help. All of us already have all the resources within ourselves that we need to change, but toxic shame blocks awareness of our strengths.

The second thing I like about this technique is that *it can be tested.* Toward the end of my work with the aforementioned client, I asked him to relax, close his eyes and go to that second grade classroom on report card day. I had him touch the first anchor he had made with his left thumb and finger. I let him feel that previously anchored shame experience and asked him to pay attention to any changes in the experience. I noticed his face and calibrated it with what I remembered before. My client reported significant change in the experience. I noted it also.

When we first made the anchor, his head dropped, he furrowed his brow, his breathing was rapid and his cheek reddened. When he tested it two sessions later, he held his head upright, his breathing was more relaxed and his skin color stayed the same. These are neurological cues that match his reported reexperience of the old pain. This technique works best with nontraumatic shame scenes. If you were sexually or physically abused, I do not recommend that you do this exercise without a knowledgeable therapist to guide you. Your vulnerable child needs protection when dealing with shame scenes.

This technique is summarized in the next section.

GIVING BACK THE HOT POTATO

1. Take three to five minutes, close your eyes and focus on your breathing. Be aware of the differences in how the air feels as you breathe in and out. Let yourself totally relax.
2. Let your mind drift back in time to a shame experience and reconnect with your inner child who survived the shame. As you feel the upset or distress of that experience, touch your left thumb to one of your left fingers. Hold it for thirty seconds. Take a deep breath; let your thumb and finger relax. Shift your awareness to something familiar, like the house you live in.
3. After focusing on something familiar, think of a resource or several resources you now have that if you had had during the shame experience you could have handled it differently. (For example, you are more articulate now. You are more assertive now. You have a resource group now.)
4. Think of a time you were using the needed resource (an actual experience from any time in your life) and go into that memory in as much detail as possible. What did you have on? What color was the other person's hair, eyes, etc?
5. When you feel that resource (you feel assertive—you are being assertive), ask your inner child if he or she feels safe enough to go back into the early shame scene with you. If your inner child does

not feel safe, do not continue! If your inner child does feel safe, touch your right thumb to any finger on your right hand. Hold for thirty seconds. Take a deep breath and let your thumb and finger relax. Repeat with any other resource you feel would have helped you in the past shame experience.

6. Let your awareness return to some current familiar scene (like your bedroom or the car you drive).

7. Now imagine that you are preparing to return to the past shame theme. Imagine you could go back in time with the present resources you have just anchored. Imagine you are going to redo the experience in a way that uses the resources you just anchored.

8. Now touch your two anchors (your left thumb and finger and your right thumb and finger) simultaneously. Go back into the shame memory and redo it. Tell the shaming person how angry you are and whatever else you want to say and do. (*Do not change any of their behavior—only your own*). Stay in the experience until your internal experience feels different. If you have difficulty doing this, come back to the present and anchor more resources. Then go back and change the memory, using the new resources. Remember to give him back his shame—the shame he avoided by acting shameless.

9. Wait a minute or two and then remember the past experiences, with no anchors, to discover by your own sensory experience if indeed this memory has been subjectively changed.

10. When the past experiences have been changed, "future pace" them. Imagine the next time a situation or context will arise that is similar to the past experiences. As you imagine the future, imagine yourself having the resources in this context. Use no anchors.

11. If your inner child does not feel safe enough to go back, start the process with another scene.

I recommend that you either memorize this sequence of instructions or put it on a tape recorder.

THE UNIVERSAL QUEST FOR THE INNER CHILD

It is important to note that the need to find the Inner Child is part of every human being's journey toward wholeness. No one had a perfect childhood. Everyone bears unresolved, unconscious issues of his family history.

The Inner Child journey is the hero's journey. Becoming a fully functioning person is a heroic task. There are trials and tribulations along the way. In Greek mythology, Oedipus kills his father, and Orestes kills his mother. Leaving one's parents are obstacles one must encounter on one's hero's journey. To kill our parents is a symbolic way to describe leaving home and growing up.

To find our Inner Child is the first leap over the abyss of grief that threatens us all. But finding the Inner Child is just the beginning. Because of his isolation, neglect and neediness, this child is egocentric, weak and frightened. He must be disciplined in order to release his tremendous spiritual power. You are the new nurturing parent who sets boundaries for the wounded child in you. As you heal your past wounds you will encounter your true self in the form of your free child. Your free child embodies all your neotenous traits. Integrating your childlike traits (spontaneity, joy, love, friendliness, curosity and fairness) is a necessary task toward your maturity.

Integrating
Your Disowned Parts

*The course of our life is determined . . . by
an array of selves that live within each of us.
These selves call out to us constantly—in our dreams
and fantasies, in our moods and maladies
and in a multitude of unpredictable and
inexplicable reactions to the world around us.*

—Hal Stone and Sidra Winkelman

As a recovering shame-based person, I have to work hard at total self-acceptance. Part of the work of self-acceptance involves the integration of our shame-bound feelings, needs and wants. Most shame-based people feel ashamed when they need help; when they feel angry, sad, fearful or joyous; and when they are sexual or assertive. These essential parts of us have been split off.

We try to act like we are not needy. We pretend we don't feel what we feel. I think of all the times I've said I feel fine when I was actually sad or hurting. We either numb out our sexuality and act very puritanical, or we use sexuality to avoid all other feelings and needs. In all cases we are cut off from vital parts of ourselves. These disowned parts appear most commonly in our dreams and in our projections. This is especially true of our sexuality and natural instincts.

Jung called these disowned aspects of ourselves our shadow side. Without integrating our shadow, we cannot be whole.

THE VOICE DIALOGUE WORK
OF HAL STONE AND SIDRA WINKELMAN

In their book, *Embracing Our Selves,* Hal Stone and Sidra Winkelman have developed a powerful approach for overcoming the self-alienation that results from toxic shame. Their work is based on the premise that our personalities are constituted by an array of selves that live within each of us. These selves are the result of the self splitting that happens naturally in the process of growing up. Since our caregivers are imperfect, none of them could have accepted us with perfect unconditional love. Each in his own way put conditions of worth on us and measured us according to his map of the world. In so doing they naturally rejected the parts of us that did not measure up to their way of viewing things. These parts were split off and, over a long childhood, become somewhat autonomous.

Each split-off part became a little self. These selves call out to us constantly. They are manifested in our dreams and fantasies, in our moods and maladies, and in a multitude of unpredictable and inexplicable reactions to the experiences of our lives. These inner selves are experienced as inner voices. The more we can become conscious of these inner voices, the greater is our range of freedom. While everyone has these voices, shame-based people have them in spades, so they have greater need than others to integrate their many selves.

As forms of energy, the disowned parts of us exert considerable influence. Shame-based people tend to be exhausted a lot of the time. They spend a lot of energy holding on to their false-self masks and hiding their disowned parts. I have compared it to holding a beach ball under water. Virginia Satir compares it to keeping guard over hungry dogs locked in the basement. The repressed parts exert lots of pressure by forcing us to keep their opposites going.

While we tend to be repelled by our disowned selves, they also hold a certain fascination for us. The underlying premise of Stone and Winkelman's work *is that all of our parts are okay*. Nothing could be more affirming and less shaming. Every aspect of every person is crucial for wholeness and completeness. There is no law that says that one part is better than another part. Our consciousness, with its many selves, needs to operate on principles of social equality and democracy.

Voice dialogue work requires lots of commitment and practice. I can only give you a bare outline of its rich structure.

Voice dialogue posits consciousness as a process, rather than an entity. Consciousness is not something we strive to achieve; it is a process that must be lived out. It is an evolutionary process, continually changing and fluctuating from one moment to the next.

According to Stone and Winkelman, there are three distinct levels of consciousness: (1) awareness, (2) experience of the subpersonalities or inner voices, and (3) ego. The awareness level is a witnessing capacity that does not judge what it witnesses. The subpersonality is the experience of self manifesting as an energy pattern. This could be physical, emotional, mental or spiritual.

A raging man, for example, could be experiencing shame-bound anger that he has repressed for years. His rage overwhelms him until he is identified with his anger. *There is no awareness.* Once he becomes aware that he is raging, he can experience his anger. Then he can use his ego to become more aware of his experience. The ego is the executive of the psyche—the choicemaker. The ego receives its information from the awareness level and from the experience of the different energy patterns. As Stone and Winkelman say, "As one moves forward in the consciousness process, the ego becomes a more aware ego. As a more aware ego, it is in position to make real choices."

This is the needed direction for healing the shame that binds us. The grandiose and disabled will I spoke of earlier is mired in shame-bound and disowned emotions. As we developed our false, perfectionistic, controlling, people-pleasing parts, our ego lost its authentic executive power and became identified with what Hal and Sidra call the protector/controller.

The protector/controller often appears as the perfectionistic, inner critic or pleaser subpersonalities. Once the ego is identified with these subpersonalities, *it loses its ability to have real choice.*

This identification of the ego with the perfectionistic protector/controller, inner critic or pleaser is what I called the false self. The crucial issue is to distinguish each of these subpersonalities from ego, which is the authentic executor of personality.

Once we become identified with any one subpersonality, we've lost any real choice. The goal is to get in touch with the energy we are experiencing and see it as one of many energy patterns that must be integrated in order to affect conscious choice leading to integrated action. All subpersonalities are parts of us—to be valued and accepted. All of us is okay. We just need to be aware that the voice we hear is only a voice. Awakening the consciousness process and expanding it is the desired goal.

Stone and Winkelman sum up voice dialogue as follows:

1. **Exploration of Subpersonalities or Energy Systems**. The subpersonalities are also referred to as voices. Voice dialogue directly engages the subpersonalities in a dialogue without the interference of a critical, embarrassed or repressive protector/controller. Each subpersonality is addressed directly, with full recognition of both its individual importance and its role as only a part of the total personality. Each subpersonality experiences life differently. The frightened Inner Child, for example, is experienced as a queasy feeling.

   These subpersonalities can also be viewed from the outside. As energy patterns, they can be seen in bodily manifestations. I have seen executives in my Inner Child workshop become transformed before my eyes: furrowed brow, taut cheeks and jaw, and narrowed lips become a wide-eyed, grinning and relaxed child.

2. **Clarification of Ego**. Voice dialogue separates the ego from the controller/protector and the entourage of subpersonalities that work with this dominant energy pattern. *Remember that control is one of the hiding places for shame-based people.* Developing the protector/controlling subpersonality is universal for all people. It was developed to take care of the vulnerable child. In shame-based people the protector/controller is rigidly identified with ego. The protector/controller energy pattern is the boss. The boss works with other subpersonalities like the pusher, critic, perfectionist, power broker and pleaser. Any of these subpersonalities can exist separately, or they can be part of a general protector/controller pattern. This will vary from one person to the next.

   When any one subpersonality begins to take over the function of ego, the facilitator will point out this takeover. He will ask the subject to move to another physical space and will engage this subpersonality directly in dialogue. In this way the ego becomes more and more differentiated, i.e., becomes a more aware ego.

What it means is that we begin to be aware of all of shame's hiding places. The protector/controller, the critic and the perfectionist are what I've called masks of the false self. They are a false self in the sense that the ego is identified with them. To see that these parts or subpersonalities were frozen in order to survive the shame we've internalized is to realize that these parts are not who we essentially are. We make no judgment that they are bad parts. They are simply parts, not the whole of us.

3. **Enhancement of Awareness.** The most crucial part of voice dialogue is awareness. Voice dialogue provides a physical space for each subpersonality, including the ego, that coordinates and executes for awareness. The physical space of awareness is separate from the other two. It is a point where one can witness and review all that is going on in a nonjudgmental way. Awareness is not about decisions or action. Nothing is to be changed. Awareness is the point from which everything is noted and accepted. In awareness one clearly observes the drama played out by the subpersonalities in relation to the ego.

One cannot do voice dialogue alone. In the beginning, one needs a facilitator. Actually, it is a mutual process and a joint venture. The facilitator and the subject cooperate in the search for subpersonalities and in the attempt to understand their functions. As one becomes more adept at facilitation, his sensitivity to changing energy patterns is more highly developed. This means his awareness is in a constant state of expansion.

(Anyone finding this work interesting can contact doctors Stone and Winkelman, P.O. Box 604, Albion, California 95410-0604. The book *Embracing Our Selves* can be ordered from the same address.)

What you can do for yourself is the following exercise. I have adapted it from the work of Hal Stone and Sidra Winkelman. I call the exercise "making peace with all your villagers." This title was suggested by the Reverend Mike Falls, an Episcopal chaplain who does superb Inner Child and shadow work at the Austin Recovery Center in Austin, Texas.

MAKING PEACE WITH ALL YOUR VILLAGERS

1. Think of people you dislike. Rank them in order according to the intensity of your feelings—the number one person being the most reprehensible and the most worthy of contempt. Write a line or two under each person specifically outlining the character and moral defects that repel you.

2. Read over each name on your list. Pause and reflect on the reprehensible aspects of that person. Be aware of your own feelings as you do this. Which one trait brings out your feeling of righteousness and goodness most intensely?

3. Reduce each's defects to what you believe is his or her one most reprehensible character trait. For example on my list:

   a. Joe Slunk—grandiose egomaniac
   b. Gwenella Farboduster—aggressive and rude
   c. Maximilian Quartz—hypocrite (pretends to help people; does it for the money)
   d. Bob Evenhouser—uses Christian facade to cover up phoniness
   e. Rothghar Pieopia—a wimp; has no mind of his own

4. Each of these personality traits may represent one of your disowned parts or an energy pattern that you do not want to integrate into your life under any circumstances. If it is one of your repressed parts, doing this exercise allows you to externalize a disowned personality trait.

5. Every disowned part has an opposite energy with which your protector/controller is identified. It takes lots of energy to keep this part disowned. This often explains the intense energy we feel about our enemies. Hal Stone compares this energy to a dam that has been built to stop the flow of this energy. Behind the dam there is an accumulation of dirty water and all kinds of debris. It is important to integrate this energy and use it more creatively.

   Ask yourself this question about each person on your list. How is this person my teacher? What can I learn by listening to this person? This person to whom you feel averse can help you look at the parts of you that you are overly identified with.

   On my list Joe helps me to see that I'm overly identified with being humble. In my case it is really more like appearing humble. Gwenella helps me to see that I'm overly identified with people-pleasing. Maximilian helps me see that I'm overly identified with being a total helper without wanting anything in return. Such helping is inhuman. It's a product of toxic shame and trying to be more than human. Bob helps me see that I'm overly identified with having to be a perfect Christian (which at times keeps me from being one at all), and Rothgahr helps me to see that I'm overly identified with my "be strong" driver. Being strong is a way I try to be more than human—refusing to accept normal human weakness. This is the way I reject my healthy shame.

6. As you go through your list, talk to the disowned part directly. Ask it what it thinks. Ask it how it would change your life if you owned it. Let this part talk to you. Listen to what it has to say. See the world through its perspective. Feel any new energy that it brings you. It's bound to be a source of new ideas. Maybe it can offer new solutions to old problems. "After all," Sidra Winkelman writes, "its views have never been available before."

You may be surprised at the new energy you receive from this exercise. You are bringing a part of you out of hiding and secrecy. You are turning your shadow into light. You do not have to become the disowned self. That would be doing the same thing you did before—identifying with one part to the exclusion of another. In this exercise you learn to speak to and listen to a shamed and disowned part of you. By so doing, you free up an energy that has been bound in shame.

THE PARTS PARTY—THE WORK OF VIRGINIA SATIR

Perhaps no one has done more pioneering work in healing toxic shame than Virginia Satir. I remember the first time I saw her work with a family. Her validation and nurturing of each person was something to behold. As she performed her mighty mirroring, I could see each person accept herself a little better. As that happened, the family moved closer together. The work was so beautiful that I actually wept while watching.

In her book, *Your Many Faces,* Virginia Satir presents the core theory of a technique that is used by therapists all over the country. It is commonly called "the parts party." I've seen this exercise adapted in various ways by different schools of therapy. In what follows I will give you my own variation of this very powerful exercise. My belief is that this work is best done with a group of people. It has more impact. I would especially recommend the work originally designed by Joe Cruse and Sharon Wegscheider-Cruse, which is now being done at Onsite in Tennessee.

THE PARTS PARTY MEDITATION

Record the following:

Close your eyes. . . . Let your mind focus on your breathing. Spend two or three minutes just becoming mindful of your breathing. As you breathe in and out, begin to see the number seven appear on a screen. It can be a black number seven on a white screen or a white number seven on a black screen. Focus on the number seven. If you can't see it clearly, imagine that you finger paint it or hear a voice say seven in your mind's ear, or do all three. Then see, finger paint, hear, the number six; then five; then four, etc., down to the number one. As you focus on the number one, let it slowly turn into a stage door and see it slowly open. Walk through the stage door and see a beautiful little theater. Look at the walls and the stage (pause). Look at the closed curtain (pause). Sit down in a front row seat and feel the fabric of the seat. Make it your favorite fabric. Feel it as you sit down. Get comfortable (pause). Look around again and make this theater be any way you want it to be. Then see the curtain beginning to open. Let yourself feel the excitement that goes with such an opening. As the curtain opens see a large sign covering the wall of the stage. It reads The [your name] Parts Review. Think of some part of yourself that you really like. See some famous person or someone you know well who represents that part walk out on the stage. (I like my humor, and I see Johnny Carson walk out.) Hear applause. Then think of another part of you that you really like, and repeat the process. (I like my charismatic speaking ability and my honesty, and I see John F. Kennedy walk onto the stage.) Repeat this until five people are on the right hand side of the stage. Then think of a part of yourself you don't like, and see that part walk onto the stage as personified by a famous person or someone you know. (I don't like my sloppiness and disorganization, and I see a very unkempt friend of mine walk onto the stage.) Hear a resounding boo as if there was an audience there. Then think of another part you don't like. (I don't like the part of me that is cowardly and afraid, and I see a person whom I imagine to be Judas Iscariot walk onto the stage.) Finally, after five parts you hate or dislike or reject are standing on the left side of the stage, imagine that a wise and beautiful person walks to the center of the stage. This person can look like an old man with a beard or a radiant youth like Jesus or a warm nurturing mother or whatever. Just let your wise person appear. Then see her walking off the stage to get you. As she approaches, notice whatever strikes you about her. Then hear her invite you to come up on the stage and review your many parts. Walk around each person who represents a part of you; look her in the face. How does each part help you? How does each part hinder or limit you, especially your undesirable parts? What can you learn from your undesirable parts? What can they teach you? Now imagine they are all interacting. Imagine them at a table discussing a problem. Think of a current problem you have. What does your humor say about it? How is that helpful? How does it hinder you? How does your disorganization help you? What would happen if you simply didn't have this part? What would you lose? How would you like to change the part you want to reject? Modify that part in the way it would be more beneficial. How does it feel to modify that part? Now go around and repeat that procedure with every single part. Modify it until it feels right for you. Then walk up to each part and imagine that part melting into you. Do this until you are alone on the stage with your wise person. Hear the wise person tell you that this is the theater of your life. This is the place you can come and review your many selves from time to time. Hear your wise person tell you that all these parts belong to you, that each has its own complementariness in your psychic balance. Make a decision to embrace your selves, to love and accept and learn from all your parts. See your wise person walk away. Thank her for the lesson. Know that you can call on her again. Walk off the stage. Be aware of yourself sitting in the theater looking at the stage whereon you play out your life. Let your mind see each of your newly modified parts float by and feel yourself as one whole organism with many aspects and interdynamic parts. Speak out, hear yourself saying, "I love and accept all of me." Say it again.

Subvocalize it as you get up to walk out of your theater. Walk through the theater doors. Turn around and see the number one, a black number one on a white curtain or a white number one on a black curtain. Finger paint it and hear it if you can. Or do any of these. Then see the number two and do the same thing. Then the number three, start feeling the life in your fingers and toes. Let it come up through your legs. See the number four and feel your whole body becoming alive. Then see the number five and know that you are coming back to your normal waking consciousness. See the number six and say, "I am becoming fully conscious." Feel the place where you are, and when you see the number seven, be fully restored to your present waking consciousness.

9

Confronting and Changing
Your Toxic Inner Voices

We are all in a posthypnotic trance induced in early infancy.

—Ronald Laing

We either make ourselves miserable or we make ourselves strong. The amount of work is the same.

—Carlos Castaneda
Don Juan, *Journey to Ixtlan*

I looked at her face. It was almost shining. She was radiant, perhaps the most beautiful woman I had ever counseled. When she walked down the hall toward my office, I was moved by her petite femininity and elegance. She was the kind of woman that Fra Angelico said you could not lust after. Her beauty was too stunning. As she began to talk about herself I thought she was putting me on, the way someone might downplay herself in order to get compliments or praise.

"I'm a terrible mother. My child deserves better. I'm about to lose my job. I can't seem to catch on to the computer system. I've always been sorta' stupid. I don't blame my husband for divorcing me. I should have married Sidney. He was blind. He wouldn't have had to look at my body." She went on and on, seemingly unable to stop. Her voice tone changed two distinct times. One tone was guttural and raspy. The other was sort of whiny and weak. The most powerful impression I had was that of a recording that couldn't stop.

I worked with her for about a year. Her name was Ophelia. A clear picture of abandonment emerged. Her real father was an alcoholic. He had left her mother when Ophelia was three years old. Her first stepfather burned her with matches on several occasions, telling her that this was a sample of what the fires of hell felt like. Another man, the stepfather's brother, used to take her for rides and do "funny things" with her. She said he was the only one who ever really paid any attention to her. He once gave her a puppy. This was one of her rare pleasant childhood memories. Her mother was a waitress in a bar and used to yell at Ophelia a lot in her rough, raspy voice. Her mother was voted the sexiest girl in her senior year of high school and constantly compared Ophelia to herself. When Ophelia was thirteen, she told her things like, "You better work on getting some tits and ass if you want the boys to take you out. I was a 36C at your age." One of her mother's boyfriends got into bed with Ophelia and made her do sexual things to him. Ophelia reported this with obvious pain, but also as if it were a triumph over her mother. All in all, this woman was severely violated. She was deeply shame-based and maintained the shame through negative self-talk, which triggered continuous shame spirals.

THE INNER VOICE

This negative self-talk is the internal dialogue that Robert Firestone calls the "inner voice." The inner voice has been described in different ways. Eric Berne referred to it as a set of parental recordings that are like cassette tapes. Fritz Perls and the Gestalt school call these voices "introjected parental voices." Aaron Beck calls them "automatic thoughts." Whatever we call them, all of us have some voices in our heads. Shame-based people especially have dominant, negative shaming, self-deprecating voices. Robert Firestone writes in *The Fantasy Bond*:

The "voice" may be described as the language of an insidious self-destructive process existing, to varying degrees, in every person. The voice represents an external point of view toward oneself initially derived from the parents' suppressed hostile feelings toward the child.

The voice may be experienced consciously as a thought. Most often it is partially conscious or totally unconscious. Most of us are unaware of the habitual activity of the voice. We become aware of it in certain stressful situations of exposure when our shame is activated. After making a mistake, one might call oneself a "stupid fool." Or say, "There I go again. I'm such a blundering klutz." Before an important job interview, the voice might torment you with thoughts like, "What makes you think you could handle the responsibility of a job like this? Besides, you're too nervous. They'll know how nervous you are."

Actually getting rid of the voices is extremely difficult because of the original rupturing of the interpersonal bridge and the resulting fantasy bond. As children are abandoned, and the more severely they are abandoned (neglected, abused, enmeshed), the more they create the illusion of connection with the parent. The illusion is what Robert Firestone calls the "fantasy bond."

In order to create the fantasy bond the child has to idealize his parents and make himself "bad." The purpose of fantasy bonding is survival. The child desperately relies on his parents. They can't be bad. If they are bad or sick, he can't survive. So the fantasy bond (which makes them good and the child bad) is like a mirage in the desert. It gives the child the illusion there is nourishment and support in his life. Years later, when the child leaves the parent, the fantasy bond is set up internally. It is maintained by the voice. What was once external—the parent's screaming, scolding and punishing voice—now becomes internal. For this reason the process of confronting and changing the inner voice creates a great deal of anxiety. But as Firestone points out, "There is no deep-seated therapeutic change without this accompanying anxiety."

In beginning this work of confronting and changing your inner voices, it's imperative that you realize how powerful these voices can be. The child, by incorporating the parent's voice, is taking on the parent's subjective, and in the case of a shame-based parent, distorted, viewpoint. And as Firestone has pointed out, the child incorporates "the attitudes the parents held when they felt the most rejecting and angry. The daughter or son incorporates feelings of loathing and degradation that lie behind their statements."

As children in shame-based families we could not help but believe that we were bad and unlovable. We simply were not capable of grasping that our parents were shame-based, needy or in some cases downright emotionally ill. The voice also has a tendency to generalize, moving from a specific criticism to other areas of our own life. If Mom transferred her shame by means of compulsive perfectionism about neatness and cleanliness, that critical perfectionism will be generalized to all other bad habits and personal defects. Children will treat themselves and others with the same ridicule, sarcasm and derision that their parents foisted onto them.

The voice is not a positive system of values. "Rather," says Firestone, "it interprets and states an external system of values in a vicious manner of self-attack and castigation." The voice can be out-and-out contradictory by both initiating actions and condemning them later.

Firestone has offered evidence that "in their most pathological form, patients who are suicidal or homicidal report experiencing 'voices' as actual hallucinations instructing them to act out destructive impulses." In less pathological form, when the voices appear to represent a parental value system, the tone is most often vindictive and leads to self-hatred rather than corrective behavior. Even when a person acknowledges a mistake or error in judgment, i.e., actually admits that she is at fault, the voice is self-righteous and punitive. The voice might say, "Sorry is not enough! You're never going to learn. You're so weak and clumsy. Face it, you're just no damn good. This proves it." The voice makes the categorical judgment that one is defective and flawed and is never going to change.

The voice is mostly created by the shame-based, shut-down defenses of the primary caregivers. Just as the shame-based parents cannot accept their own weaknesses, wants, feelings, vulnerability and dependency needs, they cannot accept their children's neediness, feelings, weakness, vulnerability and dependency. Firestone writes that the voice is the result of the "parents' deeply repressed desire to destroy the aliveness and spontaneity of the child whenever he or she intrudes on their defenses."

We must remember that the shame-based caregivers were once hurting children themselves. Their pain, humiliation and shame were repressed. Their anger toward their shaming parents could not be expressed for fear of losing the parent. That anger was turned inward and became self-hatred. The parents' defenses against their pain and shame prevent these feelings from erupting into consciousness. If the parent were to let the child express those feelings, it would threaten his own defenses. The parent must stop the child's feelings of neediness and pain so that he doesn't have to feel his own feelings of neediness and pain.

THE INNER VOICE AS AUTOMATIC THOUGHTS

It is crucial for you to learn to pay attention to your internal dialogue, your own inner voices. The most destructive aspect of your inner voice has been referred to as your automatic thoughts.

Imagine the following situation: At a crowded football game a woman shrieks loudly, stands up, slaps the face of the man next to her and rushes out of the stadium. Several people are watching. Each reacts differently. One man is frightened; a teenage boy is angry; a middle-aged man is depressed; a therapist is curious; a clergyman is embarrassed. The same event triggered very different emotions in each of the observers.

The reason lies in the automatic thoughts of each observer. The frightened man was slapped repeatedly by his shrieking mother as a child. He heard his mother's voice yelling, "What do you use for brains?"

The angry teenage boy thought, "Women can get away with hitting men. Just like my sister can hit me without getting punished. It's just not fair."

The recently divorced middle-aged man thought, "Doesn't anyone get along anymore? It's really sad."

The therapist thought, "I wonder what he said to trigger that reaction?"

And the clergyman thought, "Wasn't that woman one of my parishioners? How embarrassing!"

In every case the observer's emotion was the result of a thought. The emotional response followed a thought that interpreted the event. Our mental life is teeming with thoughts, *many of them going on unconsciously and automatically.*

Internalized shame causes you to focus on a particular group of automatic thoughts to the exclusion of all contrary thoughts. This preoccupation creates a kind of tunnel vision in which you think only one kind of thought and notice only one aspect of your environment. Aaron Beck uses the phrase "selective abstraction" to describe this tunnel vision. Selective abstraction means that we look at one set of cues in our environment to the exclusion of all others. Tunnel vision is the product of toxic shame.

CONFRONTING INNER VOICES

I hope it is clear that the negative voice fosters and intensifies toxic shame. It initiates and exaggerates shame spirals. The voice is powerful. Once the voice system is set up, it becomes the key dynamic of toxic shame's functional autonomy. Many techniques have been devised for confronting and changing the voices in our heads.

ADAPTATION OF FIRESTONE'S VOICE WORK

Robert Firestone has done pioneering work in identifying the origins and destructiveness of the voice. He has developed some powerful ways to bring these hostile thoughts into the patient's awareness. He writes that the "process of formulating and verbalizing negative thoughts acts to lessen the destructive effect of the voice on the patient's behavior."

In voice therapy patients are taught to *externalize* their inner critical thoughts. By so doing they expose their self-attacks and ultimately develop ways to change their negative attitude into a more objective, non-judgmental view. As the voice is externalized through verbalization, intense feelings are released that result in powerful emotional catharsis with accompanying insight.

Historically, voice therapy developed out of Firestone's observations of both "normal" and neurotic individuals. He especially noted how groups of so-called normal therapists became angry and defensive when told certain things about themselves that they construed as critical or negative.

"Their defensiveness," writes Firestone, "was not usually related to the accuracy or inaccuracy of the feedback they were receiving, but appeared to coincide with their own negative self-evaluations." In other words, the stronger and more reactive their defensive response, the more they were probably criticizing themselves the same way. Firestone came to the conclusion that "appraisals and evaluations from others, when they validate a person's distorted view of himself, tend to arouse an obsessive thought process." Since we are already tortured by our own critical thoughts and self-attacks, we feel very threatened whenever others attack us the same way.

METHODS FOR EXTERNALIZING THE SHAMING VOICE

Firestone's methods are mainly used in the context of individual and group therapy. I have adapted these methods so you can use them outside of therapy. I've attempted to show you how powerful your inner voices are and why you do not want to give them up. If you work on the following exercises and find yourself feeling overwhelmed, stop immediately. This means you need to do them with someone who is trained to help you.

OVERREACTION DIARY

The first method I would suggest flows directly from the early work Firestone did in testing the triggering of the obsessive critical voice process. It involves keeping a diary of your defensive overreactions. It is best done when you are involved in some kind of feedback group. But it can also be done simply in the context of your daily interpersonal life.

Each evening before retiring, think back over the events of the day. Where were you upset? Where did you overreact? What was the context? Who was there? What was said to you? How does what was said to you compare with what you say to yourself?

For example, on December sixteenth my wife and I were talking about remodeling rooms in our house. At one point in the conversation, I felt my voice tone accelerating and intensifying. Soon I was ranting about all the stresses that my current work entails. I heard myself saying, "Don't expect me to supervise this job. I can just barely keep up with my basic obligations." Later, I entered this outburst into my diary. I used the following form:

Date: Wednesday, December 16, 8:45 P.M.

Subject: My wife.

Content: Discussion of improvement of a room in our house.

Overreaction: After she said, "I'm going to need some help from you." I said in an increasingly agitated tone, "Don't expect me to supervise this job, etc."

Underlying voices: You're a rotten husband. You don't know how to fix anything. You're pathetic. Your house is falling apart. What a phony! Real men know how to fix things and build. Good fathers take care of their homes.

It's crucial to take time with the voices. I recommend you get in a relaxed state when it's quiet. Really let yourself listen to what you're saying to yourself. Write it down, and say it out loud. Be spontaneous about the expression of the voices. Once you start saying it out loud, you may be surprised at the automatic outpouring.

In Firestone's group work he encourages the person to express the sentiments aloud and emotionally. He will tell him, "Say it louder," or "Really let go." I encourage you to do the same. Blurt out spontaneously anything that comes to mind. Say it in the second person. Let yourself enter into the emotional voltage triggered by the voice.

ANSWERING THE VOICE

Once you've expressed the voice, you can start answering the voice. You challenge both the content and the dictates of the voice. In my diary entry I answered that I am a good husband and I've provided a fine home. My manhood doesn't depend on my doing anything. I work hard, and I can afford to pay someone to fix my house. I would hire someone even if I knew how. I've better things to do with my time. Many fine men are carpenters and builders. Many are not.

I repeat this dialogue the next day. I always answer both emotionally and matter-of-factly (logically). *Firestone recommends that one take action by consciously not complying with the voice or by directly going against it.* In my example, I called a carpenter I knew and told him exactly what I wanted and left him alone. I played golf and exalted that I could afford to hire someone to fix my house.

TRACKING DOWN THE INNER CRITIC

A second way to expose the shaming voices comes from Gestalt therapy. I simply call it "tracking down the inner critic."

An inner, self-critical dialogue goes on in all shame-based people. This game has been called the "self-torture" game. It is almost always so habitual that it *is* unconscious. The following exercise will help you make it more conscious and give you tools to become more self-integrating and self-accepting. I've taken this exercise from the book *Awareness,* by John O. Stevens.

Exercise

Sit comfortably and close your eyes. Imagine that you are looking at yourself, sitting in front of you. Form some kind of visual image of yourself sitting there in front of you, perhaps as if reflected in a mirror. How is this image sitting? What is this image wearing? What kind of facial expression do you see?

Now silently criticize this image of yourself as if you were talking to another person. (If you are doing this experiment alone, talk out loud.) Tell yourself what you should and shouldn't do. Begin each sentence with the words, "You should _____" or "You shouldn't ____" or their equivalent. Make a long list of criticisms. Listen to your voice as you do this.

Now imagine that you change places with this image. Become this image of yourself and silently answer these criticisms. What do you say in response to these critical comments? And what does the tone of your voice express? How do you feel as you respond to these criticisms?

Now switch roles and become the critic again. As you continue this internal dialogue, be aware of what you say and also how you say it: your words, your tone of voice and so on. Pause occasionally to listen to your own words and let yourself experience them.

Switch roles whenever you want, but keep the dialogue going. Notice all the details of what is going on inside you as you do this. Notice how you feel, physically, in each role. Do you recognize anyone you know in the voice that criticizes you and says, "You shouldn't ____"? What else are you aware of in this interaction? Continue this silent dialogue for a few minutes longer. Do you notice any changes as you continue the dialogue?

Now just sit quietly and review this dialogue. Probably you experience some kind of split or conflict, some division between a powerful, critical, authoritative part of you that demands that you change, and another less powerful part of you that apologizes, evades and makes excuses. It is as though you are divided into a parent and a child. The parent, or "top dog," is always trying to get control to change you into something "better," while the child, or "underdog," is continually evading these attempts to change. As you listened to the voice that criticized and made demands on you, you may have recognized that it sounded like one of your parents. Or it might have sounded like someone else in your life who makes demands on you, i.e., your husband or wife, a boss or some other authority figure who controls you.

This critical voice can be activated in any situation of vulnerability or exposure. Once activated, a shaming spiral is set in motion. And once in motion, this spiral has a power of its own. It is imperative to externalize this internal dialogue, since it is one of the major ways you keep yourself non-self-accepting and divided. This exercise helps make the critical dialogue conscious. This is a first step in externalizing the voice.

The second step is to take each of the critical messages and translate them into a concrete specific behavior. Instead of "You are selfish," say "I didn't want to do the dishes." Instead of "You are stupid," say "I do not understand algebra." Each critical statement is a generalization. As such, it is untrue. There are some times when everyone wants his own way. There are areas in life in which everyone is confused. By translating these generalizations (judgments, conditions of worth) into concrete, specific behaviors, you can see a real picture of yourself and accept yourself in a more balanced and integrated way.

The third step is to take these generalizations (judgments, conditions of worth) and make positive statements that contradict them. For example, instead of saying, "I am selfish," say, "I am unselfish," or, "Most of the time I'm unselfish." It is important to verbalize this and hear yourself saying it. I recommend going to someone—a person in your support group, your best friend, your husband or wife—and verbalizing the positive, self-affirming statement to him or her. Be sure that the person you go to is a nonshaming person.

STOPPING OBSESSIVE SHAMING THOUGHTS

This exercise is adapted from the work of Bain, Wolpe and Meichenbaum, and the four-steps work of Joseph Wolpe. It is most helpful in stopping a first thought or a recurring thought that triggers a shame spiral.

This technique amounts to interrupting the shaming thought with a sharp command to stop and putting a new thought, a more self-affirming thought, in its place. Shame-inducing thoughts tend to fall into three categories: self put-downs, catastrophic thoughts about one's inability to handle the future, and critical and shaming thoughts of remorse and regrets.

Shaming thoughts about future sickness and catastrophe can make one chronically anxious. The "if only I hadn't done such and such" thoughts are sure ways to trigger shame spirals. And self put-downs like "I'm too shy to make friends or get what I need," or "I'm so stupid," are ways to trigger shame spirals. Obsessions about your failures and limitations trigger spirals, resulting in severe depression. The more you obsess about something, the more intense the shame spiral. Thought-stopping seeks to stop the spiral at its source.

Pause for a moment and write down five of your most shaming thoughts. For example, the following five are thoughts I worked on while doing this exercise a few years ago:

1. Your pants are so tight, it's really disgusting. (Obsession on weight)
2. I'm a failure as a father. (Obsession on parental duties)
3. I think I'm really sick. (Obsession on physical illness)
4. What's the use. I'm just going to die. (Obsession on death)
5. You're really selfish. (Obsession on morality)

Try to find thoughts that come up over and over again and continue to shame you. Rank these on the basis of how disturbing and shaming they are to you. Rank the most shaming thought number one and the next most shaming number two, etc. Look at your numbers one, two and three. Now choose one of these shaming thoughts to work on. Don't necessarily choose the worst one. The important thing is to have a success experience, so choose the one you have a positive feeling about overcoming. Later you can go back to the more shaming ones as you acquire skill at thought-stopping.

Thought-stopping requires a real commitment to be constantly alert. You can't wish a shame thought away, you have to drive it out. It involves concentrating on your shaming thought and then quite suddenly emptying your mind. Here are the four steps for stopping an obsessive shaming thought.

Step One: Imagine the Thought

Close your eyes and create a situation in which your obsessive thought is likely to occur. Let yourself drift into that situation. If you have trouble visualizing, feel the feeling that goes with this shaming thought, or perhaps hear a voice that says this thought to you. Imagine as many details as possible relating to that scene: the clothes you have on, the colors, the smells, the feelings, the sounds of the other person(s) in the scene. . . . Now start to follow the chain of thoughts. Immerse yourself in self-talk. Be vividly in this scene before beginning step two. If you start feeling the shame, that's a good sign, because if you can voluntarily intensify the shameful feeling, you can voluntarily reduce it.

Step Two: Thought Interruption

Thoughts can be interrupted by using any number of startle techniques. Egg timers and alarm clocks are often used. I like to use a tape recorder. Turn it on and record yourself saying "STOP." Record it at varied intervals, none less than two minutes. Sit or lie down and get as relaxed as you can. Situate yourself so you are near the recorder. Close your eyes and float back into the shameful situation. Really get into the details of that scene, and let it develop all its typical associations. Recall the pictures, self-talk and people, etc., that go with the shame experience. Start your recorder after you are getting into the self-talk associated with the scene. When you hear the word "STOP" (it should be recorded with loud energy), let your mind go blank. The goal is to keep your mind completely free of the painful thoughts for thirty seconds afer hearing the shouted "STOP."

Try it again. Return to your painful thoughts, and when you hear the next "STOP," notice how long your mind is free of the painful thought. Remember, your thoughts will return, but keep doing this over and over to see if you can be free for a full thirty seconds.

Step Three: Unaided Thought Interruption

Now you need to get in a place where you can be uninhibited. You need to be able to shout the word "STOP" without worrying about it. Set an alarm clock to ring in three minutes. Return to your obsessive thought. Let yourself experience it with all the attendant feelings. When the alarm rings, shout out "STOP," and notice how long your mind stays clear of the painful thought. Now set your alarm and try it again; return to the unwanted thoughts. If you're having trouble shutting off the thoughts, try one or more of the following while you shout "STOP." You can suddenly jump up, snap your fingers, slap a desk with a ruler, hold your hand up like a traffic cop or, my favorite choice, snap a rubber band that's around your wrist. Continue with the exercise by putting the alarm on a tape recorder at about three minute intervals.

Once you can turn off the obsessive thought for thirty seconds, it's time to start saying "STOP" in a normal voice. Replay your tape recorded alarm clock. Now return to your obsessive thought. When you hear the alarm, say "STOP" in a normal voice. You can still bang a ruler, snap your fingers or pop the rubber band. Do this until you can stop the obsessive thought for thirty seconds by saying "STOP" in a normal voice. Once you can achieve stopping the thought for thirty seconds in a normal voice, start the whole procedure again, this time saying it in a whisper. Practice until you can stop the thought with a whispered "STOP."

When the whisper is sufficient, use a subvocal command to stop. Just imagine hearing the word "STOP" shouted inside your head. You might tighten your vocal chords and move your tongue as if you were saying "STOP" aloud. Do not play the recorder with the alarm clock this time. Now say "STOP" to yourself silently, just as the obsessive thought is entering your mind. You simply cut it off the second it begins, before it starts a shame spiral.

If you need to bang the ruler or pop the rubber band at first, do it. The idea of saying "STOP" silently is so you can stop the obsessive shame thought anywhere without calling attention to yourself. Now practice saying "STOP" silently. Let your mind drift, and the moment a painful thought appears, wipe it out.

Step Four: Thought Substitutions

Now you can stop the shame thought the very moment it enters your mind. But no matter how good you are at stopping thoughts, the mind will not stay blank for more than thirty to sixty seconds. Nature abhors a vacuum, so within thirty to sixty seconds the old thought may come back if you don't replace it with a positive thought.

Here are some examples of things you can say to yourself:

- This is distressing but not dangerous.
- You can only live one day at a time.
- You can only take it one step at a time.
- Take a deep breath, pause, relax.
- It will soon be over; nothing lasts forever. Let it flow over.
- Say good-bye to your past; it's okay to forget.
- Look for what you like about you.
- It's okay to be imperfect.
- It takes courage to be imperfect.
- Accomplish one thing today and you'll be all right.

These are only suggestions. You should choose ones you like and then make up some of your own. If you're in a Twelve Step program, use some of the common slogans, such as "Let go and let God," "One day at a time," "This too will pass," or "Turn it over to your Higher Power."

These new positive thoughts are called covert assertions. Using covert assertions after thought interruption was first developed by Meichenbaum. He originally called it "stress inoculation training."

Effective assertions remind you of your power to control your shame spirals and shame reactions. "You" statements are usually more effective than "I" statements. Putting your assertions in the second person imposes some distance between you and your reactions and implies a degree of outside control.

Another important key to good assertions is to focus on facts. "A pain in my chest is usually indigestion, not an impending heart attack sent by God to punish me for my past wickedness."

Above all, remember that our old shaming internal self-talk has been reinforced for years and years. You must practice stopping the shame thoughts and repeating the covert assertions. It is a skill, and like all skills, it takes time and patience. You will have setbacks. Start with a thought that is not the most shaming or difficult, like a skier on a gentle slope. I also recommend using the rubber band on your wrist. When the disturbing thought comes and you subvocalize "STOP," snap the rubber band. Then say your covert assertion.

WORK OF ALBERT ELLIS AND AARON BECK

What follows is my adaptation of the work of Albert Ellis and Aaron Beck. These men have made a great contribution to our understanding of how to change shame-producing thoughts and internal dialogue. While I do not agree with Ellis that all feelings are directly related to thoughts or internal self-talk, I do believe that his techniques are a powerful way to do maintenance work on our basic shame-based self-concept and the distorted thinking that such a belief fosters.

Our shame-based identity is predicated on the belief that we are flawed and defective. Such a belief is the foundation for shame-based thinking, which is a kind of egocentric tunnel vision, composed of the following types of distortion.

SHAME-BASED DISTORTED THINKING

CATASTROPHIZING

A headache signals an impending brain tumor. A memo to see the boss means you're going to get fired. Catastrophizing results from having no boundaries or sense of worth. There are no limits to the "what ifs" that can occur.

MIND READING

In mind reading, you make assumptions (without evidence) about how people are reacting to you. "I can tell by their faces, they're getting ready to fire me." "She thinks I'm immature, or she wouldn't ask me these questions." These assumptions are usually born of intuition, hunches, vague misgivings, or one or two past experiences. Mind reading depends on projection. You imagine that people feel as bad about you as you do about yourself. As a shame-based person, you are critical and judgmental of yourself. You assume others feel the same way about you.

PERSONALIZATION

Shame-based people are egocentric. I compare it to having a chronic toothache. If your tooth hurts all the time, all you can think of is your tooth.

You become tooth-centered. Likewise, if your self is ruptured, and it is painful to experience your self, you become self-centered.

Shame-based people relate everything to themselves. A recently married woman thinks that every time her husband talks about being tired, he is tired of her. A man whose wife complains about the rising price of food hears this as an attack on his ability to be a breadwinner.

Personalization involves the habit of continually comparing yourself to other people. This is a consequence of a perfectionistic system that fosters shame. A perfectionistic system demands comparison. "He's a much better organizer that I am." "She knows herself a lot better than I do." "He feels things so deeply. I'm really shallow." The comparisons never end. The underlying assumption is that your worth is questionable.

OVERGENERALIZATION

This distortion results from toxic shame's grandiosity. One slipped stitch means "I'll never learn how to sew." A turndown for a date means "Nobody will ever want to go out with me." In this thinking distortion, you make a broad, generalized conclusion based on a single incident or piece of evidence.

Overgeneralizations lead to universal qualifiers like: "Nobody loves me." "I'll never get a better job." "I will always have to struggle." "Why can't I ever get it right?" "No one would love me if they really knew me." Other cue words are "all," "every" and "everybody."

Another form of overgeneralization is what's called a "nominalization." In nominalization a process is made into a thing. "My marriage is sick," is a nominalization. Marriage is a dynamic process. Only some aspect of it is troubled, not the whole marriage. I heard a classic example recently. A guy said, "This country is going down the tubes." This country involves count-less dynamics, processes and people. Some aspect of all these dynamics bothers this man. But the whole country is not an entity.

Overgeneralizations contribute to a more and more restricted lifestyle. They present a grandiose absolutizing, which implies that some immutable law governs your chances of happiness. This form of distorted thinking intensifies one's shame.

EITHER/OR THINKING

Another consequence of shame-based grandiosity is polarized thinking or either/or thinking. The chief mark of this thought distortion is an insistence on dichotomous choices: You perceive everything in extremes. There is no middle ground. People and things are either good or bad, wonderful or terrible. The most destructive aspect of this thought distortion is its impact on how you judge yourself. If you're not brilliant or error-free, then you must be a failure. There is no room for mistakes. A single-parent client of mine was determined to be a perfect parent to her two children. The moment she felt confused and tired of parental chores, she began bad-mouthing herself to me. She was disgusted with herself as a parent.

BEING RIGHT

As a shame-based person, you must continually prove that your viewpoint and actions are correct. You live in a completely defensive posture. Since you cannot make a mistake, you aren't interested in the truth of other opinions, only in defending your own. This thought distortion really keeps you in the shame squirrel cage because you rarely hear any new information. You get no new data that would help change your belief system about yourself.

"SHOULD" THINKING

Karen Homey wrote about the "tyranny of shoulds." Should thinking is a direct result of perfectionism. In this thought distortion you operate from a list of inflexible rules about how you and other people should act. The rules are right and indisputable. One client told me that her husband should want to take her on Sunday drives. "Any man who loves his wife ought to take her for a drive out in the country and then to a nice eating place." The fact that her husband didn't want to do this meant that he was selfish and "only thought about himself." The most common cue words for this thought distortion are "should," "ought" and "must." A shame-based person with this thought distortion makes both himself and others miserable.

CONTROL THINKING FALLACIES

Control is a major cover-up for toxic shame. Control is a product of grandiosity and distorts thinking in two ways. You see yourself as helpless and externally controlled, or as omnipotent and responsible for everyone around you. You don't believe that you have any real control over the outcome of your life. This keeps you stuck and in your shame cycle.

The opposite fallacy is the fallacy of omnipotent control. You feel responsible for everything and everybody. You carry the world on your shoulders and feel guilty when it doesn't work out.

COGNITIVE DEFICIENCY OR FILTERING

In this thinking distortion you pick out one element of a situation to the exclusion of everything else. The detail you pick out supports your belief about your personal defectiveness. A client of mine, who was a fine management consultant, was highly praised for a marketing report he created. His boss asked if he could get the next report out in less time. My client was depressed. While questioning him, I found that he was obsessing on the thought that his boss was suggesting he was lazy. He had completely missed the enthusiastic praise in his shame-based fear of defectiveness.

Filtering is a way to magnify and "awfulize" your thoughts. This triggers powerful shame spirals.

BLAMING AND GLOBAL LABELING

Blaming is a cover-up for shame and a way to pass it on to others. Blaming lends itself to global labeling. "Your grocery store has rotten food." "The prices are a rip-off." "A reserved and quiet woman on a date is a dull wallflower." "My boss is a gutless dumbo."

Blaming and global labeling are ways to distract you from your own pain and responsibility. They are thought disorders that keep you from honestly looking at yourself and feeling your own pain. It is your pain that will move you to change.

EXTERNALIZING YOUR THOUGHT DISTORTIONS

To begin dealing with your shame-based thought distortions, you can go back to a time when you were experiencing a painful episode of shame. The following three-step procedure will help you identify your thought distortions. It will also help you to restructure your thinking. The three steps are:

1. Describe the shame-producing situation or event by writing it out.
2. Identify your thought distortions.
3. Restructure and eliminate your shame-based thinking by rewriting the distortions.

Step three seems to offer people the greatest difficulty. Our distortions are so ingrained that we have trouble knowing a more logical way to think. The following is a guide for logical corrections to the thinking distortions I have described here.

CATASTROPHIZING

The most logical counter to catastrophizing is an honest assessment in terms of realistic odds or percent of probability. What are the chances? One in a thousand (.1 percent), one in ten thousand (.01 percent), or one in a 100,000 (.001 percent)?

MIND READING

Mind reading is a form of imagining and fantasizing. In the long run you're best off making no inferences about people. Treat all your interpretations about other people as hallucinations. Use that word when you give your interpretation. Say, "My fantasy or hallucination is . . ." The best policy is to check out the evidence for your conclusion.

PERSONALIZATION

Force yourself to get evidence to prove what the boss's frown means. Check it out if possible. Abandon the habit of comparing. Make no conclusion unless you have reasonable evidence and proof.

Write on a three-by-five card "There Are No Absolutes," and put it on your desk. Challenge words like "all," "every," "never," "always," "nobody" and "everybody" by exaggerating them. Say, "Do I really mean I never, ever, ever, etc.?" Learn to use words like "maybe," "sometimes" and "often."

Check out nominalization by asking yourself if you could put it in a wheelbarrow. You couldn't put a marriage or our country in a wheelbarrow. The statements "My marriage is sick" and "This country is going down the tubes" involve the nominalization distortion.

OVERGENERALIZATION

Use a three-column technique for overgeneralizations.

Evidence for my Conclusion	Evidence against my Conclusion	Alternative Conclusion

EITHER/OR THINKING

Use your "There Are No Absolutes" card for this one. Either/or is a form of absolutizing. Toxic shame is more than human or less than human. This is the basis of grandiose thinking. There are no black-and-white judgments. The world is gray. Think in terms of percentages. "About 5 percent of the time I'm selfish, but the rest of the time I'm loving and generous."

BEING RIGHT

Own your own healthy shame. If you're always right, you stop listening and learning. The key to overcoming being right is to become an active listener. Carl Rogers did pioneering work in developing this skill. As an active listener you listen for content as well as process. You learn to listen with your eyes as well as your ears. You learn to give feedback and check things out.

By listening and clarifying we learn to see things as another person sees them. The checking-out process helps us grasp the other's point of view. It is important to remember that others believe what they are saying as strongly as we believe our own convictions. I like to ask myself, "What can I learn from the other person's opinion?"

"SHOULD" THINKING

Use the words "should," "ought" and "must" as red flags. Flexible rules and expectations don't rely on these words because there are always exceptions and special circumstances. Rigidity is the mark of mental illness; flexibility is the mark of mental health. Without flexibility, there is no freedom.

Think of at least three exceptions to your rule—and then consider all the exceptions you can't even imagine.

CONTROL THINKING FALLACIES

Aside from acts of God, you are responsible for what happens in your world. I suggested earlier that neuroses and character disorders are disorders of responsibility. Learning to be responsible and to allow others that privilege is to live in reality. Ask yourself, "What choices have I made that resulted in this situation? What decisions can I now make to change it?" Also remember that respect for others means letting them live their own lives, suffer their own pains and solve their own problems.

COGNITIVE DEFICIENCY OR FILTERING

Stop using words like "terrible," "awful," "disgusting," "horrendous," etc. Write out the phrase "No need to magnify. I can cope. I can stand it." My favorite phrase of all comes from Abraham Low. Say to yourself, "This is distressing, but not dangerous."

To stop filtering, you have to shift focus. Place your attention on coping strategies to deal with the problem rather than obsessing on the problem itself. Focus on a theme such as danger or loss. Then think of things that represent safety, or think of things you have that are valuable.

BLAMING OR GLOBAL LABELING

Accept responsibility for your own behavior and choices. Focus on your own problems. Look at the beam in your own eye, rather than the speck in your brother's eye. When you start labeling, ask yourself, "What am I trying to avoid?" If you find you are not avoiding, be specific rather than global. "My boss is often conservative. He is rarely a risk-taker." This is accurate. Calling him a gutless dumbo is about your need to vent anger at having to answer to him.

CHANGING INNER VOICES
THROUGH POSITIVE AFFIRMATIONS

This is literally a positive brainwashing technique. It attempts to replace old, negative, judgmental and critical shaming tapes with new, realistic and positive affirmations. Since most of the old, critical voices came from someone else's opinion of you, they represent a subjective opinion about you, rather than who you really are. New affirmations will help you change your internal self-talk, so you can be the person you want to be.

The technique of affirmations involves writing a positive statement about yourself fifteen to twenty times (ideally, twice daily). Once the positive statement is written, wait for the first spontaneous response that comes to you. Usually these responses will be negative. Wait about a minute. If no response comes, continue the affirmations, writing exactly the same statement as before. The purpose of the response is to externalize all the negative shaming messages in the unconscious.

The monotony of writing over and over again catches the shame-control mechanism off guard. It is important to remember that some of the most shamed parts of our self-image were told to us repeatedly. For example, "Why can't you be like your sister/brother?, etc.," or "You are so sloppy, lazy, stupid, etc." Always put your own name in the affirmation. The outline for affirmations is as follows:

Affirmation	Response
I ____am often loving and kind.	Wait for first spontaneous response
I ____ am often loving and kind.	Whatever comes.
I ____ am often loving and kind.	Whatever comes.
Repeat above statement.	Whatever comes.

This is to be done for twenty-one days. Research has shown that this amount of time is needed to be optimally effective.

MAKING AFFIRMATIONS WORK FOR YOU

Work with the same affirmation every day. The best times are just before sleeping, before starting the day and especially whenever you feel "bummed out."

1. Write each affirmation ten to twenty times.
2. Say and write each affirmation to yourself in the first, second and third persons, as follows:

"The more I ____ love myself, the more others love me."
"The more you ____ love yourself, the more others love you."

"The more she/he, loves her/himself, the more others love her/him."

Writing in the second and third person is very important since your conditioning came to you in this manner.

3. Continue working with the affirmations daily until they become totally integrated in your consciousness. You will know this has happened when your mind responds positively and when you begin to experience mastery over your goals. You will be using your mind to serve you.

4. Record your affirmations and play them back when you can. I very often play them while driving the car on the freeway or when I go to bed.

5. It is effective to look into the mirror and say the affirmations to yourself out loud. Keep saying them until you are able to see yourself with a relaxed, happy expression. Keep saying them until you eliminate all facial tension and grimaces.

6. Use visualizations with your affirmations.

As the responses accumulate over time, you may see patterns of negative voices. You may also experience a voice you had not been previously aware of. These negative voices can become sources for new, contradicting positive affirmations.

10

Choosing to Love and Forgive Yourself for Your Mistakes

You do not need to be loved, not at the cost of yourself.
The single relationship that is truly central
and crucial in a life is the relationship to the self. . . .
Of all the people you will know in a lifetime,
you are the only one you will never lose.

—Jo Courdet
Advice from A Failure

Toxic shame's greatest enemy is the statement "I love myself." To say "I love myself" can become your most powerful tool in healing the shame that binds you. To truly love yourself will transform your life.

CHOOSING TO LOVE YOURSELF

Scott Peck has defined love "as the will to extend myself for the sake of nurturing my own and another's spiritual growth." This definition sees love as an act of the will. This means that love is a decision. I can choose to love myself, no matter what the past has been and no matter how I feel about myself.

EXERCISE: THE FELT SENSE OF SELF

Try this experiment. Sit in your favorite chair. Get really comfortable and relaxed. Now close your eyes and imagine the person you currently love and respect the most is sitting across from you. (Don't pick someone you're in emotional pain about). The person can be a spouse, lover, child, parent, friend, hero, etc. Close your eyes and see that person. Take three or four minutes.

223

Now get in touch with the feelings you have when you experience that person with you. I felt warm and vitalized and appreciative when I saw my best friend. This is my felt sense of that relationship.

Now close your eyes and see yourself sitting across from you. Stay in the experience three or four minutes.

The first time I did this experiment, I felt myself begin to criticize myself. This happens to me occasionally when I look at myself in the mirror. Just notice what you felt when you looked at yourself. One person I was working with recently saw her cheeks as too fat and felt bad about her posture. Most of us have some negative feelings about ourselves. If you're shame-based and you've done nothing to heal your shame, you will probably feel intense feelings of rejection. The rejection of self is the core of toxic shame.

ACCEPTING YOURSELF UNCONDITIONALLY

To counteract these negative feelings about yourself, make a decision to accept yourself unconditionally. You do this by an act of choice.

"I love myself. I will accept myself unconditionally."

Say this out loud and often. This amounts to unconditional love.

I can remember vividly the first time I truly accepted and loved myself unconditionally. It was awesome! I later read a book by Gay Hendricks where he talked about the same thing (see *Learning to Love Yourself* by Gay Hendricks). He described how he would confront people in his workshops with the simple question, "Will you love yourself for that?"

When I first read the transcript of one of his therapeutic interventions with a group member, I was taken aback. Surely there are things we do that are unworthy of love. As Gay went on and on, asking the person if he could love himself no matter what he did or didn't do, I realized that our love needs to be for who we are, not for what we do. You are lovable, period.

Remember that toxic shame turns you into a human doing because toxic shame says your being is flawed and defective. If your being is flawed and defective, nothing you do could possibly make you lovable. You can't change who you are.

Understanding the distinction between being and doing is one of the great lessons of my life. I tried so hard to achieve and do better and better. But no matter what I did, I still felt the deep sense of defectiveness that is the mark of internalized shame. Saying "I love myself for whatever. . . ." is a powerful counteraction to the voice of shame. Saying "I accept myself unconditionally" can transform our lives.

One of the best therapeutic successes I ever had was dealing with a woman's weight problem. The success came as a result of this exercise. She felt she was twenty-five pounds overweight. She was contemptuous of her body and put herself down with comparisons and self-labeling. I worked with her for several months, continually challenging her comparisons and put-downs. I'd ask her, "Will you love and accept yourself for that?"

No matter what she said, I'd challenge her with that statement. Gradually she began to accept herself just as she was. I refused to talk about diets or exercise. I knew that until she accepted herself exactly as she was, she would never change. She couldn't lose weight by continually shaming herself. How can a problem that is organized and motivated by toxic shame be cured by increasing the toxic shame? Every time my client compared herself or put herself down with a negative label, she started a shame spiral. The shame spiral intensified the toxic internalized shame, which set her up to eat more as a way to mood-alter the pain of the shame. Self-labeling and odious comparisons are the way to stay overweight, not the way to lose weight.

In order to heal the shame that binds you, you have to begin with self-acceptance and self-love. Love creates union. When we make the decision to love ourselves unconditionally, we accept ourselves unconditionally. This total self-acceptance creates "at-one-ment." We are at one with ourselves. Our full power is available to us because we are not dissipating our power by having to guard our hungry dogs in the basement (our split-off parts).

CHOOSING TO LOVE OURSELVES IS POSSIBLE, EVEN IF WE HAVE NEGATIVE FEELINGS ABOUT OURSELVES

I have often disliked one of my children, but that didn't mean I stopped loving him or her. If we make the decision to love ourselves unconditionally, we will start feeling differently about ourselves.

As we choose to love ourselves, our self-value will be enhanced. Years ago Sidney Simon and Kirschenbaum wrote a book called *Values Clarification*. They suggested that a value is not a value unless it has seven factors in it. The seven factors are:

1. It must be freely chosen.
2. It must be chosen from a consideration of alternatives.
3. It must be chosen with clear knowledge of the consequences.
4. It must be prized and cherished.
5. It must be publicly proclaimed.
6. It must be acted on.
7. It must be acted on repeatedly.

Choosing to love yourself is a free choice. It is a simple decision. The alternatives are a shame-based lifestyle with disastrous consequences. I'm encouraging you to say, "I love myself," out loud, to proclaim that you love and accept yourself unconditionally. If you act on such a belief repeatedly, you will grow more deeply self-loving and self-valuing.

GIVING YOURSELF TIME AND ATTENTION

If you decide to love yourself, you will be willing to give yourself time and attention.

Scott Peck's definition of love implies that love is hard work. It involves expansion; it means we have to extend ourselves. To extend yourself requires work.

The work of love involves giving yourself time. How much time do you spend with yourself? Do you take time for proper rest and relaxation, or do you drive yourself unmercifully? If you're a human doing, you drive yourself. You need more and more achievement in order to feel okay about yourself. If you're willing to love and accept yourself unconditionally, you will allow yourself time to just be. You will set aside times when there's nothing you have to do and nowhere you have to go. You will allow yourself solitude, a nourishing time of aloneness. You will take time for hygiene and exercise. You will take time for fun and entertainment. You will take vacations. You will take time to work at your sex life. You will be willing to give yourself pleasure and enjoyment.

The work of love is the work of listening to yourself. You listen to yourself by monitoring your feelings, needs and wants. You need to pay attention to yourself. This may mean learning techniques for getting in touch with your feelings. It may mean joining a share group where you get feedback. The work of paying attention to yourself requires discipline.

Again, as Scott Peck has pointed out, discipline allows us to enhance life's pleasure. If you love yourself, you're willing to delay gratification so that something else more conducive to your growth might take place.

When I was a shame-based drinking addict, I could not even think of delaying gratification. Like most children of trauma and dysfunction, I never thought there was going to be enough. I wouldn't delay gratification because my shame-based self didn't trust that I could get any more.

Discipline demands telling the truth and being responsible for my own life. If I love myself, I will live in reality. I will commit to telling the truth and being responsible. Those behaviors increase my self-esteem. If I love those behaviors in others, why wouldn't I love them in myself?

We have a saying in the recovery community: "Fake it till you make it." Sometimes we just decide to act ourselves into a right way of feeling, rather than trying to wait until we feel like changing. This applies to loving yourself. Make the decision. Say it aloud. Act like you love, value and accept yourself unconditionally; you will begin to feel more self-loving and accepting.

BECOMING SELF-ASSERTIVE AND GIVING YOURSELF PERMISSION TO MAKE MISTAKES

Another action and work of love that will enhance your self-love and heal your toxic shame is to become more assertive. Assertiveness is based on self-love and self-valuing. This is different from aggressiveness. Aggressiveness is usually shame-based behavior. To become aggressive is to win at any cost. It often involves shaming another person. Shaming someone else cannot enhance one's self-love.

I consider self-assertion and assertiveness training to be a powerful way to heal the shame that binds you. As the shame internalization process took place in your dysfunctional family, your needs became bound by shame.

After a while you no longer knew what you needed. There was no way to learn how to ask for what you wanted. As your dependency needs were violated, you came to believe that you couldn't depend on anyone. You lost all sense of your rights as an utterly unique and unrepeatable human being.

Assertiveness training is a way to learn how to get those needs met. In assertiveness training you learn how to say no and ask for what you want. You learn to build new physical, emotional, volitional and intellectual boundaries.

Books like *When I Say No, I Feel Guilty,* by Manuel Smith, *Do You Say Yes When You Want to Say No?* by Fensterheim, and *Your Perfect Right,* by Alberti and Emmons, are all useful to learn how to stand your ground and get your legitimate needs met. The methods presented in these books require practice.

Each of us needs to create our own Bill of Rights. We need to have total permission for our rights. Manuel Smith in *When I Say No, I Feel Guilty* sets forth the following list of rights (you may add your own):

- You have the right to judge your own behavior, thoughts and emotions, and to take responsibility for their initiation and consequences.
- You have the right to offer no reasons or excuses for justifying your behavior.
- You have the right to judge if you are responsible for judging other people's problems.
- You have the right to change your mind.
- You have the right to make mistakes and be responsible for them.
- You have the right to say, "I don't know."
- You have the right to be independent of the goodwill of others before coping with them.
- You have the right to be illogical in making decisions.
- You have the right to say, "I don't understand."
- You have the right to say, "I don't care."

In loving yourself, think about how you loved that person in the exercise The Felt Sense of Self at the beginning of this chapter. If someone was hurting or hassling the person you love, what would you do? If you saw him hurting or shaming himself, what would you do to take care of him? Think of the work and energy you have exerted in loving your children. Will you love yourself the same way? You really are worth it. There has never been anyone like you. Nor will there ever be anyone like you again. You are unique, unrepeatable and of precious worth.

REFRAMING MISTAKES

A shame-based person tries desperately to present a mask to the world that says, "I'm more than human," or "I'm less than human." To be more than human is to never make a mistake. To be less than human is to believe you are a mistake. Dealing in a healthy manner with our mistakes is crucial for the maintenance of self-love. Reframing our mistakes is a way to handle them.

Reframing, as I'm using the word, means changing your interpretation or point of view. You put a new frame around a picture or an event to change the way you look at it. This new frame will change its meaning for you. Reframing mistakes means learning to think about them in ways that remove their catastrophic qualities. Instead of awful catastrophes, you view your mistakes as natural and valuable components of your life. This is exactly the purpose of your healthy shame. When you are connected with your healthy shame, you know you can and will make mistakes and use your mistakes as occasions for learnings or as warnings to slow down and look at what you're doing.

MISTAKES AS WARNINGS

Mistakes are like the buzzer in your car that warns you of the dangers of driving without a seatbelt. If you get a speeding ticket, it can be a warning to drive slower and concentrate on your driving. Such a warning could ultimately save your life.

Toxic shame, with its mask of perfectionism, changes the warning into a moral indictment. You become so preoccupied with defending yourself against the inner critical voices that you miss the opportunity to heed the warning of the mistake. Get into the habit of reframing the mistake as a warning. Focus on the warning, rather than the culpability.

MISTAKES AS ALLOWING SPONTANEITY

To know you can and will make mistakes allows you to live your life with vitality and spontaneity. Healthy shame is a condition of creativity. Knowing you will make mistakes allows you to seek new information and new solutions. It keeps you from believing that you know it all.

The fear of mistakes kills your creativity and spontaneity. You walk on eggs, always afraid to say what you think or feel. McKay and Fanning write:

> If you're never allowed to say the wrong thing, you may never feel enough to say the right thing, to say you love someone or that you hurt or want to give comfort.

MISTAKES AS TEACHERS

There is no way you can learn any task or skill without errors. The process of learning has been defined as "successive approximation." Watch children learning to walk. They literally learn to walk by falling down. Each time they fall, they adjust their balance and try again. Each failure creates a successive approximation. Finally they can walk.

Mistakes are a form of feedback. Every error tells us what we need to correct. As we correct each mistake, we get nearer to the behavioral sequence that works best.

As a teacher I know that students who fear making mistakes have trouble learning. They are scared to tackle new material because of the possibility of not understanding it. Such students go on to take the first job they are offered. They often stay in that job for a lifetime. They are too scared to get a new job because they would be faced with new procedures and challenges. They won't get new and advanced training because the inevitable mistakes are just too painful.

Again McKay and Fanning say it beautifully:

> Framing mistakes as *necessary* feedback for the learning process frees you to relax and focus on your gradual mastery of the new task. Mistakes are information about what works and what doesn't work. They have nothing to do with your worth or intelligence. They are merely steps to a goal.

COMMON CATEGORIES OF MISTAKES

There are common categories of mistakes. Ten of the most common are:

1. **Errors of Data.** You write down a phone number as 529-6188 when it was actually 529-6185.
2. **Errors of Judgment.** You decide to buy the cheaper shoes, and they lose their form in six months.
3. **White Lies.** You say you're sick, and you run into your boss at the grocery store.
4. **Procrastination.** You keep putting off the visit to the dentist. Now it's the weekend, and you have a raging toothache.
5. **Forgetfulness.** You go out for a fun shopping trip and forget your money.
6. **Missed Chances.** The gold you decided not to buy at $48 an ounce is now $432 an ounce.
7. **Overindulgence.** You ate the whole thing, and you're sick all night.
8. **Wasted Energy.** You work on a manuscript entitled *Places in the Heart,* and a movie comes out with that exact title. (It happened to me.)
9. **Failure to Reach A Goal.** You're on the summer trip to the beach, and you're still fat.
10. **Impatience.** You try to flip the fish over the side of the boat, and it spits out the hook.

Many more categories could be added to the list. These are human issues. They are natural. The common thread running through all of these examples is this: a mistake is always the product of hindsight. McKay and Fanning write:

> A mistake is anything you do that you later, upon reflection, wish you had done differently. This applies to things you didn't do that you later, upon reflection, wish you had done.

Hindsight is what you see so clearly later on. The key word is "later." It is the later interpretation that turns the action into a mistake. A mistake is a label you apply in retrospect.

At the time you always choose the action that seems most likely to meet your needs. At the time, the benefits seem to outweigh the disadvantages. The action in any given moment depends on our awareness. McKay and Fanning define awareness as follows:

> Awareness is the degree of clarity with which you perceive and understand, consciously or unconsciously, all the factors relating to the need at hand.

Mistakes are the result of a later interpretation. Hence, mistakes have nothing to do with self-esteem. If you label your choice "bad" because it was a mistake in the light of later awareness, you end up punishing yourself for actions you couldn't help performing. Better labels for your past mistakes would be "unwise," "not useful" or "ineffective." These terms are a more accurate assessment of your judgment.

Expanding awareness is an obvious corollary to the problem of mistakes. If you are mistake-prone, you might consider expanding your awareness as you approach a course of action. This is the most useful solution. Vowing never to make the same mistake again is not useful because you will make the same mistake again if you do not expand your awareness.

Saying that you have always made the best decisions available to you does not relieve you of being responsible for your mistakes.

Responsibility means accepting the consequences of your actions. There is a consequence for every action. Becoming more responsible means expanding your awareness to be more aware of the consequences of your choices.

As you externalize your shame, your awareness increases. A shame-based person has a very low level of awareness because blocked and bound emotions bias one's ability to think and be aware. Internalized shame creates a kind of tunnel vision, which in turn narrows awareness and is manifested in distorted thinking. As one heals one's shame through the various externalization processes, awareness increases. You start getting your "brains out of hock."

THE HABIT OF AWARENESS

McKay and Fanning describe a simple procedure they call "the habit of awareness." They suggest certain questions to ask yourself when considering the likely consequences, both short- and long-term, of any significant decision you are to make. Here are the questions:

- Have I experienced this situation before?
- What negative consequences might be expected to come from the decision I plan to make?
- Are the consequences worth it, given what I expect to gain?
- Do I know any alternative with fewer negative consequences?

The chief ingredient of the habit of awareness is to make a commitment to yourself. You commit to examining the probable consequences of every significant act you do. This is a decision to love yourself. It is a decision to take the time to weigh and evaluate the consequences of your choices. After all, your choices are the fabric of your life!

11

Dealing with Toxic Shame in Relationships

*For there is but one veritable problem—the problem
of human relations. We forget that there is
no hope or joy except in human relations.*

—Antoine de Saint Exupéry
Wind, Sand and Stars

A common joke among Twelve Step recovering people is the oft-quoted statement: "We don't have relationships; we take hostages." This is one of those jokes that is aimed at lightening the pain experienced by shame-based folks trying to establish intimate relationships. Indeed, I would say that *intimacy is the number one problem resulting from internalized shame.* It certainly has been for me.

Intimacy requires the ability to be vulnerable. To be intimate is to risk exposing our inner selves to each other, to bare our deepest feelings, desires and thoughts. To be intimate is to be the very ones we are and to love and accept each other unconditionally. This requires self-confidence and courage. Such courage creates a new space in our relationship. That space is not yours or mine; it is ours.

As a shame-based person all this was impossible for me. I had no relationship with myself. I was in hiding, not only from you but also from myself. I was a human doing because I could not go inside myself.

There was no one there. I had no self. My relationship with myself was rejecting and contemptuous. What I feared most of all was exposure. I had no self to give to anyone.

235

ADULT CHILD CODEPENDENCY ISSUES

I suggested earlier that codependency and toxic shame were the same reality. In looking at relationships, the word "codependency" defines the problem very accurately. The phrase "adult child" also helps us see the problem.

ATTACHMENT AND BOND PERMANENCE

Because of abandonment trauma, shame-based people become adult children who form codependent relationships. These relationships are dominated by the fear of abandonment. They are the result of the "bond permanence" Alice Miller speaks of. Such relationships are dominated by attachment issues, either overattachment (enmeshment) or being underattached (isolation).

As an adult child it's hard for me to let anything go. I have notes I took in my first year of college fifty years ago! I have boxes full of odds and ends I've been keeping for years. Change for me is extremely difficult. Having been abandoned gives me a feeling of scarcity. I'd better hold on to what I've got because there may not be any more. It's hard for me to delay gratification for the same reason. There may not be any more.

I have had a hard time being flexible in my relationships. I have a monumental time giving up control. I have tried to set relationships up in such a way that I become so important to the other people that they cannot leave me. But ultimately I would start getting too close, and my commitment phobia would be triggered. Then I would leave the relationship. Others have the opposite problem; they cannot leave a relationship once they are in it.

CONTROL

Control is the great enemy of intimacy. By definition, intimacy excludes one person controlling the other. Control is the product of your disabled will. It is an attempt to will what cannot be willed. You cannot change another person. You cannot fix your parents, spouse, lover or children. You cannot control their lives or their pain.

ENMESHMENT

Having no authentic self, you look for a relationship with the only self you feel you have, your false self if you are a victim. The only relationship you know anything about is with a persecutor. The opposite is true if you are a persecutor. I was my mom's Surrogate Spouse and the Family Caretaker. As my mom's Surrogate, I always looked for women I could take care of.

What this amounts to is a reenactment of the fantasy bond I spoke of earlier. The fantasy bond is an enmeshed, codependent entrapment. It's based on the bond permanence that was set up by the abandonment trauma. Once fantasy bonded, we only have one relationship, and we repeat it over and over again.

The way out of all of this is through the original pain and Inner Child work, the basic grief work. Our bond fixation resulted from our authentic self being frozen by the unresolved abandonment trauma. Each time we reenact with a new fantasy bond relationship, we are trying to do the grief work. We choose the same kind of person in order to have another chance at resolution. Each new partner represents aspects of one or both of our parents. We try to make our partner into our parent(s) so we can resolve the conflict and move on. Since we are no longer children, it never works.

The only way out is to do the legitimate suffering that the grief work demands. To do this we have to give up the false self and leave home. That is the only way we can gain our true self.

OVERINVESTMENT OF POWER, ESTEEM AND EXPECTATION

Because any adult/child relationship is an immature child's relationship, it results in an overinvestment of power and esteem in the other person. Such an investment flows from the abandoned child's need to have a nurturing parent. Expecting one's partner to provide what one's parent failed to provide is a delusion. It is an unrealistic expectation and ends in disappointment and anger.

PROJECTION OF DISOWNED PARTS
OF SELVES ONTO RELATIONAL PARTNERS

One of the most damaging aspects of shame-based relationships is the projecting of our disowned parts onto our partner. In the movie *Terms of Endearment,* the fascination and repulsion of disowned selves was portrayed artfully. Jack Nicholson portrayed a man who was totally identified with his wild, impulsive, sexually indulging self. Shirley MacLaine portrayed a sexually repressed, perfectionistic, overly controlled, moralistic widow who lived next door. Each incarnated the extreme polarities of toxic shame. Jack Nicholson was dissipated and acted less than human. Shirley MacLaine was "holier than thou" and acted more than human. The couple had a lot to teach each other as they danced back and forth between attraction and repulsion. Finally each helped the other to integrate the self that had been disowned. He allowed her to embrace her sexual self, while she acquainted him with his conservative and nurturing self.

When I counsel people in destructive relationships, they usually are relating through their disowned parts. Generous men often marry selfish women; perfectionistic women marry sloppy men; nurturing women fall in love with emotionally unavailable men. Instead of learning from each other by incorporating their disowned selves, they live with these selves expressed in their mates. Since each disowns the part expressed by the mate, they are judgmental and angry about that part in their partner.

The integration of all the parts of self is primarily a process of self-acceptance. Wholeness and completeness result from total self-acceptance. Wholeness is the mark of mental health. Total self-acceptance means that every part of our self is okay. It's equivalent to unconditional love.

ATTRACTION/REPULSION COLLAGES

A variation of the exercise "making peace with your villagers" was suggested by Reverend Mike Falls. Mike has been counseling for some thirty years. He is a highly gifted and intuitive counselor. When a person comes in with relational problems, Mike often has them do the following.

He tells them to go through a series of magazines and select all the pictures of the people they feel attracted to. Next they are to make a collage of these pictures on a large poster board.

Then they go through the magazines and select the pictures of people they feel repulsed or turned off by. They also make a large poster board of those pictures. The collage of pictures that attracts you is more than likely the parts of you that you are overly identified with. The pictures that turn you off may very likely be composed of parts of yourself that you disown. Once you are aware of the parts that turn you off, you can dialogue with the disowned parts in the manner described in Chapter Four. I've used this procedure many times with outstanding results.

It's good to do the poster-board exercise with same-sex turnons and –offs as well as opposite-sex turnons and –offs. Men are often ashamed of their femininity and women of their masculinity.

Carl Jung believed that a part of each person's shadow was his contrasexual opposite. Every man and woman is the union of male and female hormones. Men have minority female hormones and majority male hormones. Women have minority male hormones and majority female hormones. The feminine shadow side of the male Jung called his "anima." The male shadow side of the woman he called her "animus." Integration of the anima/animus shadow is crucial for full human integration.

I have pointed out how our rigid cultural sex roles are ways we develop a false self, i.e., overidentify with one part of ourselves. Men are shamed for being feminine by being called names like "sissy" or worse. Women are shamed for being masculine.

I've mentioned *Terms of Endearment* as a movie that dramatically portrays the male-female polarity. Another movie, *The African Queen*, which stars Humphrey Bogart and Katharine Hepburn, is a brilliant portrayal of the male-female polarity. Bogart, as overidentified masculine energy, and Hepburn, as overidentified feminine energy, dramatize the fascination/repulsion dynamic of disowned parts of self. Eventually there is an integration of the disowned selves by each person in the movie, and each character is transformed by the addition of the energies represented by the other. Both movies were Academy Award winners. It would be interesting to see how many Academy Award winners portray this universal struggle for integration and wholeness.

DANGEROUS RELATIONAL SITUATIONS

Certain relational situations seem to be more vulnerable to shame induction than others. Criticism and rejection are painful for anyone. They are excruciating for shame-based people. I will deal with each of them separately. For now, let me describe certain situations that can regularly trigger shame spirals. These situations should be prepared for and kept on the tip of our consciousness. They are as follows:

TALKING TO PARENTS

Since parents are our source relationships, they present an ever-present risk of triggering old shame spirals. If you've been severely shamed in the past, be wary of casual talk with your parents. If you're working hard on shame reduction and you've done your stage II work, you will be well prepared to avoid getting hooked. If you haven't done such work, you are in danger. Just talking on the telephone can trigger old auditory imprints.

AUTHORITY FIGURES

One of the common characteristics of children of alcoholics is fear of authority figures. This almost always relates to the shaming abuse in a person's source relationships. It can also relate to shaming incidents in school. I know a psychology professor who begins to experience shame if he sees a policeman driving along the street. His mother used to threaten him by telling him that the police were going to pick him up and take him to jail. Such a practice is not uncommon. Many shame-based people experience overreactions of shame inducement just by the mere presence of a boss or authority figure.

NEW RELATIONSHIPS

Shame is often triggered in new relationships. The most common form it takes is in critical self-talk, which usually starts immediately after the other person has gone away. The shaming voices will suggest things like "Boy, you bungled that one!" or "Nice job, Mr. Clutch," or "You with that mumbled conversation." New relationships are risky because they expose us to someone we've never been exposed to before.

WHEN YOU OR THEY ARE ANGRY

Most shame-based people have anger deficits. We do not know how to express anger, and we are extremely vulnerable to being manipulated by anger. I'm thinking of a guy whom I really dislike. One day he expressed anger to me in a totally off-the-wall transaction. I was actually praising him. Several other people had told me that he was jealous of me. When I praised him, he reacted with anger. He heard something totally different than what I said to him. I ruminated over this incident for weeks. I wanted to call him and make everything okay. I used lots of self-assertive positive self-talk to stop myself. His anger was about him and his personal history. It had nothing to do with me.

Most of us were shamed with anger and rage. When someone expresses anger, our first reaction is fear. The various techniques in the section on criticism can help a lot in handling anger.

WHEN YOU ARE HURT OR YOU HURT SOMEONE

Because we've been hurt so badly, we fear hurting others. We often don't handle it well when we are hurt. If you had parents who manipulated you with hurts, you are especially vulnerable to hurts. Shame-based parents manipulate their children with hurts whenever the child's behaving in a way they dislike. "You kids will never know how you've hurt your father," or "I don't know if I can ever forgive you. You've hurt me so badly." A lot of hurts are pure manipulation. They are used to get one's own way. Healthy relationships are accountable. If I've hurt you, I want to own my part in it. I also know that some of it is about you and your history.

SUCCESSES

In *Man Against Himself,* Karl Menninger describes a number of people who had complete breakdowns after they achieved success. Some even killed themselves. Shame-based people do not believe they have the right to be so happy. Deep down, their toxic shame tells them they have no right to money or fun when other people are poor and suffering. The success is not limited to material prosperity. You can feel toxic shame after being rewarded with any kind of honor. Often this is a family system issue. If the other members of the family are still in their old, frozen, rigid roles, and one member breaks out and creates a unique life of her own, that member may feel shame for being so different and successful. Remember, in dysfunctional families no one is supposed to leave her role in the family.

RECEIVING AFFECTION AND STROKING

Shame-based people have great trouble with compliments and praise. Deep down the toxic shame cries out, "You don't have the right to be loved and receive all this attention." If you've worked hard at the material I've presented in Chapter Five, you will know that you are lovable. Your own unconditional loving relationship with yourself will be the basis of your accepting all love and praise as your just due.

CRITICISM

Years ago I wrote half a book about how to live with a critical person. Somehow I never got around to finishing the book. I felt that criticism was a major blight on human relationships and that people needed help in defending themselves against it. Certainly shame-based people are repelled and pained by criticism. They are also attracted to it as a way to interpersonally transfer shame to others.

I've never believed there was any value in so-called "constructive criticism." In our share groups we give each other *feedback*. Feedback is high quality, sensory-based observation *without interpretation*. In a group setting, feedback can be enormously helpful. But criticism, as I define it, is always a subjective interpretation based on one person's experience and grounded in that person's personal history. As such, it is not very useful.

I encourage shame-based people to avoid being critical, and I offer the following techniques as ways to handle a critic.

The main principle in handling criticism is *Never defend yourself.* If you defend yourself, you're taking on the toxic shame. To help you remember these techniques I've named each of the ways to handle direct criticism with a word starting with the letter C. My techniques are: clouding, clarifying, confronting, Columboing, confessing, confirming, comforting and confusing.

CLOUDING

Clouding is an adaptation of a technique taken from assertive training. Manuel Smith calls it fogging. In this technique you acknowledge the truth, the possibility of the truth or the probability of the truth. You do not defend. You simply let the critic's statement go through you like a cloud. For example, you are talking to your mother on the telephone. She says, "Your children are undisciplined. They are going to get in trouble at school." You answer, "You're right. They may get in trouble at school." You acknowledge the possibility of the truth of your mother's statement. Then she might say, "Well, when are you going to give them more discipline?" You say, "I'll give them more discipline when they need it." This is vague enough, and it acknowledges the truth of the statement.

CLARIFYING

Clarifying is a way to pin your critic to the wall and expose the shame-transferring intention of the criticism. Let's imagine your spouse says, "You're not going to wear those brown pants are you?" You answer, "What is it about these brown pants you don't like?" No matter what the critic says, you ask for clarification. If the critic says, "They look cheap." You say, "What is it that you don't like about cheap pants?" or "Why do cheap pants bother you?" These questions force your critic into an adult part of her personality. The adult is not contaminated by repressed feelings. The adult is oriented toward logic and objectivity.

The usual outcome of this technique is a dissipation of the critic's energy. One question after another will smoke out the real issue that lies behind the criticism. The real issue is either purely subjective or an attempt by the critic to cover up his own shame and pass it on to you. This technique does not always work. None of them always works. However, the more techniques you have, the more protective choices you have.

CONFRONTING

Confronting means what it says. You confront your critic. It is a form of assertiveness. In confronting, I recommend that you follow these guidelines:

1. Stay under your own skin. Say what you perceive (see and hear), what you interpret, what you feel and what you want.

2. Use "I" messages. Be responsible for what you perceive, interpret, feel and want.
3. Use sensory-based behavioral detail rather than evaluative words.
4. Look the person right in the eyes. This has to be practiced. I teach people who are severely shame-based to stare at a spot between the person's eyes.

I had an example of confronting recently. I had just bought a new BMW convertible. It is the most expensive car I've ever owned. I have some cultural shame around growing up poor. Whenever I get around someone who is rich, my shame comes out. I start feeling inferior, like I don't belong. This same shame comes out when I have something (like a new BMW) that costs a lot of money. It is especially bad if I'm around someone who has very little money. Although I've worked hard on this, it still happens from time to time.

When I showed my car to one of my relatives, he gave me a left-handed, critical comment. He said, "Wow, that's a beauty. I bet a whole family could live for a year on what you paid for that car." When I heard the statement my mind went blank. I started to feel shame. A voice said to me, "You could have got something for half the price and given some money to the poor and needy." I've worked hard on my voices. I countered with, "I love myself for celebrating my life with a fine new car." I looked at my relative and said, "When you make comments like that, I interpret that you feel bad about my good fortune. Somehow my good fortune triggered your shame. I'm sorry you have that shame, and I'm going to send you a copy of my new book on healing shame." At that point my relative began a long, defensive diatribe about my sensitivity. He allowed that he meant no harm and that I misinterpreted him. He said he was very happy for me, that I deserved it. I agreed and drove away! Confrontation may trigger rage in your critic. In that case, I simply say, "I'll be happy to talk to you when you stop raging," and I leave. Withdrawal is an assertive behavior in the face of a bully or offender type criticism.

COLUMBOING

Columboing is taken from the antics of the TV detective Columbo. Detectives come in all sizes, shapes and styles. Columbo is sloppy and unkempt. He is constantly asking questions. He seems in awe of the people he interrogates. He seemingly doesn't know enough to come in out of the rain. Yet there's a profound brilliance in his apparent ineptness. He never misses the most insignificant detail. He checks everything out. He is a master of concrete, specific detail.

When you Columbo your critic, you play dumb and ask a lot of questions. You say, "Now let me see if I'm getting this straight. . . .You think I should stop wearing my hair this way. . . . What is it about my hairstyle that you don't like?" When they answer your question, you go through the same routine. The goal is to get to the bottom of it, to expose their subjectivity. The criticism is usually about their toxic shame, and not about your hairstyle. By Columboing you avoid defending yourself and get the other person out of his critical parent cover-up.

CONFESSING

This response is useful if you have clearly and unequivocally done what you're being criticized for. If you spilled the milk, you say, "Yes, I did spill the milk." Simply make an acknowledging statement. *Do not* add things like, "How stupid of me!" The tenth step in Twelve Step programs states, "When we were wrong, we promptly admitted it." This is a maintenance step. Its aim is to keep us focused on our healthy shame. We can and will make mistakes. We need not apologize for them. They are part of the human condition.

CONFIRMING

This is a technique you can use when talking to a parent. It can be used when talking to any critical person. I like to use it on the telephone. As you are talking and the other person becomes critical, put your hand over the telephone mouthpiece and say aloud, "No matter what you say and do to me, I'm still a worthy person." Repeat this statement over and over again.

You can also anchor this positive statement. As you say it aloud, visualize yourself as standing tall, looking confident and looking the other person in the eye. As you feel the strength and power of this, touch your left thumb and left finger together. (It doesn't matter what hand you use.) Hold the touch until you feel the power of confirming yourself. Later on, sitting in your boss's office, or in some context where an authority figure is criticizing you, you can fire your anchor by touching your left thumb and finger together. You can hear your own confirming voice as you look at the authority figure.

COMFORTING

I use this method when I've inadvertently and unintentionally violated another person's boundary. The goal of comforting is to allow the other person to express his feelings, not to blame or defend yourself.

Comforting is exactly the same behavior as active listening. Let's say my car was blocking the driveway. I am away from the house. I've gone jogging. When I return, my wife is upset and angry. She says, "I have a dental appointment, and I'm late. You should have asked if I needed to use my car." I say, "Gosh, I hear that you're upset and angry. I'll move the car right now," or "I hear your frustration," or "I know how upsetting that is."

Comforting is a form of accountability. It allows us to acknowledge another's upset concerning our unintentional trespass and to make reasonable amends. What it avoids is triggering a shame spiral by putting ourselves down. Unintentional hurts are part of the human condition.

WHEN ALL ELSE FAILS—CONFUSING

This is a technique I advise using in nonintimate relationships. It is a technique to use when you've tried other methods. Confusing is a way to get someone off your back. Use it when you feel vulnerable and you can't seem to confront or clarify.

In confusing, you use either a big word or a made-up word, out of context. For example, a fellow employee scolds you for taking too much time on your lunch hour. You do not want a confrontation or hassle. You've been through this situation before with this person and it ended in a unresolved harangue. So you look at him and say, "Boy, the traffic was otiose today." The use of an unfamiliar word, or a word out of context, is often a real stopper. You can see the perplexed look on the other person's face. His mind is now involved in a search for the meaning of what you just said. You just smile and walk away.

This technique involves the fun, childish part of you. You can feel gleeful as you see the other person's perplexity. It puts you in control. Remember, criticism is a cover-up for shame and a way to control another person. Confusing is a technique that allows you to maintain control. It can afford you a moment of pleasure rather than defensiveness.

Nothing works all of the time. If one of these techniques does not work, try another. They form an arsenal of support to protect you from the inter-personal transfer of shame.

REJECTION

There is no greater potential for painful shame than rejection. This is a truism for all relationships. But for shame-based people, rejection is akin to death. We have rejected ourselves; when someone on the outside rejects us, it proves what we fear the most: that we are flawed and defective as persons. Rejection means we are indeed unwanted and unlovable.

There are degrees of rejection, ranging from the store clerk not smiling to being rejected and left by a cherished lover. The pain of the latter rejection is physical as well as emotional. It feels like a knife in our chest. I've only experienced it once; I certainly would not want to repeat it. I've been with scores of clients as they go through the pain of this kind of separation.

All the techniques I've outlined can be useful while going through the grief of a broken heart. The more one has done the original pain work and left one's fantasy bonded family enmeshments, the better one will be able to handle rejection. If one is still fantasy bonded and enmeshed, the rejection is equivalent to death. For a fantasy bonded person, the rejection impacts the hurt and lonely child who has never resolved the original grief. So I heartily recommend that *you do original pain and Inner Child work* as a way to lessen the pain of future potential losses. The more you have differentiated and separated, the better you can handle separation and aloneness.

I once thought of writing a book called *I Grieve, Therefore I Am.* I wanted to show that to live well is to grieve well. Everything you have ever done has ended. Life is a prolonged farewell. Grief is the process that finishes things. The end of grief work is to be born again. So to live well is to grieve well.

When going through the grief of personal rejection, you need legitimization, social support and time. You need a loving and significant other to be with you. You need your feelings mirrored and affirmed. It's better if you have more than one significant other. This is the advantage of having a Twelve Step group or any kind of support group.

Grief goes through all the stages I've described: shock, denial, bargaining, depression, anger, remorse, sadness, hurt, loneliness, etc. You need time to go through your grief stages. The worst thing you can do is rush into a new quick-fix relationship. I've seen this happen disastrously. The new relationship covers up the grief core, and another layer of unfinished grief accrues. Grieving a rejection takes time. Stay close to nourishing and supportive relationships. You are a worthy and precious person, in spite of the other person's leaving you.

Finally, remember that your internalized shame resulted from your childhood abandonments. Your worst fear (rejection) *has already happened and you survived it.* You were a needy, vulnerable and immature child and you survived. Wow! You can and will survive again.

MAKING A "SHAME SIREN"

Lesser rejections are part of the "terrible dailiness" of life. I use an adaptation of a technique I first heard Terry Kellogg describe to deal with the everyday rejections of life. It involves developing a "shame siren." A shame siren is a kind of anchor. When someone slights you, overlooks you, gives you an evaluation or out-and-out rejects you, do the following:

1. Imagine that you have a siren you can turn on by pulling your ear. (Either ear is okay.) When you pull your ear, you hear a siren that shrieks out, "Shame, shame, shame, shame, shame, shame." Hear it loud and clear.

2. Say to yourself, "Oh, it's only a feeling. . . . I'm really a worthy person." Say this several times to yourself. In this way you externalize the internalized shame. You transform it from a state of being back into a feeling. Feelings rise and fall. They are over and done with.

3. Call at least one person in your most significant support group (or actually see him or her if that's possible). Ask that person to verify your goodness and lovableness. Say, "Tell me I'm a lovable and beautiful person." This restores the interpersonal bridge.

If you get in the habit of using the "shame siren" it will become second nature to you. I've found that I have less and less overreaction to being slighted and being evaluated by others when I use my shame siren.

LOVE IS WORK

There are many other things I've done to work on shame in my inter-personal relationships. I've spent many hours learning and practicing effective communication techniques. I've done several assertiveness training and awareness seminars. All of these have enhanced my relationship skills.

THE COUPLES JOURNEY

The work of love involves commitment. This means I have to make a decision to hang in there. Remember that shame-based people have an all-or-nothing core of grandiosity. If it's not going my way, I'll leave. It's all or nothing!

Marriage is a journey. A superb coach and therapist, Susan Campbell based her book *The Couples Journey* on a long study she had done of a large number of couples who had been together in excess of twenty years. She found that each of these couples had gone through similar stages and struggles in the journey to intimacy.

ROMANTIC STAGE

Each couple had been in love. This was the romantic stage. That stage was characterized by a fusion of boundaries. It felt oceanic and powerful. The couple felt they could conquer all! When they married, a new stage soon began.

POWER STRUGGLE

In this stage the boundaries bounced back. There was no longer a fusion of differences. Each person's family-of-origin rules came into play. The Hatfields and McCoys had to battle it out. This was a stage of really coming to know each other's differences. Rules about money, sex, sickness, socializing, celebrating, household maintenance and, with the arrival of children, parenting had to be negotiated. This took ten years for most of the couples. It was followed by a stable period of settling down. All was quiet and routine for a while. But soon aging, the empty nest and the individuation process ushered in a third stage.

OWNING PROJECTIONS AND ACCEPTING PERSONAL RESPONSIBILITY

This stage was characterized by a soul-searching journey of personal responsibility and a quest for ultimate meaning. Each partner owned his/her anima/animus projections. The men became individuated by embracing their female side. The women owned their masculine side. They embraced their generative needs for self-actualization. As each partner became more and more complete, a new and fruitful stage began.

PLATEAU INTIMACY

Because the partners were complete within themselves, they could come to their partner out of desire rather than neediness. There was no longer any patching up of each other's deficits. The new bond was based on choice and decision, rather than fantasy bonding out of neediness.

Each could love more generously. Each gave because he/she really wanted to. A new plateau of intimacy emerged. Some of the qualities of the in-love stage returned. Each was fascinated with the other's uniqueness and differences. Each became the other's cherished friend. Each was bonded out of deep respect and appreciation of the other.

The journey toward intimacy is marked by the following: healthy conflict, learning to negotiate and fight fair, patience, hard work and the courage to risk being an individual. Above all, it is marked by a willingness to embrace a disciplined love.

The bottom line is that achieving love and intimacy in a relationship is a dynamic process. Such a process ebbs and flows. It is marked by conflict and individuation. In the end it is all worthwhile. I believe with Saint Exupéry that "there is no hope or joy except in human relations."

PART III

Spiritual Awakening—
The Discovery
Process

It is the wounded oyster that mends itself
with the pearl. . . .
—*Ralph Waldo Emerson*

What am I, an infant crying in the night,
Crying for the light
And with no language but a cry.

                 —Alfred Lord Tennyson

Introduction:
Healthy Shame as the Source and Guardian of Spirituality

Now that the biblical scholars have demythologized the word "diabolic," which comes from the Greek word diabolos and literally means "to tear apart," we have to consider the danger of holding on to words like "Devil" and "Satan" and conceiving of our moral spiritual life as a struggle between two polarized absolutes. Doing that tears us apart because it makes one person or one group either all good or all evil. In our battle with Muslim terrorists, they call us the Great Satan, and we call them the Great Satan. Nothing can come of such polarization except annihilation and destruction. I have no love of the theological stance of Muslim fundamentalists, but I have no love of the theological stance of Christian fundamentalists.

With healthy shame we look at the log in our own eyes; we make every effort at nonviolent solutions.

John Sanford, the great Jungian Episcopal theologian, once said:

> Deliver me from people who want to "do good"—because in their zeal they overlook the impact their good is doing to individuals and the ultimate consequences of their actions.

The demonic is fostered by toxic shame and its cover-ups, righteousness, blame, speechlessness, fear, conformity and the loss of autonomy.

Healthy shame moves us to polarity—polarity is not all or nothing, it is both/and. In Vietnam we sometimes exhibited as much brutality as the people who horrified us with their brutality. With healthy shame we own our shadow, our prejudice, our disgust and dissmell.

Symbolic and Spiritual

The psychiatrist Rollo May has pointed out that diabolic is the antonym of symbolic. The word "symbolic" comes from sym-bollein, which means to unite or throw together. May comments that "there lies in these words tremendous implications with respect to an ontology of good and evil." The symbolic is the natural language of true religion and spirituality because true religion and spirituality aim at uniting and reconciliation. They speak of that which cannot be reduced to the literal. They deal with awe, mystery, love and transcendence. Thoreau, Gandhi and Martin Luther King, Jr., not to mention Jesus Christ, have shown us the life-transforming power of nonviolence.

Evil and good coexist as possibilities in each of us. Their creation depends on free will. Goodness depends on sound ethical judgment, which as Jung points out (as did Aristotle long ago) is not black and white. Good and evil are not polarized absolutes but depend for their existence on the choices we make.

When we've developed a refined and mature sense of shame we are in awe of the mysteries of life and death, good and evil. We are in awe of God, understood as our Higher Power. Our shame tells us we are not God—we are finite and our judgments are prone to mistakes. Our healthy and mature shame brings with it our sense of humility.

I've outlined a rough sketch of how healthy and mature shame naturally leads us to a generative place from which good human judgment and choice can ensue. The fruit of mature and healthy shame is spirituality in the full sense of the word. Spirituality is nourished by symbol. It is an inner life characterized by rigorous honesty—an honesty that is profoundly aware of its strengths and weaknesses. Spirituality is about love and union, it aims at reunion, compassion, service and forgiveness. Toxic shame is the source of righteousness, self-contempt, self-hate and violence. Toxic shame is the foundation of evil. It cannot be fully healed without a "spiritual awakening."

12

Spirituality and Sexuality

Lovers look into each other's eyes, not at the other parts of their bodies. For in the eyes shame (aidos) dwells.

—Aristotle

We find the spiritual marriage not beyond the sensual, but through it, by means of it. The lover explores the body of his beloved and discovers himself at his source. His partner has brought out his erotic potential and given it the opportunity for realization: but what is exposed to real love is always the deep soul, never only what mentality we intend or understand.

—Thomas Moore
The Soul of Sex

During the time I was engaged in formal counseling, I noticed that many people who had sexual problems really had spiritual problems, and that many people with obsessive spiritual problems really had sexual problems.

"THE SECOND COMING"

I remember sitting in my counseling office waiting for a new client. I could look out on Main Street from my office window. I saw a woman walking down the sidewalk toward my office. The woman was literally stopping traffic. Car horns were honking, guys were putting their heads out of the windows of their cars and giving catcalls to the woman. As she drew closer, I could see she was dressed in a way that grossly emphasized her breasts, hips and, as she passed, her buttocks. To my surprise, when I went into my waiting room, there she was. She was the client I was waiting to see.

255

As she seductively sat across from me, she said, "I'm involved in several Christian Bible discussion groups," and, as she stretched to show off her huge bosom, "I want to know if you believe in the Second Coming." I felt a long pause of shame and realized that at that moment, I was thinking of the third and fourth coming!

It turned out that this woman, obsessively involved in church services and Bible discussion groups, had three lovers and was the mistress of the head of a hospital board who was subsequently indicted for fraud and embezzlement of hospital funds. She was also given jail time for a part she had played in the embezzlement. Without going into any more details about her dysfunctional family of origins, it should be obvious this woman had a real split between her sexuality and spirituality (really her religiosity). She was purportedly involved in religious activities and Bible study, but she really was spiritually bankrupt. Her obsessive religiosity covered up her sexual addiction.

In my book *Creating Love,* I present a diagram that describes any addiction as a pseudo form of religion. Shakespeare described alcoholism as a kind of idol worship that transforms the alcoholic into "a beast." Every addict worships a false god (alcohol, cocaine, sex, etc.). I based my pseudoreligion model on the toxic shame cycle (page 37) which I adapted from Pat Carnes's book *Out of the Shadows,* where he describes the squirrel cage that is the outcome of sexual addiction. The addictive system that Carnes presents can be used to understand any addiction. The sex addict's ultimate concern is sex. Paul Tillich, the Lutheran theologian, pointed out that when you find a person's most energetic and ultimate concern, it is there you find their god.

If we look at the addictive system described by Dr. Carnes, we can see that every sex addict has a god, a belief system (their dogma and doctrine), a mantra or prayer (their obsessive preoccupation with sex), and rubrics and rituals (the acting-out ritualization). The ecstatic climax is a kind of atonement (an "at-one-ment" produced by the analgesic mood alteration of orgasm). Unmanageability comparable to being a sinner (the consequence of meta-shame, a neurotic immorality guilt) pushes the addict deeper into their dogma or doctrine of impaired thinking and pseudoworship *(I'm flawed and defective and my savior—my greatest need—is sex).*

The sex addict's dogma is that "without sex my life is hopeless." During the acting-out cycles a person obsessively ruminates over their particular drug of choice: pornography, compulsive masturbation with pornography, cruising the Internet, indecent phone calls, affairs, molestation, rape or whatever. Then comes the rubrics or rituals that are part of the acting-out cycle. This may involve cruising the shopping malls or hustling partners in singles bars or on the Internet. More time is spent in the rubrics and rituals of sexual addiction than in the culmination of the addiction, which is the ecstatic orgasm.

The moment of ecstasy gives the addict a feeling of "at-one-ment" with the split shame-based self. But it is abortive and short-lived because the meta-shame and life-damaging consequences soon follow.

Recovering addicts of all kinds often move from their addiction to some kind of strict religiosity—they simply transfer one addiction for another. God can easily become a drug. In healthy recovery, addicts move toward a true spiritual awakening and a spiritual life. Part of a healthy spiritual life is healthy, soulful sexuality.

SEXUAL SHAME—THE AGONY AND THE ECSTASY

My colleague Dr. Pat Carnes, one of the pioneers in helping us clinically understand and treat sexual addiction, and I have given a seminar for the past three years entitled "Sexual Shame: The Agony and the Ecstasy." In this workshop, Dr. Carnes describes how toxic shame forms the various categories of sexual addiction. He outlines how to work with and treat sexual addiction that is based on toxic sexual shame.

My part in the workshop is to describe how healthy shame is the foundation for healthy sexuality. My work is derived from the German philosopher Max Scheler, who has outlined how "healthy shame forms, directs and fulfills" the healthy human sex drive. I also spend some time showing the relationship between healthy sexuality and spirituality. Indeed, healthy, soulful sexuality is a manifestation of spirituality. Let me briefly expand on Scheler's work and healthy sexuality as a manifestation of spirituality.

MAX SCHELER

The German philosopher Max Scheler wrote a book entitled *Über Sham ünd Schlamgefühl*. It was translated into French in 1952 under the title *La Pudeur*. I'm indebted to Carl D. Schneider's discussion in his book *Shame, Exposure and Privacy* for my understanding of Scheler's work.

Max Scheler outlines his belief that healthy shame forms, directs and fulfills the human sex drive. While toxic shame is the source of depersonalized sexual addiction, healthy shame is the source of truly awesome and reverent intimate sexuality.

In Figures 12.1A and 12.1B, I've made a rough outline of Scheler's work based on my reading of Carl Schneider's book. If you look at the chart on the developmental stages of healthy sexuality, you can see how the sex drive is formed from birth to puberty. The full emergence of the sex drive occurs at puberty, which is the time that the feeling of shame is most acute. I described shame as an affect auxillary—a boundary and limit that monitors our feelings of pleasure and excitement. The human sex drive is designed to be the most exciting and pleasurable of all the human drives.

As children begin full locomotion, they invariably discover their genitals and experience the pleasure they offer. A parent can affirm her child's genitals and gently remove the child's hands from playing with herself, letting the child know that public display of her genitals, as well as public display of masturbation, are not appropriate. Young children will naturally experience shame as their curiosity and pleasure are curtailed. Shame serves as a first boundary or inhibition of autoerotic excitement.

By three and a half to four years old, the dominant hemisphere of the brain is awakening, marking the beginning of the extensive use of language. At this stage a child's guardian needs to name things for the child. A boy is bound to ask why he has different genitals from his sister and vice versa. Sigmund Freud had a theory about this period, calling it the Oedipal period. He suggested that little boys, loving their mothers, want to replace their fathers and gain their mother's full love.

He believed that little girls, seeing that they had no penis, felt a kind of inferiority (only a man could conceive this). He called it the castration complex. Freud felt that both the Oedipal and castration complexes produce great guilt. Freud further fantasized that boys realize they are no match for

FIGURE 12.1A
Developmental Stages of Healthy Sexuality

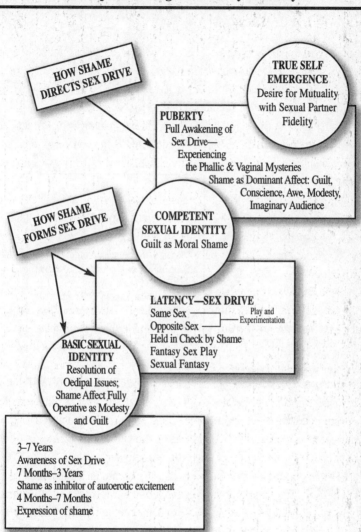

References:

Shame, Exposure and Privacy—Carl D. Schneider

The Evolution of Modesty—Havelock Ellis

The Justification of the Good—Vadimir Soloviev

Uber Scham ünd Schamgefuhl—Max Scheler (Fr. translation *La Pudeur*—McDupuy)

Paris: Aubier, 1952

FIGURE 12.1B
Developmental Stages of Healthy Sexuality

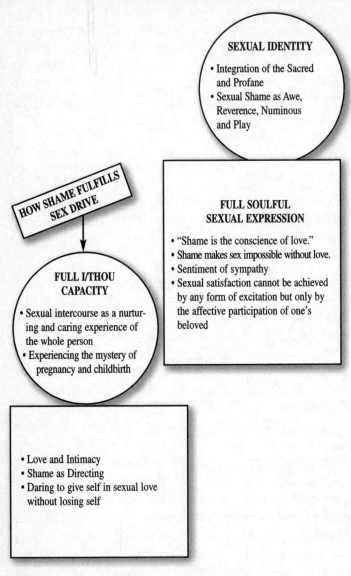

SEXUAL IDENTITY

• Integration of the Sacred and Profane
• Sexual Shame as Awe, Reverence, Numinous and Play

HOW SHAME FULFILLS SEX DRIVE

FULL SOULFUL SEXUAL EXPRESSION

• "Shame is the conscience of love."
• Shame makes sex impossible without love.
• Sentiment of sympathy
• Sexual satisfaction cannot be achieved by any form of excitation but only by the affective participation of one's beloved

FULL I/THOU CAPACITY

• Sexual intercourse as a nurturing and caring experience of the whole person
• Experiencing the mystery of pregnancy and childbirth

• Love and Intimacy
• Shame as Directing
• Daring to give self in sexual love without losing self

References:
Shame, Exposure and Privacy—Carl D. Schneider
The Evolution of Modesty—Havelock Ellis
The Justification of the Good—Vadimir Soloviev
Uber Scham ünd Schamgefuhl—Max Scheler (Fr. Translation *La Pudeur*—McDupuy)
 Paris: Aubier, 1952

their fathers, and girls believe they are inferior because of castration.

This is a fantasy theory. The fact is that little boys and girls are sexual and begin to form their earliest sexual identity between three and a half to eight years of age. What is perhaps most important for healthy sexual identity is their parents' good modeling of their sex roles, as well as their loving sexual relationship, guided by modesty, privacy and good boundaries. Genetic inheritance is also important for sexual identity.

GAYS, LESBIANS AND TRANSGENDERED

It seems clear that gay, lesbian and transgendered children have a different genetic inheritance than do heterosexuals. The following statement on the "gay brain" is taken from a recent book, *Mapping the Brain* by Rita Carter.

> In 1991 the prestigious journal *Science* published a study showing that the brains of a group of homosexual men who had died from AIDS were structurally different from the brains of heterosexual men. The nucleus in the hypothalamus that triggers male-typical sexual behavior was much smaller in gay men and looked more like that in the brains of women. The author, Simon LeVay, then associate professor at the Salk Institute for Biological Studies and adjunct professor of biology at the University of California, was immediately attacked by gay activists, who feared that the recognition of homosexuality as a physical-based condition might lead to it being restigmatized. LeVay, who is himself gay, then went on to discover that the corpus callosum differs between gay and straight men, too—in gays it was found to be bigger. Three years later a study led by molecular biologist Dean Hamer of the National Institutes of Health in Washington, DC, found evidence that a specific gene carried on the maternal line influenced sexual orientation in men. Put together, these studies provide strong evidence that homosexuality is rooted in biology, and hostility to the idea has largely disappeared.

I would add that common sense should tell us that no one would choose to be gay or lesbian. In a society where churches condemn them to hell, where they are the continuous butt of comedians' jokes and their very lives are threatened by warring fundamentalists, including mainline "redneck" homophobics and white supremacists, why would anyone choose to be gay or lesbian? "Coming out" simply means that a person is clear about his or her sexual orientation and has the courage to own it.

LATENCY

Freud called the juvenile period from eight to early puberty the latency period because he felt that the sexual issues of boys and girls were dormant until puberty. That has simply not proven to be true. There is natural curiosity, opposite-sex play and experimentation during the latency period. There is also a degree of sexual fantasy during this period.

If shame develops well and is consistent with the cognitive stages of development, it is experienced as modesty that is a natural part of sexual development. Modesty guards the realm of the private. We have natural behaviors of concealment. Children are often overexposed, i.e., toxically shamed, because their parents have no respect for their own or their children's privacy. Families need to have good generational boundaries. Mom and Dad need a private space of their own to share, to be intimate and sexual. Children also need privacy. They need to be able to lock the door in the bathroom. They will blush if their parents' nudity is too much for them. Parents need to guard their discussions and jokes about sexuality. Severe toxic shame is transferred by making jokes about their children's bodies, especially their genitals—the size of their son's penis or their daughter's breasts and buttocks. There is strong clinical agreement that this kind of joking and teasing constitutes sexual misconduct.

GUILT

Guilt is also developed during the juvenile period. Children often have an excessive sense of guilt due to what the Swiss psychologist Piaget called moral literalism or moral realism. As much as parents might try to soften their rigidity, their moral rules are thought of as concrete absolutes during the juvenile period. Children need a healthy sense of guilt, but parents, teachers and clergy persons do not need to be excessively rigid, especially about sex. Well-formed guilt and conscience are important elements in the development of healthy sexuality.

NO GENITALS

In my family there were no genitals! I cannot imagine my parents or grandparents having sex. I was caught in a chinaberry tree with a girl my age who lived down the block. I had shown her mine, and just as the great moment of her showing me hers was about to come, I heard my mother's booming voice saying, "Get down from there." She shamed me for days and weeks to come, trying to be sure I'd never do it again. I was told that what I had done was a mortal sin, one that condemns you to hell's fire! I was seven years old and had just made my first confession, a Catholic sacrament in which the priest you confesses to supposedly has the power of Jesus Christ to forgive your sins. My mother dragged me to the confessional. I was terrified! What if the priest refused? I'd be doomed. Thank God the priest was more enlightened and gentler than my mother.

PUBERTY

At puberty we experience the full awakening of the sex drive. To experience the pleasure of masturbating and reaching climax for the first time is an awesome and mysterious experience. I can remember the scene of my first awakening as if it just happened. I was in the bathroom and emptied my semen into the toilet! My scene has all the elements of toxic shame surrounding it. Immediately after the amazing pleasure, I felt the piercing eyes of God, who I had been taught was always watching us. I felt moral judgment and heard a chorus of mixed voices telling me I had committed a terrible sin. One voice told me to look for a wart on my hand. I looked, and thank God, my hands were both okay! Then I blinked several times to see if I was going blind. My eyes were okay! Then I heard voices saying that sex was good—a holy gift from God. What a confusion! The shame spiral fired like a Fourth of July fireworks show.

My sex education at Catholic parochial school had certainly not prepared me for the joy of my first experience of healthy sexuality. In the fifth grade, Sister Rogata used to read the examination of conscience before going to confession. At the place where she read "did I touch myself impurely," her voice would tremble. She could hardly say the words. I remember thinking how bad it must be to touch your penis if this holy woman of God was so upset by the very words describing it.

SEXUAL SHAME—THE ECSTASY

Few of us have been educated in a way that would allow us to experience the ecstasy of sexual shame as a sacred and holy mystery. With the exception of the Jewish bar and bat mitzvah we've lost the ritual of celebrations called "puberty rites." In the past, the advent of the sex drive was celebrated! There was a rite of passage whereby a man or woman moved from childhood to sexual adulthood. Human sexuality was considered mysterious and sacred.

Today our technology and scientism tend to see the facts of life without their human dimensions. Today sex is relegated to the world of facts, and it is divorced from value. Today we seem to have lost a sense of public modesty. "Modesty," says Carl Schneider, "is the emotional expression of our soul which knows everything has an unknown depth—a symbolic character."

The adolescent's mind is capable of experiencing this more abstract and symbolic value of modesty. Sexuality is a prime area of vulnerability and exposure—a sense of shame safeguards the individual from the public observance of private experience. Pornography is precisely the public exposure of sexual matters that belong to the private sphere.

I once counseled a sex addict whose drug of choice was pornography and compulsive masturbation. He told me that he lived alone, and that even though no one else was there he locked himself in his room and turned the lights to their lowest level when he viewed the pornography and masturbated. Cybersex, with its nineteen thousand new sites a day, is the perfect place to hide from exposure. The porn industry, according to Dr. Pat Carnes, has taken over the Internet. Cybersex is gaining new addicts by the day.

Anthropology points out there are rules for concealment of the genitals and restrictions on the time and manner of genital exposure in almost all primitive people. Sexual intercourse is conducted on the whole in private. In communal living, the sex act usually takes place outside the dwelling in the field, bushes, forest or beach.

MODESTY

Modesty, the developed form of healthy shame, safeguards a private place for sex. Modesty also regulates sexual relationships. Its purpose is to restrain us when love and intimacy are not present.

MODESTY—THE CONSCIENCE OF SEXUAL EMBRACE

For Scheler, healthy shame as modesty is "the conscience of love." When there is no sense of modesty at the beginning of sexual love, when there is no blush, there is only technique, role and repetition.

We humans are the animals who make love face to face, gazing into each other's eyes. The sex act is the fruition of an "I and thou" encounter, in which two subjects are moved toward sexual physical union in order to be as fully connected as possible. Carl Schneider suggests that we have lost the sense of shame as modesty. He writes: "The reduction of sexuality to temporary pleasure or adult play is due to the general dismissal of shame as the artificial inhibition imposed by a misdirected socialization."

Sexual shame as modesty and blushing safeguards the depersonalization of human sexuality, the so-called "cold fuck."

When depersonalized, the other is no longer a unique, unrepeatable subject, an "I," but is an object to be used and enjoyed. Pornography is an attempt to stimulate sexual feelings and a sexual relationship without the presence of a chosen loved one, i.e., another human being. Pornography is sexual obscenity. It is a depersonalized form of self-sex. If you think about sexual fetishes, pornographic pictures of naked men and women in demeaning sexual postures, phone sex, cybersex, indecent liberties, sex in massage parlors with a stranger, or sex with a male or female hooker—all amount to having sex with oneself. There is no relationship, no "I and thou," no intimate caring in such relationships.

TEENS GONE WILD

Our teenagers are bewildered by cybersex and the shameless excesses of pornography. It's little wonder "teens have gone wild." Without healthy shame as the "conscience of love" there are no boundaries to restrain the pleasure of sexual orgasm. Sexual shame is not there to restrain them when love is not present.

I'm not suggesting that masturbation or the exploration of one's genitals during adolescence is shameful or wrong. In fact, most clinical studies agree that a certain amount of sexual exploration and experimentation with oneself is normal. Certainly courting and kissing are a normal part of adolescence. But if people's sexual shame were developed in a healthy manner, they could talk about sex, even at home in early adolescence. If parents modeled and spoke of their sexuality as beautiful, wonderful and sacred from children's earliest days, then sex would be something less toxically shameful, although it would still be something private.

SEX EDUCATION

Adolescence is the time when formal sexual education is most appropriate. If parents, teachers and clergypersons are to perform their responsibilities to prepare those in their care for living their lives well, how could anything be more important at the developmental stage in which the sex drive emerges than sex education? Why are the elders so ashamed about such matters? Certainly we have to take into account religiously zealous parents who oppose any form of sex education. They pose a huge problem that I'm not capable of solving. I can say that as a high school religion teacher (I taught at two Catholic high schools), I saw this suppression as enhancing the young people's toxic shame. When I taught in college, I saw many of these toxically shame-based kids throw caution to the wind and go sexually berserk. There were many exceptions, of course, but the impact of early pregnancies and irresponsible, immature youngsters trying to raise children is a true disaster. Think of Felicia and Jerome, Max and Bridget and the early pregnancies their children reenacted. The problem of sexual promiscuity and early pregnancies is multigenerational and is a serious threat to the family as the foundation of society.

THE SOUL OF SEX

Thomas Moore, in his superb book *The Soul of Sex,* talks about the phallic and vaginal mysteries. Moore is one of the most profound spiritual writers of our time. He is a Renaissance man who has a vast knowledge of ancient mythology. The Greeks used the word "aidos" when speaking of the shame appropriate to sexuality. Aidos has the connotation of awe, as is evidenced in the text from Aristotle's *Eroticus,* which I used as an epigraph for this chapter. Aristotle described lovers as gazing into each other's eyes in aidos (awe), not at the other body parts. There is an avoidance of depersonalization and objectification expressed in such a statement.

Thomas Moore's work could be used as an important tool to help teenagers get a larger view of their emerging sexuality. He writes:

> The women of ancient Greece waved huge wooden phalluses during religious processions. They weren't advertising for bigger penises, they were celebrating the phallic potency in life, the divine power that grants a more than human passion for life.

Most people know from their own experience that penis or breast or buttocks size is not really important, yet wanting big penises, breasts and buttocks may be important because of the larger symbolism they embody. Our genitalia symbolize a particular aspect of life's mysterious power and possibility.

MEANING OF THE SEX ORGANS

Our secular way of thinking objectifies men and correlates sexual potency and personality with the size of the penis. Moore writes:

> From a less secularized point of view, the penis represents life's potency in the largest sense, something we all need and crave.

When we objectify and literalize the meaning of the penis solely as an aspect of male psychology, we miss the larger symbolic and value-laden idea that a soulful search for a bigger penis might be looked upon as a search for the phallus, the "source of erotic vitality." In some cultures, the phallus is an image of *divine potency.*

According to Moore, the ancient Greeks placed phallic images at gravesites, "presumably because Hermes, an especially phallic god, guided souls to the underworld." For the Greeks, this image of divine power had healing properties.

Moore asks why sex can't be symbolically looked upon as healing. "The phallus," says Moore, "represents life itself—procreative, pleasurable, rising and falling, penetrating, healing and enduring." Understood spiritually and symbolically, our powerful attraction to the penis, breasts and buttocks "may simply serve to spur us on to living a lively and abundant life."

A VAGINAL WAY OF BEING

"The vagina," writes Moore, "represents symbolically and in fact the originating sea out of which life is born." Because of our overemphasis and fetishlike obsession that associates the size of the penis with personal power, we have simply overlooked the symbolic and deeper significance of the vagina. In art, folk legend, Greek myth and psychoanalytic literature, the vagina symbolizes "a haven from the threats and cares of life, the goal of a regression toward our peaceful origins." In our aggressively heroic world of competition, success and "don't let the bastards churn you down," the vagina offers a contrary objective. In the symbolism of antiquity, the vagina is the holy of holies, the container in which life germinates and blossoms. Moore says, "This (the symbol of the vagina) is the realm of soul par excellence . . . containing, creating, warm and assuring."

I have written of toxic shame forcing us to become human doings and ignoring us for just being. Perhaps the fear men have of the feminine secret, the concave, nurturing vagina as a haven of nurturing and being, is related to our fear of just being.

All in all, we cannot understand our sexuality with awe and reverence if we reduce it to a valueless fact and eliminate the profound and deep mysteries associated with it.

The Greek playwright Artistophanes wrote *The Acharnians,* a play in which a grievous sexual sickness called satyriasis attacked the men of Athens because they refused to honor the Greek god Dionysus. Satyriasis was a disease of compulsive sexuality. The Greeks also used the word "priapism" after the phallic god Priapus, for a condition in which a man cannot get rid of an erection (long before Viagra). Moore suggests that the Greeks understood that when sexuality is objectified and depersonalized it loses its soul and becomes a metaphor for sexual addiction. "Could our so-called satyriasis," Moore asks, "be due to the neglect of the religious aspects of sex?" When sex is disengaged from awe, reverence and mystery (healthy shame), it becomes a sickness of soul and falls into the hog pen of spiritual bankruptcy. "Pornographic penises," writes Thomas Moore, "are symptomatic of our need to rediscover the phallus, with its religious appreciation of life's mysterious potency."

PUBERTY, MENSTRUATION, GENITALIA— THE MYSTERIES ASSOCIATED WITH THE BIOLOGY OF HUMAN SEXUALITY

The psychologist Abraham Maslow has written magnificently about the full human dimension of sexuality. In his book *Religion, Values and Peak Experience,* he shows how all human behavior must have the polarity of fact and value. There is an earthy dimension to sexuality and a spiritual, symbolic and deeper dimension along with it. Both must be present in understanding human sexuality.

Maslow writes, "Rather than being a local and temporary nuisance, menstruation can be seen as a biological drama that has to do with the very profound biological rhythm of reproduction, life and death. Each menstruation, after all, represents a baby that could have been." Most men see this strictly as something that they don't experience, something they don't know about, something that is altogether women's secret. Men tend to view it as a nuisance. What if it was understood as a mystery, making it a holy ceremony, rather than a messy accident or curse?

For practically all primitives, these biological sexual matters are seen in a more pious, sacred way, as rituals, ceremonies and mysteries. The ceremony of puberty, which we make nothing of, is extremely important for most primitive cultures. Maslow writes, "When a girl menstruates for the first time and becomes a woman, it is truly a great event and a great ceremony, and it is truly, in the profound and naturalistic human sense, a great

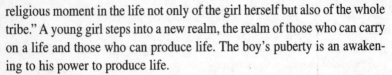

religious moment in the life not only of the girl herself but also of the whole tribe." A young girl steps into a new realm, the realm of those who can carry on a life and those who can produce life. The boy's puberty is an awakening to his power to produce life.

Maslow comments, "After all, menstruation, male ejaculation, marriage, pregnancy, new life, are in truth mysteries. If we lose our sense of the mysterious or the numinous, if we lose our sense of awe, of humility, then we have lost a very real and basic human capacity and are diminished thereby." The basic capacity is healthy shame.

Perceiving with healthy shame can also be a powerful self-therapy. "Practically every simple culture," says Maslow, "makes a very big fuss over the woman and her childbearing function and everything that has to do with it." To us moderns, their ceremonies over the placenta, the umbilical cord, menstrual blood and the various cleansing ceremonies may look ridiculous and superstitious. Yet the fact remains that by these methods they keep the whole area of the mythological, poetic and symbolic alive and sacred. Such a woman must think her menstruation and her menstrual blood can be powerful and dangerous. She must, therefore, think of herself as a pretty powerful person who is capable of being dangerous. She matters. She is important.

"We could see man's sexuality better," writes Maslow, "if all his mysteries were taken as true mysteries, e.g., the fact that he can produce erections and ejaculate spermatozoa, that these live, that they swim, that in some mysterious way they can penetrate the ovum and make a baby grow, etc."

His ejaculation is not just some casual or shameful spilling out of something, as mine was. Rather Maslow suggests, "It becomes as much a ceremony, a mysterious, awe-inspiring, piety-producing ceremony as any high religious ceremonies like the Mass, the Sun Dance, etc."

Imagine if we could teach this to our young men and our young women. Every boy would become the bearer of a holy thing, of a scepter, given to him by nature. We supply him thereby with an ultimate and irreducible self-esteem that is his simply by virtue of being a male, a man with a penis and testicles, which should at times awe the woman and the man as well. This attitude should help him think of his orgasm as a holy experience, a symbol, a miracle and a religious ceremony. This kind of thinking and imagining is a far cry from my experience with the toilet!

YOUNG ADULTHOOD—LUST,
ATTRACTION AND ATTACHMENT

If we had our adolescents study ancient mythology as part of their sex education, if parents had this spiritual and religious sense of sexuality as symbolic of an even deeper sense of creation and life's amazing power, our youngsters might better be able to handle their emerging sexuality.

If our sense of healthy shame could be preserved and we could view each other with healthy polarity, we could see a woman as a Madonna, a Priestess, as Mother Earth with nurturing breasts, as the uterus in which life is formed, and at the same time a chatty Kathy, sometimes empty-headed, too plump, horny, ordinary, sweaty, having to go to the toilet—then we could embrace her in her true human personhood. She would be hard to lust after or be attracted to if she were only a goddess or a Madonna, but she'd become an object to be used if she was robbed of her mystery and sacred uniqueness. In my high school you never thought of having sex with a "nice" girl.

The same with the male. If he could be viewed as the Hunter who brings home food and nourishment, the Conqueror of Nature, the one who knows about the outside world of things, the ruler, protector of the weak and inno- cent, *and* at the same time as controlling, unemotional, ogre father, making a meager living, not meeting the cultural images of physical prowess or success—then he could be loved in his perfectly/imperfect human polarity. If he is only the mythic rich hero, the knight in shining armor, the all-pow- erful conqueror of nature—then he can't be made love to, he must be revered and adored. Or if he is the deficient one, not living up to our cultural obsession with money making or athletic prowess, he is to be disdained. Much of the disgust in male/female relationships comes from sexual polarization of the kind I'm describing. When couples fall in love they tend to see only the sacred aspects of their partner, ignoring completely their profane status—nature wants life to go on and to expand, so nature pushes us to meet, mate and procreate. The chemistry of being "in love" is power- ful. It causes infatuation that is by definition foolish, shallow love. The chemical phenylalanine (PEA) triggers dopamine, the pleasure neurotrans- mitter, as well as norepinephrine, the chemical that triggers a sense of urgency. When couples have "in-love" sex they are flooded with oxytosin—

the same chemical that is found in the nursing mother's milk, which bonds the baby and the mother.

If we have a broken interpersonal bridge, a dysfunctional attachment, we are sitting ducks for love addiction and the pseudoconnection caused by the chemistry of the in-love state.

The PEA/dopamine cocktail wears off in eighteen to thirty-six months and the couple returns to their normal hormone levels. Creating a healthy, secure attachment will depend on how much each person has developed his/her sense of selfhood and emotional literacy and grieved their wounds from the past. In Susan Campbell's study of the couples' journey that I described in Chapter Ten, the second stage of the journey involved the working through family-of-origin differences, learning to argue well, learning to express needs and wants, listening, gifting, putting one's self aside in kindness and compromise, and developing an "I and thou" kind of respect for each other as unique, incomparable persons. When they achieved this, it spilled over into their sexual relations. This stage took some ten years for most of the couples to negotiate. As they grew as individuals, their love grew and their sexuality reached a satisfactory balance. This was the *fulfilling stage* of sexuality.

SEXUAL FULFILLMENT

Couples fulfill their sexuality by having a healthy sense of shame, which gives them a sense of awe and reverence for each other, respecting each other's perfectly imperfect humanity. As I will discuss in the next chapter, when two people in a relationship have a solid sense of themselves, real individualities, awareness of themselves that includes knowing and accepting their own strengths and weaknesses, they can accept each other as whole people. Each person has integrated their healthy shame as the permission to be human. Knowing and loving their own deficiencies as part of human nature, neither partner projects his or her deficiencies on the partner.

Their sexual relationship moves into the realm of value and is spiritual. Each person has the ability to love in an "I and thou" embrace. Subject to subject, with equality and intimacy, sexual intercourse becomes a nurturing and caring experience of each other as whole human people.

SPIRITUAL AND SOULFUL SEX

Soulful sex is grounded in sexual shame as aidos (awe and reverence). Shame as aidos makes sex impossible without love and empathy for each other. Sexual satisfaction cannot be achieved by any technique or form of excitation, but only by the affective participation of one's beloved.

Shame as awe and reverent modesty protects human sexual relations from degradation and profanation. I counseled many couples whose sexuality was marred by the sexual compulsivity and addiction of one of the partners. This often involved one partner "acting out" sexuality with the other, such as a husband demanding "blow jobs" or "hand jobs" without any concern for his partner's satisfaction.

I saw couples involved in the other polarization of sexual addiction—sexual anorexia. Sexual anorexia is a phobic avoidance of sex after the couple is married and/or committed. It often comes from the polarization I described earlier where one partner has toxically shaming messages about "having sex with someone you love or respect." Many people carry such toxic sexual shame that they cannot function when sex is not dirty and forbidden.

Soulful sexuality between two committed human beings can be playful, experimental, earthy and as erotic as whatever the templates of arousal are for each other. As long as love and valuing, affection and moral considerations are in their intentions, the sexual relation is fully human and therefore deeply soulful and spiritual.

DISGUST

Healthy shame as aidos inhibits the sexual response until the whole self responds to the other person in their wholeness. To ignore the restraints of healthy shame is to invite powerful negatives. Disgust is the most common negative response. "Without heeding the restraint of modesty," writes Schneider, quoting Max Scheler, "disgust is aroused." Healthy shame as modesty and aidos (awe and reverence) appears as a resistance in any sexual occasion that involves only the services of the other and not the genuine giving of the self. Max Scheler goes so far as to say "that shame (modesty, awe) resists physical intimacy, even in relationships where two people love each other, if the moment of desire is not accompanied by a loving attitude."

I saw a great deal of disgust turned into hatred in relationships that came to me at the point of divorce. Most often the disgust and hatred were caused by one or the other's violation of their partner's healthy shame.

The beauty of couples in fulfilled sexual relationships is rooted in a core of mutuality and spirituality. Healthy sexuality is indeed a form of deep spirituality. It has nothing to do with the frequency of the act but everything to do with respect, friendship and a sense of the true mystery of sexual intercourse between two people who are deeply committed to each other in love.

Thomas Moore comments on the fact that everything in life suffers when our vision of it is too small. "Sex," he writes, "is the religion of marriage. It is its contemplation, its ritual, its prayer and its communion." And in another place, commenting on spiritual depths in sexuality, Moore says, "Sex purifies. In various stages of mutual generosity . . . gazing, touching and being touched, the individuals lose defendedness and discover what it means to be present in another, body and soul."

13

Shame as Revelatory and Revolutionary: Discovering Your Spiritual Destiny

When death finds you, hope that it finds you alive.

—Source unknown

Exposure to oneself lies at the heart of shame.
We discover in experiences of shame
the most sensitive, intimate and vulnerable parts of ourself.

—Anonymous

Each mortal thing does one thing and the same. . . . myself
it speaks and spells, crying, "What I do is me: for that I came.

—G. M. Hopkins

I've referred to the "true self" as the indestructible center of the self. Major spiritual traditions have always referred to this core of self as the soul. Many religions teach that the soul is immortal. I don't know about that, but there is scientific support for the self's intuitive ability to use the outer environment for its own survival. The shame-based false self is a necessary adaptation for a person's survival.

THE ADAPTIVE DESIGN OF THE HUMAN PSYCHE

The psychologists Malcolm Slavin and Daniel Kriegman, in their book *The Adaptive Design of the Human Psyche*, have presented an argument for the evolved adaptation of a "true self" in all humans. Slavin and Kriegman write:

275

We have from the very beginning some form of implicit intuitive capacity to "know" certain givens about ourselves. We have a class of motivations that are largely independent of the shaping and regulating influence of the relational world. We could never be designed in a way that permits the claim that motivations arise solely from lived experience.

Slavin and Kriegman's argument rests on the question of "inclusive fitness." What must the human child accomplish psychologically in order to enhance its own inclusive fitness? If life has an edge and only the fittest survive, how does a tiny, helpless infant ensure its survival in a world of cultural biases? In Chapter Four we discussed the part played by the "consensus reality"—religion, family and the school system—in inducing toxic shame. How do we overcome these obstacles to our true selves?

The neotonous drive in all humans pushes us to maintain the childlike and juvenile qualities of the true self, but we must be intuitively capable of self-interested deceit in order to survive. Slavin and Kriegman write:

> In order to have adapted, the human psyche must be equipped to deal with the normal biases and deceptions of the "good enough average developmental environment," i.e., a normal environment. There is a built-in human capacity to experience the world in a self-interested manner. We are biological organisms that have evolved to actualize our own self-interest with others.

In my toxically shaming family, I learned early on that I would best survive by being a caretaker of others, especially my mother's pain. I also used my true self's talents to be the Star and to superachieve.

High achievement and leadership strengths are a part of my true self. But I learned to adapt by using my talents to take care of everyone else, not myself. Deep down I learned to feel the toxic shame that caused me to pit my false self against my true self. My own feelings and need for self-care and nourishment were judged not okay, so I repressed them and used my natural ability to deceive in developing my false self.

DECEPTION FOR SURVIVAL

The natural ability to deceive is part of our true self's ability to survive. No one would morally judge a Jew for lying to a Nazi in order to survive. The renowned biologist Robert Travers writes:

> Since deceit is fundamental to all animal communication, there must be a strong selection to spot deception, and this ought in turn to select for a degree of self-deception rendering some facts and motives unconscious so as not to betray—by the subtle signs of self-knowledge—the deception being practiced. Regression of the true self is an evolved adaptation used by the child as a deceptive tactic and developmental strategy.

REPRESSION

Slavin and Kriegman have recast the terminology used by Freudian and neo-Freudian psychology. Slavin and Kriegman redefined repression. Repression, for example, is not concerned with our instinctual drives for pleasure or destruction, as it was for Freud. Rather, repression is the defense our true self uses to put its desires, needs and feelings aside in order to survive.

The child must maximize the amount of investment (love, time, interest, guidance) provided by an environment (parental and otherwise) that is biased by its own self-interest and its own level of functionality. The child, in order to survive, needs to develop an internalized map of reality that includes an accurate guide to the relational world, but he must be able to correct and compensate for parental biases so he can build crucial aspects of his own unique self. The evolutionist wants to know how the human child evolved the basic structural dynamic capacity to maintain and promote an unbiased sense of his or her own self and self-interest throughout a long developmental process that involved a biased and often deceptive set of interactions.

Slavin and Kriegman write, "Some of the answer lies in the evolved ability to 'repress' crucial dimensions of meaning related to personal experience." And when repression is understood in this revolutionary context, it is seen as a mechanism to ensure the dynamic function of the true self.

From this evolutionary viewpoint, repression is a state in which something is missing in a person's "experience of him- or herself." Some crucial dimension of meaning is absent in the child's account of his or her own experience. "Missing but not necessarily lost forever," write Slavin and Kriegman, "by using the adaptive mechanism of repression, the child is thus an active strategist of his or her own development." Repression is a way to safeguard the child's true self, his or her own version of reality, including his or her own wishes when they conflict with their parents' identities and view of reality. Once again, Slavin and Kriegman write:

> Repression allows the reality of the true self to be put out of consciousness and to be held in reserve so that it can be allowed to reenter the child's repertoire when conditions change and the need for repression is lessened and can be retrieved, as the child's true self is needed to fulfill his or her unique interest and destiny.

REENTRY OF THE TRUE SELF

Once our toxic shame is embraced and we come out of hiding, we begin the uncovery process I described in Part II. As our ego strength is rebuilt and we gain mastery by developing a solid sense of selfhood and self-esteem, our true selves are ready to reveal themselves. If we are willing to pursue it, the revelation of the "true self" will lead to the revolutionary discovery of our spiritual destiny and calling. Each of our true selves is a unique manifestation of our Creator, and each true self manifests something of the Creator that we alone can manifest. I like to say that the whole world is a library and each person is one unique book in that library so that by my knowing and loving you, I learn something of our Creator that I could not have known any other way. When any one of us dies, our unique story lives on in the hearts of those who have known and loved us. This is the joy of our spiritual destiny. It is also the stage of great tragedy for those toxically shame-based people who die having never come out of hiding.

THE NATURAL DRIVE FOR CONNECTEDNESS

While we may have to pretend and use a deceitful false self to survive (a mostly unconscious process), we also have an innate desire for attachment and empathic mutuality. Our true self desires to belong to a community and be empathically connected to others. Life does not permit us to be connected to a large number of others, but we need to find a secure attachment figure and a few good friends. Doing that requires the work of love and our willingness to invest the energy required to do this work.

UNCONDITIONAL SELF-LOVE

We cannot love others if we don't love ourselves. We can be no more honest with others than we are with ourselves. What does it mean to love ourselves unconditionally? Besides what we talked about in Chapter Nine, it means that we embrace our healthy shame, our perfectly imperfect humanity.

Once I had done my grief work and given back my carried shame, I could embrace my true self. I like the metaphor of the Inner Child as a way to feel the connection with myself. I keep a picture of myself at four years old by my bedside in my writer's cottage. My editor at Bantam Books put this picture on the back cover of the paperback edition of my book *Homecoming*. I respect and honor the child. In doing so I reconnect with myself.

OWNING MY DISTORTED BEHAVIORS

My precious Inner Child is beautiful, but he was wounded by carried and induced shame. My shame-based self did many things I'm not proud of and that I feel genuine guilt about. My conscience calls me to be aware of the immoral things I've done. Those behaviors are part of me, and I can't be whole if I try to block them out. The psychologist Sheldon Kopp writes, "I cannot rid myself of my demons without risking that my angels will flee along with them."

EXERCISE

Imagine you are sitting in your favorite room. Create one, if you're not completely satisfied with the one you've got. Put the colors you like in the room. Put in the furniture you like (leather, velvet, etc.). Make your floors out of wood or marble or whatever you like. If you like rugs, put beautiful rugs in your room. Put in flowers with fragrant smells, and fill the room with the music you like (or let it be silent). Imagine that all the likeable parts of you are incarnated in the room with you. I see a guy in his Valentino baby blue suit doing his Inner Child meditation on *Oprah*. I see a guy holding the *New York Times* bestseller list and pointing to being number one. What is it that you really like about yourself? Perhaps you have an infectious, hearty laugh. Imagine you see yourself dressed in an attractive way and you hear yourself laughing heartily. Continue finding incarnated parts of yourself that you really like.

After you've assembled your entourage of personality traits and talents, let yourself feel connected to them. They are you, and it's wonderful to enjoy these parts of yourself!

Now hear a knock on the door. Open it and see someone who looks like a disliked part of yourself, dressed in a way that is consistent with your behavior at the time. If you had a period of promiscuity in your life, imagine yourself dressed in a bawdy way, as a hooker or a gigolo. Invite that disliked part of yourself into your room. Let yourself feel whatever you feel. I see a seminarian who cheated on his theology test when the class was put on their honor. He is dressed in a dirty black cassock and a stained white Roman collar. While I don't condone his actions, I remember how pressured he felt. He was driven by toxic shame to be the valedictorian of his class. He felt he had to be perfect. He was lonely and felt disconnected at the time. Nothing condones immoral behavior, but what I know for sure is that I am capable of such behavior.

Let people come to your door until you can no longer produce another person. Empathetically view each of your despised and disdained parts. They represent the shadow side of your consciousness. The more you avoid thinking about these parts of yourself, the more they become unconscious. The more unconscious they are, the more you will project them on others by criticizing, blaming and judging. This keeps you alienated from others.

The more you accept the unwanted parts of yourself, the more you become *one* with yourself and become rigorously honest with yourself. Rigorous honesty with yourself allows you to be whole. Carl Jung once said, "I'd rather be whole than good." In fact, the Greek word "telios" as used in the Bible and usually translated as "perfect," really means to be finished, complete or whole.

Unconditional love of myself means that I love all of me, my strengths and my weaknesses, my successes and my failures. I love myself in my perfectly imperfect humanity. Unconditional self-love is rooted in healthy shame as the permission to be human. Healthy shame is about polarity, not polarization. All humans are both/and rather than either/or. We have our goodness mixed with our badness. We are never all good or all bad.

When I'm loving all of me, all of my perfectly imperfect self, I become whole. When I love myself unconditionally, I have the potential to love others unconditionally. Knowing my own faults, seeing the log in my own eye, I will not be focused on the faults of others or finding the speck to criticize in others. Unconditional self-love allows me to be kind, forgiving, compassionate and accepting of others.

SHAME AS THE SOURCE OF SPIRITUAL DESTINY

As I love myself unconditionally, I allow my true self to flourish. There is a great deal I do not know about myself because the internalization of shame closes the door to the expansion of my personality. Living defensively, in secrecy and hiding, limits my life drastically. When people are always on the defensive, they cannot be authentically present and are unable to view the novelty that the world presents minute by minute. To live in a defended way precludes adventure and discovery. We cannot really have new experiences and encounters with the world because we view everything with the frozen eyes of our defended selves. The poet David Whyte says that when our "eyes are tired, the world is tired also." The world cannot present itself to us because we are so defended we can't see what is in front of us. We'll talk about how our consciousness can expand in the next chapter.

THE WATER OF YOUR BELONGING

According to Slavin and Kriegman, the true self is negotiated and re-negotiated throughout our lives. They define the true self as a unique constellation of universal and individual characteristics, "the maxim of which is known in each individual's experience through a sense of vitality, aliveness and a fit within a relational context."

In Rilke's poem "The Swan," he talks about how awkward the swan walks until she lets go of the ground she lands on and enters the water. Suddenly, as the swan enters the water, she is transformed into the most graceful creature. The water moves her "while the swan, marvelously calm, is pleased to be carried minute by minute, more like a king or queen." When the swan enters the water she has found the water of her belonging, the *water of her life.*

What the poem suggests is that when we find the water of our belonging we will have found our bliss, our grace, our spiritual destiny, our fully actualized true selves.

In my own journey, I've looked at the places in my life that are graceful. They bring me alive. Standing in front of an audience, being a teacher, brings me alive in an extraordinary way. My calling and destiny is to be a teacher. I've taught at every level of schooling for twenty years, and in the last twenty years to the public at large.

Ask yourself, "Who are the people who make me feel most alive when I'm with them? What is it that I love to do, that when I'm doing it I feel energy and vitality? What is my heart's desire in life? What does it feel like when my heart's passionate and on fire? Where do I feel most at home?"

These are the questions that your healthy shame allows you to ask. And when you've found answers to these questions, you've found your bliss, your spiritual calling and your destiny. Your calling does not have to be surrounded by the bright lights of the celebrity. It can be very simple. It may be something you've been doing all along. I know women who love home, gardening, and nurturing their children and others. I know a man who is passionately proud of his ability as an electrician. In one of his poems, "Sweet Darkness," the poet David Whyte tells us that the world was made to be free in. He urges us to give up any place where we do not really feel like we belong. He suggests "that anything or anybody that does not bring you alive is too small for you." Finding what truly brings you vitality, passion, spontaneity and full aliveness is finding your bliss, your true spiritual calling.

14

Seven Major Spiritual Blessings
That Come from Developing Healthy Shame

Invoked or not invoked, God is present.

—Written over the entrance to Carl Jung's home in Switzerland

In Figure 1.1, I describe how, when it is properly nurtured, the innate feeling of shame is experienced as the core of the life cycle. As we reach full maturity, shame is experienced as our sense of dignity, honor and ethical sensibility. Mature shame is also experienced as a sense of awe, reverence, modesty, mystery, the holy and numinous. Mature shame is the source and guardian of our spirituality. Of the many blessings that this mature spirituality brings, the following seven seem to be the most important:

1. Sound choosing, using your "grand will"
2. Secure attachment to your Higher Power
3. Silence and solitude, prayer and meditation
4. Solidarity with all things, unity consciousness
5. Sacrament of the present moment (authentic presence)
6. Synchronicity (ordinary miracles)
7. Serenity, service and a sense of humor

1. SOUND CHOOSING

We were born to be masters of our own unique destinies. As we embrace our toxic shame, we begin to discover our true selves, which have their own unique agendas for our spiritual callings and destinies. I've already described how you can track down clues to discover your spiritual calling with a fully functioning will. We can begin to explore those energetic areas that will lead us to our true selves. We have to be willing to follow the path that is calling us, even if it is Robert Frost's less-traveled road. We can respond only when we've dropped the defensive armor we used to hide our feeling of toxic shame. Joseph Campbell, one of the world's prominent scholars in the field of mythology, describes what he calls the hero's journey in his book *The Hero with a Thousand Faces.* The hero's journey is the symbolic story of the journey each person must take in order to find his or her bliss. In his PBS series *The Power of Myth,* Campbell describes how, when you've found your bliss or spiritual calling, "you put yourself on a kind of track that has been there all the while waiting for you." Once you're there you bypass your ordinary will and move into the realm described by the philosopher Martin Buber as the "grand will." Buber believed that the truly free person gives up his "puny, arbitrary will."

He writes, "Freedom and destiny are solemnly promised to each other and linked together in meaning."

With our puny, arbitrary will we try to change things we cannot change and constantly react to forces outside our control. Your grand will is one with your destiny. The precondition of owning your grand will is your willingness to give up trying to control everyone and everything. You must stop living from the outside, governed by "impression management." You have to quit worrying about what other people think and trust only that which brings you truly alive. When we use our grand wills we make up our own mind, but our sense of identity has shifted. When we say yes to the call of spiritual destiny we do what we do like the swan; we feel like we're riding the crest of the waves. Buber says, "This is not what we 'ought' to do; rather, we cannot do otherwise." With our grand will our freedom and destiny merge together.

2. SECURE ATTACHMENT TO YOUR HIGHER POWER

The mysteries and overwhelming immensity of life cause us to experience our littleness and finitude. When I look into endless space and I'm told our universe is one of many galaxies, I feel like a bubble on the vast oceans of the earth. Experiencing the death of my loved ones, both my parents, has left me bewildered and wondering. At times of grief I hear the poet Alfred

Lord Tennyson saying, "What am I, an infant crying in the night, crying for the light, and with no language but a cry."

I felt an overwhelming sense of littleness when I was recovering from quadruple bypass heart surgery. They had sawed my chest open and taken my heart out of my body. I felt fragile and vulnerable in a way I had never felt before. I remember reading the Bible in my youth and thinking the psalmist I was reading overdid it in his praise of God. I remember the line that triggered the reaction: "I thank you God for every breath I breathe." Now I pray that line daily. Now I live as if today is the last day of my life! My bypass surgery fully connected me with my healthy sense of shame. I felt how powerless I was in terms of my family history of coronary artery disease, and how little I really knew about the meaning of life. I have faith in the revelation of Jesus about the joys that God has in store for those who love him/her, but faith is faith and not knowledge—I'm often like the unbelieving disciples. I do believe that my life is an awesome gift. And I believe with Gabriel Marcel that life itself is a "mystery to be lived," not a problem that can be solved. This awe, reverence and appreciation of my life is a spiritual gift flowing from my shame.

When we know our limitations, we know there is something greater than ourselves. In the Twelve Step programs this greater something is called the Higher Power or God as you understand God. I personally choose to call this power God. I further believe that such a power cannot be less than personal. The apex of human life is personhood shared in the embrace of intimate love. If God is a Higher Power, God cannot be less than our human fulfillment. I believe that spirituality involves a personal union with a personal God.

BEYOND EGO CONTROL

For a shame-based person, "spiritual awakening" is impossible until the "externalization" work is done. Without such work, our ego self remains ruptured and alienated.

FULL HUMAN CONSCIOUSNESS

All the exercises I've described in the previous chapters have to do with reconstructing your ego self and integrating your alienated energies.

This is essential work on our journey toward wholeness. But you need to know that the ego self is not your true self. Figure 14.1 is a common way of representing the fullness of human consciousness. The small circle in the center is the ego self. It represents your core psychosocial boundary. It is narrowed consciousness and deals with establishing a sociocultural identity. The ego's main concern is survival and balance. It is the executor of the personality. The ego's primary purpose is the fulfillment of our dependency

FIGURE 14.1
Full Range of Human Consciousness

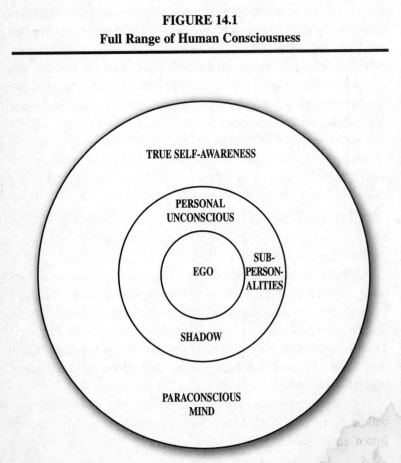

and survival needs. When our ego is strong, we know we can get our basic needs met. We know we are able to get enough food, clothing, warmth, love and protection. A strong ego is essential for survival.

The second circle has to do with storing both current and past experience. It also represents the storehouse of our forbidden feelings, needs and drives. The circle is called the personal unconsciousness or subconscious. All the parts of us that have been toxically shamed and split off reside in the subconscious. The subconscious is the abode of what Stone and Winkelman called our subpersonalities. Once we have integrated our shadow, we are ready to expand. Expansion leads to the full range of consciousness. In Figure 14.1 the outer circle represents this full range of consciousness. Stone and Winkelman call this the level of awareness. Transpersonal psychologists often refer to this circle as the paraconscious or higher conscious mind. It is also called unity consciousness. The paraconscious is the realm of our true beingness and selfhood. Once achieved, this level of consciousness is transforming. On this higher level of consciousness we see and experience everything differently. This is the level of pure novelty and discovery. Here we find a new self, not a better self. The new self is the self of our spiritual calling.

SPIRITUAL AWARENESS

This expanded consciousness is a way to describe "spiritual awakening," which is about the growth and expansion of awareness. Spirituality is about wholeness and completeness.

It is dangerous and counterproductive to work on this expansion until the lower self (ego) is unified. Spiritual masters often speak of ego integration as the journey into the desert. In the Christian Scripture, Jesus goes into the desert for forty days and forty nights before beginning his spiritual work. The mystics speak of "the dark night of the soul." The dark night of the soul is the stage of preparation before entering the "unitive way." The unitive way is the way of bliss—the state of true intimacy with God.

The spiritual masters also tell us that if the ego work is not finished, we will be drawn back to it. Much of the ego work is about the bound and frozen energy caused by developmental arrest. Unless that energy is unfrozen and unbound, it will draw us back to it. You have seen that one of the major ways your frozen and shame-bound energy is recycled is through reenactment. This can even happen with spirituality if the ego work is left undone.

SPIRITUAL REENACTMENT

I've shown you how piety and righteousness can be a cover-up for toxic shame. The offshoots of pious righteousness are perfectionism, judgment and blame. For me, one of the surest ways to know that a given style of spirituality is not true spirituality is to apply the following criteria to it: How blaming and judgmental is it?

Years ago I wondered about the judgmental rambling of both Jim Bakker and Jimmy Swaggart. As I listened to them, their words were divisive. It was always "us" and "them;" they condemned and accused others. They saw the specks but never the log. They hid from their shame. Their unresolved shame was ultimately acted out sexually. They were covering up their own unresolved ego issues and shame by blaming and judging others. They acted like spiritual leaders but their ego issues were unresolved.

No matter how much prayer and good work we do, if the ego needs are unmet, they will continually draw us back to the level where the unmet need exists until that need is met.

In my own case, even though I was ten years sober, teaching adult theology and probing the realms of ancient spiritual wisdom, I was still compulsive. *I was compulsive about my spirituality.* My Inner Child was still bruised and unhealed. I was still on an "insatiable quest" to fill the empty hole in my psyche. Such a quest is quite different from a healthy longing for God. The issue in compulsivity is unresolved grief and the issue of unmet ego needs. Although saints may look compulsive, compulsivity is not what their yearning for God is about. Their yearning for God flows from a higher human need. It is a being need. Such a need arises when our dependency needs have been adequately met. Figure 14.2 gives you my adaptation of what Abraham Maslow called the hierarchy of human needs.

FIGURE 14.2
The Hierarchy of Human Needs

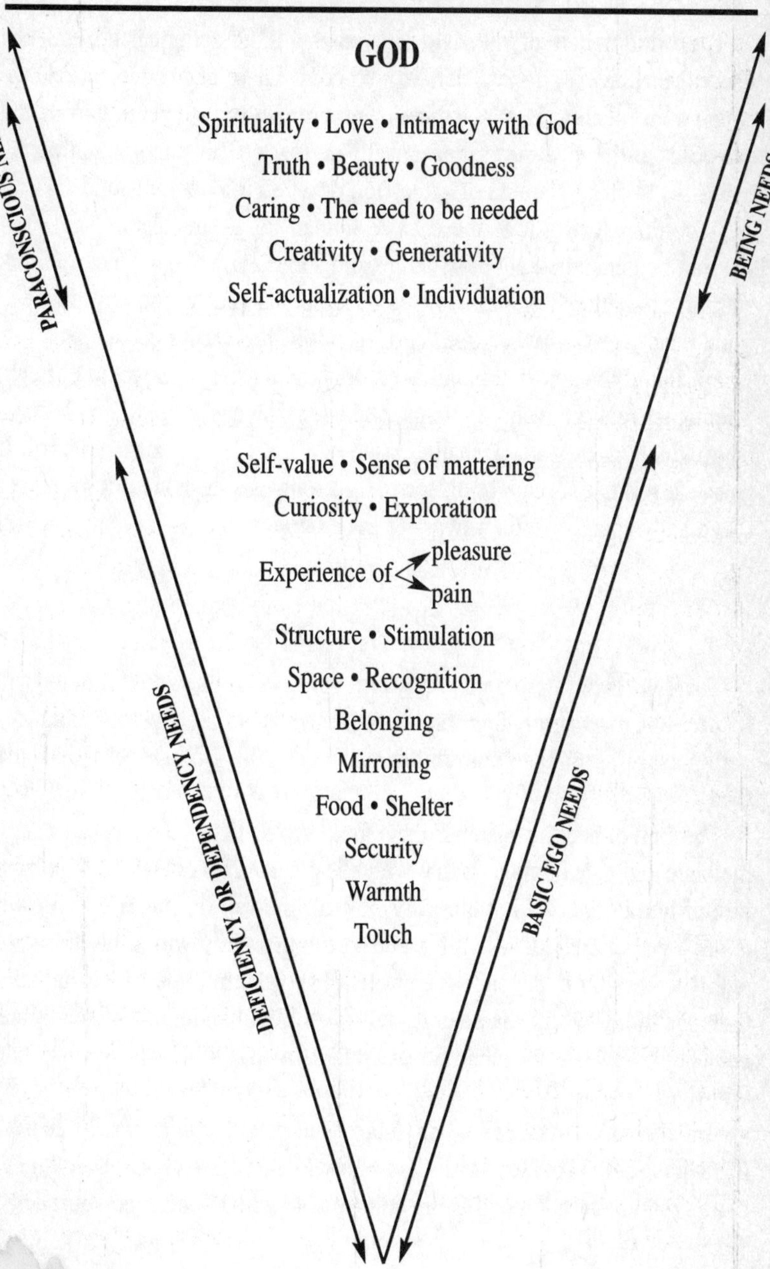

GOD

Spirituality • Love • Intimacy with God
Truth • Beauty • Goodness
Caring • The need to be needed
Creativity • Generativity
Self-actualization • Individuation

Self-value • Sense of mattering
Curiosity • Exploration
Experience of ⟨ pleasure / pain
Structure • Stimulation
Space • Recognition
Belonging
Mirroring
Food • Shelter
Security
Warmth
Touch

PARACONSCIOUS NEEDS

BEING NEEDS

DEFICIENCY OR DEPENDENCY NEEDS

BASIC EGO NEEDS

The bottom half of the pyramid represents your human dependency needs. Maslow called these deficiency needs. These needs depend on others for their fulfillment. When these needs are unmet, the energy that should accrue from the meeting of these needs is frozen. This energy continually expresses itself in patterns of projection or repetition compulsion.

According to Maslow, these basic human needs are hierarchical. You will not be concerned about structure and stimulation if you have no food, warmth or shelter. The same is true of the being needs. You will not seek truth, beauty or God when your ego has unfinished business.

Spirituality is a basic human need. It is the reason we develop our ego. The higher reality always explains the lower. The ego serves as a platform from which to expand. A shame-based ego fears letting go of control. It guards lest it is ever caught off guard. A strong ego structure allows you to let go and expand like the sawn. We must *let go in order to grow.*

CONSCIOUS CONTACT

The Twelve Step programs transform our toxic shame and end in the call for spiritual awakening. Step Eleven urges us to commit to prayer and meditation as a way to keep our conscious contact with God as we understand God.

The fruit of healthy shame is the humility to realize that we need to pray, meditate and give homage to that which is greater than ourselves. This posture of humble prayer is supportive of growth, even if your Higher Power is not a personal God. A humble person living solidly within the frame of reality knows he is dependent and gladly shows gratitude to all that supports his life. Healthy shame urges us to work on maintaining a "conscious contact" of awe, reverence and gratitude for that which is greater than ourselves.

It makes my life more joyous to pray and meditate and work at achieving a "conscious contact" with God as my Higher Power. Prayer and meditation require creating and being comfortable with silence and solitude.

3. SILENCE AND SOLITUDE

Each of us is alone. This is the hard-and-fast boundary of our material condition. Aloneness is a fact of life. How we embrace our aloneness determines whether it will be toxic or nourishing. Toxic aloneness is fostered by toxic shame. It is a consequence of being self-ruptured. Nourishing aloneness is a fruit of blissful spirituality. It flows from the secure attachment to a Higher Power, which gives us a greater sense of security. Feeling secure, we delve into self-love and discovery. Because you love and value yourself, you want to spend time alone. This is called solitude. When you know the joys of solitude, you want more of it. You also want it for the ones you love. Instead of your own shame-based possessiveness, you will become a protector of your own and your beloved's solitude.

Solitude is possible because you have done your ego work, especially the original pain work. With the completion of that work, you accepted your separateness. The fear of separation is why you stayed "fantasy bonded" in the first place. The fantasy bond is an illusion, the illusion that you will always be protected by your parents.

Once you've accepted your separation and aloneness, you come to believe that your ego is strong enough to take care of you. Your ego is strong enough for you to survive alone. This is also the precondition for meditation. As you come to experience a blissful union with God through meditation, you come to know your true self. You also come to know there is a place where you are never alone. With such awareness, solitude is most desirable.

SUFFERING AND SOLITUDE

Some of my life's most liberating experiences and moments of pure grace came from times when I was most wounded and broken. I think of getting on the bus with almost nothing to my name after my voluntary commitment to Austin State Hospital. During my stay there I had to experience myself in a unique solitude that occured when everything familiar collapsed around me. I was in a state of heightened anxiety and terror during the seven-day commitment, yet the anxiety and terror brought me face to face with myself in solitude. The state of solitude gave me the chance to draw on untouched resources within myself. Albert Camus wrote, "In the midst of winter, I found within me an invincible summer." It was a new experience during which I had to reach deep into my true self to discover the strength to go on. A new power and a new compassion came to me as a result of that experience.

MEDITATION

Meditation, a vehicle for consciousness expansion, demands a strong ego. To meditate well you must be willing to give up ego control. A strong, integrated ego is like a first-stage booster rocket, allowing you to go into the outer space of higher consciousness. Meditation is a way to create silence within yourself. Silence is a unitive state. If you cut silence in half, you still have silence.

One way to achieve inner silence and higher consciousness is through meditation. True meditation is the ultimate overcoming of toxic shame. Meditation aims at an immediate union with God. Physical love gave you an awareness of union. True love brought you into the chambers of the source of all union. Prayer allows you to dialogue with the source of union. And meditation allows you to be united with the source of union in a relationship of bliss.

MEDITATION TECHNIQUES

There are many ways to meditate. Each involves a technique. It is important to understand that the techniques of meditation are not the goal of meditation. There is no "goal" for meditation in the usual sense of the word.

Meditation is a search for immediate intimacy with God. The various techniques aim at creating the conditions for such intimacy. The main condition for this intimate union is called "the silence." Whatever the meditation technique, it aims at creating the silence. The techniques range from simple breath exercises to the exercises of the whirling dervishes. In between there are mandalas, mantras, music, manual arts, mental imaging and message exercises. The choice of technique depends on your personal preference. No one technique has greater value than any other. Each technique aims at distracting your mind and absorbing all your consciousness.

After much practice you can create a state of mindlessness. This state is called the silence. Once the silence is created, *an unused mental faculty is activated. It is a form of intuition. With this faculty one can know God directly.* Spiritual masters present a rather uniform witness on this point. They speak of this intuitive knowing as "unity consciousness," God consciousness or higher consciousness. It is direct union with God. In this union one also knows oneself as one really is. This knowing is unmeditated. With such inner vision one has new insights and *enlightenments.*

TWO WAYS TO SILENCE AND HIGHER CONSCIOUSNESS

In what follows, I will outline two approaches to higher consciousness (Higher Power meditations). For best results, I recommend that you record the meditation instructions on your tape recorder.

REFRAMING YOUR LIFE THROUGH THE EYES OF YOUR FREE CHILD

Figure 4.1 (page 103) shows the various layers of cover-ups for toxic shame. In the center circle there is a diamond. This diamond represents your "free child." The free child is another way to describe our true self, a psychic energy that withstood the onslaught of toxic shame. The free child emerges when the wounded Inner Child is embraced and nourished.

As the reparenting process takes place, you recognize there was a part of your authentic self that endured. This is the part of you that bought this book and leads you to seek recovery from the shame that binds you. The free child is that part of you that can laugh amid the pain, that can have fun and enjoy rich moments in life in spite of your toxic shame.

As a theologian, I see the free child as the image of God within us. It's the part of you that is Godlike. In creating you, God looked at all the possible ways his reality could be manifested. You became the incarnation of one of those ways.

The way of thinking is mythical. Myths are the ways we structure meaning about realities that are transcendant. We use myths and symbols when speaking about God. All God talk is mythical and symbolic.

The question of God cannot be avoided. It is demanded by our healthy shame. As the statement written over the entrance to Carl Jung's home says, "Invoked or not invoked, God is present." We cannot avoid speaking about God.

ALL GOD TALK IS SYMBOLIC

Paul Tillich used to scold his students for saying God talk is only symbolic. Symbols participate in the reality they try to describe. Symbols are more holistic then logic. Over half of the Judeo/Christian Scripture is written in symbols, (e.g., visions, dreams, parables, psalms, etc.). Symbols are the stuff of myth.

In my myth, each of us is a unique and unrepeatable creation of God, and each of us incarnates some aspect of the divine reality. Each of us came into the world in order to manifest that unique part of God's reality. We do that by being ourselves. The more we are truly ourselves, the more we are truly Godlike. To truly be ourselves, we need to accept our eternal mission and destiny. This consists in manifesting in a fully human way our Godlikeness. I follow Jesus Christ because he is for me the perfect expression of this.

Our destiny is known by the free child as our true selves. Once we've done our shame reduction work, we have our free child available and we can continue our journey to selfhood and true beingness. Our abandonment trauma pushed us off track. We momentarily lost our way. Our free child pushed us to do our recovery work. As we resolve our grief, we resume our journey. We reintegrate our ego self and establish our ego boundaries. This forms our human identity. However, even when our ego identity is fully restored, even when it is positive and life-affirming, it is socially and culturally limited. It is time bound; it is limited by language and constricted awareness. Our true self endures. It persists throughout all changes. It survives as our free child.

Using that mythology, I invite you to expand your consciousness with your free child. Since this part of you has been alive but hidden, it is now time for expansion and unfolding. The following meditation is one way to continue this unfolding.

FREE CHILD MEDITATION

Find a quiet space where you will not be interrupted. Take the phone off the hook or turn off the ring signal. Find a comfortable chair. Sit in an upright position. Do not cross your arms and legs. Choose a time when you're not too tired.

Meditation is most effective when your mind is producing alpha and theta brain waves. Alpha and theta brain waves create an altered state of consciousness that resides between waking and sleeping. This is the proper context for meditation.

Record the following:

Start by focusing on your breathing. Breath is life. It symbolizes the most fundamental rhythm of life, holding on and letting go. As you breathe in and out imagine an ocean with the waves rising (as you breathe in) cresting and spilling over (as you breathe out). Hear the power of the ocean as the waves spill over and wash onto the shore. Do this for two minutes. Now let your mind become full of breathing. Be aware of your chest as you breathe in and as you breathe out. Just be mindful of breathing (one minute). Now be aware of the air as it comes in and as it goes out. Be aware of the difference in the air as it comes in and as it goes out. Is it cooler or warmer as it comes in? As it goes out? (One minute.) Now breathe into your forehead and feel any tension that may be there and breathe it out. Repeat. Now breathe in around your eyes; look for any tension and breathe it out. Repeat. Now breathe in around your mouth and jaws; look for any tension and breathe it out. Repeat. Continue this process with your neck, shoulders, arms, hands and fingers, chest, stomach, buttocks, knees, calves, feet and toes. Now let your whole body relax. Relax every muscle and every cell. Imagine that you are hollow on the inside, like a human bamboo stalk. Breathe in a warm, golden sunlight through the top of your head and breathe it down through your whole body and out through your toes. Repeat this several times. Now imagine you are standing at the base of three stairs leading to a door. Place all your worries in an imaginary ball of sunlight. Make the ball with your hands. Put all your worries in the ball of sunlight and bury them. You can have them back later on. Walk up the three stairs and open the door. You will see three more stairs leading to a door. Make another ball of sunlight and place all your presuppositions and rigid beliefs in the ball and bury it. You may have them back when you're finished. Walk up the next three stairs and open the door. You will see three more stairs leading to a door. Now imagine another ball of sunlight by cupping your hands together. This time place your ego in it. Include all the roles you play. Put them in the ball one by one. Now open the door and walk out on a porch. Imagine that you are looking into the abyss of outer space. Look straight ahead and see a stairway of light beginning to form. When it is completely formed, look to the top of the stairs. Your free child will appear there. The child will begin walking down the stairs toward you. Notice everything you can about this free child. What does the child have on? Look at the child's face as the child comes near. Notice the child's eyes and hair. When the child steps onto the porch, embrace the child. Feel the connection with this powerful part of yourself. Talk things over. Imagine the two of you could review your life. The moment you were conceived, what was your mother's emotional condition? What about your father? See their union and your conception from God's point of view. Ask your free child about your purpose. Why are you here? Who are you? What is your specialness and uniqueness? What unique part of God do you manifest? What is it about you that makes a difference? Accept whatever your free child tells you. The answer may come in words. You may receive a symbol or a collage of symbols. You may have a strong feeling. Just accept what you receive, even if you cannot make sense out of it. If you do get a clear answer to your sense of purpose, review your life from that perspective. See the significant people who affected your life. You may see someone who seemed to be a negative influence in the past as an integral part of your plan or divine purpose. You may also see someone who seemed to be a positive influence in the past as less important for your true destiny. Go through all the events of your life step by step. View them all as part of a larger plan and purpose. See them from your free child's point of view. Let the film of your life run up until the present moment. Reflect on what you are experiencing now. Feel the presence of your Inner Child. Get a sense of the unity and coherence of your life. See it all from a more expanded point of view. See it all, your whole life, differently than ever before (one minute). Embrace your free child. Tell your child when you will meet with her again (sooner rather than later). Hear your child assure you that she is there to guide you. Your child is your ally. She has been there holding on to you through all the bad times. Now is the time for ripening and expanding. See your child walk up the magic stairway of light. Take two minutes to reflect on what has transpired. Let yourself dream a dream of integration. Let all your life come together in one unified purpose. Feel your willingness to commit to your purpose. Now for just two minutes of clock time, which is all the time in the world to the unconscious, dream your dream (allow two minutes on the recorder). Now begin to feel the place where you are located in the room. Feel your clothes on your body, the air on your face, the sounds in the room. Let feelings of your worth and value flow over you. Tell yourself that there has never been anyone like you (ten seconds), nor will there ever be anyone like you again (ten seconds). Make a decision to go forth and share yourself with others (ten seconds). Go back through the door and down the stairs. Pick up the ball of sunlight with your ego in it. Reintegrate your ego. Feel yourself coming back to your normal waking consciousness. Walk through the next door and down the stairs. Decide whether you want your old beliefs and presuppositions. If you do, take them out of the ball of sunlight. If not, walk through the third door, down the stairs and pause. Decide if you want your worries back. Remember that many worries are forms of fear and have a quality of wisdom about them. It is wise to fear certain things. You decide if you want some or all of your worries. Take the ones you want out of the ball of sunlight. Leave the rest buried. Walk to some beautiful place you know about and gaze into the sky. See the white clouds form the number three. Feel your feet and hands. Feel the life coming back into all of your body. Feel every cell and muscle awake. See the clouds blow away the number three and new clouds form the number two. Feel yourself returning to your normal waking consciousness. See the clouds blow away the number two and new clouds form the number one. When you see the number one, open your eyes and be fully awake.

Always sit for a few minutes after you've meditated. Let yourself integrate the experience. Meditation is an inner experience. It feels strange, even weird at first. The inner life has its own language. Inner experience is expressed in images, symbols and feelings.

As a shame-based person I had rarely been in my inner castle, as it were. I was busy guarding and defending myself lest I be found out. I was so busy guarding the outside that I never went inside. I lived peering out of a locked front door.

Meditation takes time and practice. My grandiosity and impulsiveness wanted it all at once. I wanted the floodgates to open and for God to appear. My free child has often punctured my grandiosity. I use my free child as an inner guide. I remember once asking him what I needed to do to resolve a spiritual dilemma I was having. His answer was, "Start by cleaning off your desk!" I was terribly disappointed with this answer. I wanted him to tell me to go to a monastery or fast for seven days. Clean off your desk? Come on! The way of the spirit is very simple. It is simple but difficult. The way of the ego intellect is complex and complicated. Analyzing and intellectualizing are complex but easy.

The answer to the purpose of my life was very simple. I found that the life I ought to be living was in fact the life I had been living for thirty-five years. It was the life of a teacher. It's the only thing I do not have to work at. To be me is to love myself in the ways I've described. This includes loving others, since I couldn't really love myself without wanting to expand and grow, and that can only happen through love.

BLISS

Joseph Campbell tells us that all the mythical stories of the hero's journey are stories of people finding their spiritual calling and destiny. When people are doing what they want with their one and only life, they have found their bliss.

MINDLESSNESS—CREATING THE SILENCE

This meditation aims at enhancing your "beingness." When you are in touch with your beingness, you are one with everything that is. There is no longer any separation. Without separation there is no object or event outside of you to achieve.

One meditation master, Suzuki Rashi said, "As long as you are practicing meditation for the sake of something, that is not true practice." In meditation we simply let ourselves be. The more we stop thinking and doing, the more we just are. Since God, as I understand God, is being itself, to let ourselves be is to enter into union with God.

In this meditation you can begin to experience pure moments of just being here. These moments feel open and spacious because they are devoid of personal needs, meanings and interpretations. This larger space is one way to describe the silence. Meditation can teach us how to contact this larger space (or silence). Since this space lies beyond the constant search for personal meaning, it can affect a radical transformation in the way we live. In shame-based lingo, this means you will give up your hypervigilance and guardedness. Meditation can lead you to this larger sense of aliveness. Such a sense of aliveness is not about anything we do; it's about who we are. As Jacquelyn Small says, "There is nothing that has to be done; there is only someone to be."

Creating the state of silence or mindlessness involves discipline. It is best compared to water dripping on a rock. Over the years the rock gets eaten away. This is one of many ways the state of mindlessness can be approached.

Begin this meditation using the instructions for the free child meditation. Creating a state of mindlessness involves following your awareness wherever it goes. Start with your breathing and let your thoughts come and go. Do not try to control them or direct them in more pleasant directions. Whenever you become aware of your thoughts, gently bring your awareness back to focusing on your breathing.

Start by becoming aware of the sensation of air passing through your nostrils. Feel its touch. Notice in what part of the nostrils you feel the touch of the air when you inhale, and in what part of the nostrils you feel the touch of air when you exhale. Become aware of the warmth or coldness of the air. Breathe into your forehead and become aware of any sensations in your forehead.

Continue to be aware of any sensation around your eyes, around your mouth, in your neck and shoulders. Just be aware of the sensation. Continue through your whole body. Omit no part of you. You may find some parts of you completely devoid of sensation. Keep focused on those parts. If no sensation emerges, move on.

Once you get to your toes, start over again. Do this for about ten minutes. Then become aware of your body as a whole. Feel the whole of your body as one mass of various types of sensations. Now return to the parts—

focusing on your eyes, mouth, neck, etc. Then once again rest in the awareness of your body as a whole.

Notice now the deep stillness that has come over you. Notice the deep stillness of your body. Go back to a part and come back to the stillness.

Try not to move any part of your body. Each time you feel an urge, don't give in to it, just be aware of it as sharply as you can. This may be extremely painful for you at first. You may become tense. Just be aware of the tenseness. Stay with it and the tension will disappear (one minute).

Let the whole horizon become darker and darker until there is nothing but darkness. Gaze into the darkness (one minute). Begin to see a candle flame in the center of the darkness. See the light from the flame growing brighter and brighter until the whole landscape is illuminated. Gaze into a field of pure white light; let yourself be absorbed by the light. Let yourself flow into the light. Be aware of nothing. There is nothing, only a great abyss and emptiness. Flow into the "nothingness" (three minutes).

Slowly begin to see the number one on the horizon; then the number two. Very slowly see the number three, number four, five, six; when you see the number seven, open your eyes. Sit in reverie for a few minutes.

To be mindless is to be free of any mental content. In the silence, you stop all the inner voices. You turn off your mental chatter. The mind is emptied and focused on nothing (no-thing). Such a state is a state of pure being. Being is the ground of all the beings that are. There are human beings, animal beings, tree beings. Each is a specific form of being. Each is a thing. When the mind reaches a state of nothingness, it goes beyond all things to the ground of all things. When you get beyond anything, you arrive at a place beyond any form of being. You arrive at pure being. So to get to the nothingness, you actually get to the ground of everything. You become united to being itself. In such a state you are connected to everything.

4. SOLIDARITY WITH ALL THINGS— UNITY CONSCIOUSNESS

Creating a sate of mindlessness is the way to achieve unity consciousness. The physicist David Bohm wrote a book entitled *Wholeness and the Implicate Order.* Bohm is considered by many the heir apparent of Einstein.

Bohm argues that both the material world and the world of consciousness are part of a single unbroken totality of movement. The implicate order is a level of reality beyond our normal everyday thoughts and perceptions and beyond the picture of reality presented by scientific theory, which is the explicate order. Everything in the universe affects everything else because they are all part of an unbroken whole. The old concepts of space, time and matter no longer apply. The old way of thinking causes us to think of individuals and groups as "other" than ourselves, leading to isolation, separation and wars. Bohm says, "We are all one." In the state of unity consciousness there is no division or separation. All the dichotomies are synthesized. There is a coincidence of opposites. The veils of appearance break down. You see the interconnection of all consciousness. In this state, everything is transformed. All your egoic understandings are transcended. You do not become a better self; you become a different self. You see your whole life as perfect, as something that had to be. You get a view of the whole puzzle, not just the pieces of the puzzle.

TOTAL ACCEPTANCE OF SELF AND OTHERS

With unity consciousness you totally and unconditionally accept yourself. Erikson writes: "It is the acceptance of one's one and only life cycle as something that had to be. . . . The possessor of integrity is ready to defend the dignity of his own lifestyle against all threats" (*Childhood and Society*).

With total integrity you can truly say, "If I had my life to live over, I'd do it all the same!" *Integrity is total self-acceptance, the complete overcoming of toxic shame.* Once such a state is experienced, it has no opposite. You thirst for it. It is a "land more kind than home," according to Thomas Wolfe.

SYNTHESIS OF OPPOSITES

In a state of bliss you no longer see things in opposites. There is no "us" and "them." You experience unity. The ego boundaries you worked so hard to establish have become the very structure that allowed you to transcend all boundaries. The naive mysticism of your free child has expanded into

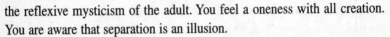

the reflexive mysticism of the adult. You feel a oneness with all creation. You are aware that separation is an illusion.

Living in the state of unity consciousness brings you to the highest levels of human compassion and kindness. Very few achieve this state fully—Mother Teresa, Albert Schweitzer, the great mystics, sages and holy ones. We can all have glimpses of it and achieve varying degrees of it. Prayer and meditation are the best vehicles to get us there with our perfectly imperfect humanity.

5. SACRAMENT OF THE PRESENT MOMENT (AUTHENTIC PRESENCE)

Prayer and meditation enhance our ability to embrace ourselves and experience some degree of our unity consciousness. They are spiritual practices (there are many others) that bring us to a state of "authentic presence." Authentic presence is a profound state (although every small child has it if not engulfed by toxic shame). In the state of authentic presence, the explicate order becomes a sacramental altar. Every moment has the potential to bring an experience of the implicate order. Every moment can become a *kairos* moment, a moment when the sacred breaks through the illusive barriers of time. Great music and poetry have the power to move us into transcendence, where we experience the timeless, the eternal. Catholic theologians refer to the sacrament of the present moment.

The sorcerer Carlos Castenada talks about a cubic centimeter of chance that pops in front of our eyes from time to time. The person who has some degree of unity consciousness is alert and present to this possibility. The deeper the level of unity consciousness, the greater the authentic presence. In the moment of the cubic centimeter, new insight is possible within oneself. It is in these moments I believe that God or our guardian angel, or the spiritual helper that Plato referred to as our *diamon,* offers people grace or calls us to our destiny or effects a spontaneous healing. Whatever way we try to explain it, something interrupts our ordinary way of looking at things, and we are changed.

To live in the dungeon of toxic shame is to live in the past or the anxious, catastrophic future. It is to be so defended and guarded that we cannot see what is going on around us. We look but we don't see. In so many ways, toxic shame is a living hell, a kind of living death. And we can go to our deaths never knowing who we are. When death finds you, hope it finds you alive. "Authentic presence" prepares us for what has been referred to as "ordinary miracles."

6. SYNCHRONICITY

Carl Jung defines "synchronicity as a meaningful coincidence of two or more events, where something other than the probability of chance is involved." (Synchronicity: an acausal connecting principle) Synchronicity is one of the fruits and rewards of the implicate order and unity consciousness. It has been witnessed over and over again by people who know their spiritual destiny and live by the "grand will." It is most often seen in retrospect as a person experiences higher consciousness. I knew it had happened to me long before I understood the meaning of synchronicity. Once I made certain commitments, unexpected things started happening. I wanted to do a TV series on the family. Beth and Charlie Miller appeared out of nowhere and offered to fund the series. I had met them before in a couples conference at the Houstonian years earlier. Liz Kaderli, a lady in my Sunday school class who worked for PBS, told me she wanted to do a ten-part series. She directed *Bradshaw On: The Family,* a series that generated hundreds of thousands of letters, fifty thousand a month during its first three years. These letters were thank-yous for the program and attested over and over again to transformations in peoples' lives.

When a person is authentically present and committed, doors open and people and money appear as if from nowhere. There is a coherent field of collective consciousness where the individuals in the field may not even be aware of one another. Somehow, several times in my life, my individuality seemed to disappear, and I became part of a generative order of action. Joseph Campbell described it as invisible hands coming together. He told Bill Moyers on his PBS special that "if you follow your bliss, you put yourself on a track that has been there all the while, waiting for you. . . . you begin to meet people who are in the field of your bliss, and they open the doors to you. . . . follow your bliss, and don't be afraid, and doors will open where you didn't know they were going to be."

ORDINARY MIRACLES

The mystics and physicists tell us that in the state of bliss, we have a Higher Power available to us. Being connected to all consciousness gives us resources of insight and knowledge that are more powerful than any we've ever imagined. The only condition required for such knowledge is the letting go of all ego control. A slogan in Twelve Step groups says, "Let go and let God." Another says, "Turn it over." Both slogans urge you to let go of ego control.

MIND OVER MATTER

The physicists also tell us that both mind and matter are forms of energy. Matter is a less radiant form of energy; it vibrates at a lower frequency. Mind or consciousness is a higher frequency energy; it can ensconce matter and powerfully affect it. This may involve phenomena like psychokinesis.

Delores Kieger has taught thousands of people how to alleviate pain through the laying on of hands. This phenomena is achieved through concentration and the development of kinesthetic sensory acuity. Anyone can learn to do this. The mind can create events outside itself through the use of imagination. This includes the creation of wealth. It also includes the power of mind to heal the body.

THE INTENTIONALITY OF CONSCIOUSNESS

All consciousness is intentional. This means it is purposeful. "Nothing walks with aimless feet," says the poet. I've suggested that "people make sense" no matter how bizarre their behavior may appear to us. When we are in higher consciousness, we are united to all consciousness. We share in the purposefulness of all consciousness. Many physicists and transpersonal psychologists believe there is a "plan" for our lives. As we look back over our lives, it is often clear there was such a plan. I foresaw things at twelve years of age that have acutally happened in my life. Over the years it has become clear to me that if I get out of the way and quit trying to control things, they always work out. Barry Stevens calls this "flowing with the river." Our ego, with its limited vision, can't see the proverbial forest for the trees. To "let go and let God" is to turn it over to higher consciousness.

NONATTACHMENT

Spiritual masters and saints have always practiced letting go. They call it nonattachment. They tell us that our suffering stems from our attachments. What we are emotionally invested in is what causes our pain. Since all human events have an ending, emotional pain is inevitable as long as we are emotionally invested.

In the movie *Zorba the Greek,* Zorba exhibited this nonattachment when he met with calamity. He had totally committed himself to the project of building a lumber conduit down a mountainside. No one could have worked harder or been more committed. After months and months of hard work, the project was ready to be tested. As the lumber flowed down the mountain, the momentum created too great a force and the conduit collapsed. Zorba was stunned. He took it all in. Then he began to laugh! He laughed and laughed! Then he began to dance! He danced and danced! The laughing and dancing were a kind of cosmic chuckle and cosmic dance. From the perspective of unity consciousness, no single event has importance. What is important is the whole.

The whole is what wisdom is all about. "The mountain to the climber is clearer from the plane," says the poet. We can only understand the parts when we see the whole. As Sri Aurobindo says, "You must know the highest before you can truly understand the lowest." Unitive vision and nonattachment are the fruits of bliss.

There are other fruits that flow from spiritual bliss. Some of these are serenity, service and a sense or humor. Each is manifested differently in accord with each person's unique life.

7. SERENITY

Serenity is characterized by what Robert Frost called "riding easy in harness." With serenity, your life will become less problematic and more spontaneous. You will act without analyzing everything and without ruminating. You will quit trying to figure it out. You will stop overreacting; your hypervigilance will diminish greatly. You will enjoy each and every moment as it comes along. You'll quit believing in scarcity and give up your impulsiveness and need for instant gratification. You'll accept the richness of life moment by moment. You'll see what you see, hear what you hear, know what you want and need, and know that you can get your needs and wants met. Serenity changes life into a childlike vision where "meadow, stream and every common sight" take on a newness. Those who are serene love the earth and all things. Life is its own splendid justification.

8. SERVICE

Spiritual bliss synthesizes life's polarities. The more solitude you come to know and enjoy, the more you will want to serve others in ways that enhance their spirituality. As Ken Wilber says in *No Boundaries:*

> To intuit and know your true self is a commitment to actualize that self in all beings, according to the primordial vow. However innumerable beings are, I vow to liberate them.

Service may also mean a commitment to worshiping in a way that fits your own beliefs. You may want to go back to your old church and religious denomination. If you return, you will have a new outlook and an expanded awareness. You can then see worship and ritual as ways to incarnate the "pooled memories" of your religious tradition. If your religious preference is a sacramental church, you can participate in the commemoration of the mighty acts of God as you understand God. As you participate in the symbolic reenactments of your ancestors' collective memory of their God, you can experience yourself as part of the past and part of a living tradition. You can experience your actions in the now as bringing the past into the present and the present into the future.

Service means caring for others and giving back what you have received. Step Twelve urges its participants to carry their spiritual awakening to others who suffer from toxic shame. All of us who have come out of hiding need to bring the light to others. Carrying the message is done by modeling, not by moralizing. It is done by those who "walk the walk as they talk the talk." This means there are no gurus. There are only those who have walked a little farther down the path. Anytime you make someone into a guru, you have relinquished your own power. Service and love for others flows directly from service and love for ourselves. We truly cannot give what we haven't got. We cannot teach our children self-valuing if we are shame-based. We cannot take our clients where we have not been as therapists.

Service is a true mark and fruit of spiritual bliss. In bliss we know what Paul Claudel meant when he wrote:

> There is no one of my brothers . . . I can do without. . . . In the heart of the meanest miser, the most squalid prostitute, the most miserable drunkard, there is an immortal soul with holy aspirations, which deprived of daylight, worships in the night. I hear them speaking when I speak and weeping when I go down on my knees. There is no one of them I can do without. Just as there are many stars in the heavens and their power of calculation is beyond my reckoning so also there are many living beings. . . . I need them all in my praise of God. There are many living souls but there's not one of them that I'm not in communion in the sacred apex where we utter together the Our Father.

EMPOWERMENT

Bliss engenders empowerment. We move from our childish belief that we will always be victims to a childlike spontaneity and optimism. We embrace our imagination and creativity. We refuse to be victims any longer. We become the artistic creators of our own lives. We take risks. We go after the things we really want.

As you come to the end of this book, my most sincere hope is that you have come a long way in healing the shame that binds you. In so doing you've opened yourself to the awesome, but limited, possibilities of your human nature. Such possibilities are modeled by the magnificent outpouring of human creation. Our great musicians were limited by the laws of the musical scale, but within those limits the variety of their compositions are almost unbelievable. Our great painters were limited by their canvas, but walking through a museum of fine art can be an awesome and overwhelming experience. Within our human limits, there are still miracles to come. You are one of the miracles!

Toxic shame, with its more-than-human/less-than-human grandiosity, is a problem involving the denial of human finitude. Being human requires courage. It requires courage because being human is being imperfect. Alfred

Adler first used the phrase "the courage to be imperfect." You need the courage to be imperfect. As I've tried to show, our families, religions, schools and culture are based on perfectionistic systems. We are set up for being measured, which in turn sets us up for perpetual disappointment. Perfectionism is without boundaries. There are no limits. You can never do enough. It takes courage to do battle with these perfectionistic systems. But it's worth it!

9. SENSE OF HUMOR

The courage to be imperfect engenders a lifestyle characterized by spontaneity and humor. Once you've accepted that mistakes are natural products of limited human awareness, you stop walking on eggs. You take more risks and feel freer to explore and be creative.

Most important, you will laugh more. *A sense of humor may be the ultimate criterion for measuring a person's recovery from internalized shame.* Being able to laugh at events, other people and ourselves requires true humanness. To have a sense of humor you have to straddle the more-than-human/less-than-human polarity. This demands that you be a paradox juggler.

A sense of humor is based upon the juxtaposition of the incongruous. To have a sense of humor is to take life less somberly and more seriously. As Walter O'Connell has so well written, "Humor results from resolution of human paradoxes." Every human paradox has two extremes. It is by reuniting these extremes that we gain energy and hope. These are the fruits of our humor. It also gives us perspective and balance. It lets us laugh at both our overinflated egos and our flaws. Give yourself permission to enjoy every minute of every day. Ride easy in harness, as Robert Frost would have it. Go for enlightenment. You'll know you're there when you lighten up!

Epilogue

Looking at Yourself Through the Eyes of Your Higher Power

This meditation is a short one. It can be done in ten to fifteen minutes. It allows you to look at yourself from the point of view of your higher consciousness or Higher Power.

Use your own experience of God as you understand God.

Record the following instructions on your tape recorder:

Close your eyes and focus on your breathing (ten seconds). Be aware of your breath as it comes in, and as it goes out. Focus on the difference in the feeling of the air as it comes in and as it goes out. Is it cool as it comes in? It it warm as it goes out? Feel the difference as completely as you can (thirty seconds). Now take several very deep breaths. As you breathe in and out begin to see the number five (twenty seconds). Then see the number four (twenty seconds). Then see the number three (twenty seconds). Then see the number two (twenty seconds). Then the number one. See the number one turn into a door and see it open (ten seconds). See a long, winding corridor leading to a field of light. Walk down the corridor, noticing that there are doors on either side. Each door has a symbol on it. Walk toward the field of light (ten seconds). Walk through the light field into an ancient church or temple (ten seconds). Look around this holy place (twenty seconds). Sit down in a comfortable place and allow some symbolic image of your God or Higher Power to enter the church or temple. Allow the image to come toward you and to sit across from you. Be aware that this is the presence of truth, beauty, goodness and love. Imagine that you can float out of your body into this presence. When you can see yourself sitting across from you, make a kinesthetic anchor with your thumb and a finger on your right hand. Hold the anchor.

Imagine that you are your Higher Power. You are the creator of life, love and all the humans on earth. You are looking at you this very moment. You see yourself through the eyes of love itself. You are in the very heart and mind of love itself. You can see yourself completely and perfectly. You begin to recognize qualities and aspects of yourself that you've never seen before (twenty seconds). You see and hear what your Higher Power cherishes about you (twenty seconds). You feel yourself totally and unconditionally accepted (thirty seconds). Holding all that your Higher Power loves and cherishes about you, especially those aspects of yourself you were unaware of with your own eyes, slowly come back to your own body. Be totally you. Let go of your thumb and finger anchor.

Feel all the love and value that is you. Thank your Higher Power and walk out of the place where you are. As you come to the entrance, see a scene of natural beauty. Walk out into it. Feel yourself part of the universe. Feel yourself as a necessary part of nature. You are supposed to be here (thirty seconds). Look up in the sky and see the clouds form the number one. Tell yourself you will remember this cherished feeling. See the cloud become a two, then three; feel your hands and feet. Be aware of your body. See the clouds form the number four; know you are coming back to your normal waking consciousness. See the number five, and slowly open your eyes.

This meditation came to me as a kind of synchronicity. After I experienced it I was unable to reject myself again. I felt the unconditional love and acceptance of myself in all my perfectly imperfect humanity. I am loved and accepted unconditionally by my Higher Power. Who do I think I am to ever refuse this love?

Sources

The author gratefully wishes to acknowledge the following books. I enthusiastically recommend them to the reader.

Alberti, Robert, and Michael Emmons. *Your Perfect Right.* San Luis Obispo: Impact Publishers, 1990.

Bach, George, and Herbert Goldberg. *Creative Aggression.* New York: Doubleday & Co., 1974.

Bandler, Leslie. *They Lived Happily Ever After.* Capitden: Meta Publications, 1978. (Now published under the title *Solutions: Future Pace.*)

Beck, A. T. *Cognitive Therapy and Emotional Disorders.* New York: New American Library, 1979.

Black, Claudia. *It Will Never Happen to Me.* New York: Ballantine, 1990. Dr. Black is my colleague at The Meadows. She is one of the great pioneers of the adult child movement. She can be contacted at The Meadows in Wickenberg, Arizona.

Bohm, David. *Wholeness and the Implicate Order.* London: Rourledge & Kegan Paul, 1980.

Bradshaw, John. *Bradshaw On: The Family.* Deerfield Beach: Health Communications, 1988.

____. *Creating Love.* New York: Bantam Books, 1992.

____. *Homecoming: Reclaiming and Championing Your Inner Child.* New York: Bantam Books, 1990.

Buber, Martin. *I and Thou.* New York: Charles Scribner's Sons, 1958.

Campbell, Joseph. *The Hero with the Thousand Faces,* Princeton, N.J.: Princeton University Press, 1968.

____.*The Power of Myth with Bill Moyers.* Betty Sue Flowers, ed. New York: Doubleday, 1988.

Campbell, Susan. *The Couples Journey.* San Luis Obisbo: Impact Publications, 1980.

Carnes, Pat. *Out of the Shadows: Understanding Sexual Addiction.* Minneapolis: CompCare Publications, 1985.

Carter, Rita. *Mapping the Mind.* Berkeley: University of California Press, 1999.

Cermak, Timmen. *Diagnosing and Treating Co-dependence.* Minneapolis: Johnson Institute.

Darwin, Charles. *The Expression of Emotions in Man and Animals.* City: publisher, date.

Dwinell, Lorie, and Jane Middelton-Moz. *After the Tears.* Deerfield Beach: Health Communications, 1986.

Ellis, Albert. *A New Guide to Rational Living.* North Hollywood: Wilshire Books, 1975.

Ellis, Havelock. *The Evolution of Modesty* (Studies in Psychology of Sex). New York: Random House, 1936.

Erikson, Erik H. *Childhood and Society.* New York: W. W. Norton, 1950.

Farber, Leslie. *The Ways of the Will and Lying, Despair, Jealousy, Envy, Sex, Suicide, Drugs and the Good Life.* New York: Basic Books, 2000.

Firestone, Robert. *The Fantasy Bond.* New York: Human Sciences Press, 1985.

Forward, Susan. *Betrayal of Innocence.* (Rev. ed.) New York: Penguin Books, 1988.

Fosha, Drana. *The Transforming Power of Affect: A Model for Accelerating Change.* Dallas: Behavioral Sciences Research Press, May 2000.

Fossum, M. and M. Mason, *Facing Shame.* New York: W. W. Norton.

Hendricks, Gay. *Learning to Love Yourself.* Englewood Cliffs: Prentice Hall, 1982.

Jaworski, Joseph. *Synchronicity,* Betty Sue Flowers, ed. San Francisco: Berrett-Koehler, 1998.

Jung, C. G. *Synchronicity: An Acausal Connecting Principle*—Vol 8, Collected Works.

Kaufman, Gershen. *The Psychology of Shame.* New York: Springer, 1989.

____. *Shame: The Power of Caring.* Cambridge: Schenkman Books, 1992.

Kopp, Sheldon. *Mirror, Mask and Shadow.* New York: Bantam Books, 1982.

Kriegman, Daniel, and Malcom Slavin. *Adaptive Design of the Human Psyche.* New York: The Guilford Press, 1992.

Kritzberg, Wayne. *Adult Children of Alcoholics Syndrome: From Discovery to Recovery*. Deerfield Beach: Health Communications, 1988.

____. *Gifts for Personal Growth and Recovery*. Deerfield Beach: Health Communications, 1988.

LeDoux, Joseph. *The Emotional Brain: The Mysterious Underpinnings of Emotional Life*. Reprint edition. New York: Simon and Schuster, March 1998.

Lowen, Alexander. "In Defense of Modesty." *Journal of Sex Research*. Madison: University of Wisconsin, 1968.

Lynd, Helen Merrell. *On Shame and the Search for Identity*. Eugene: Harvest House Publications.

Maslow, Abraham. *The Farther Reaches of Human Nature*. New York: Penguin Books, 1976.

____. *Religion, Values and Peak Experiences*. New York: Viking Press, 1970.

Masterson, James. *The Narcissistic and Borderline Disorders*. New York: Brunner/Mazel, 1981.

Meichenbaum, D. *Cognitive Behavior Modification*. New York: Plenum Press, 1977.

Mellody, Pia, Andrea Miller and J. Keith Miller. *Facing Love Addiction*. San Francisco: Harper, 1992.

Mellody, Pia and Lawrence Freundlich. *The Intimacy Factor*. New York: Harper, 2004. Pia's tapes on shame are extraordinary. Call the Meadows Treatment Center, Wickenberg, Arizona (800-240-5522).

McKay, Matthew, Martha Davis and Patrick Fanning. *Thoughts and Feelings: The Art of Cognitive Stress*. New Harbinger Publications, 1981.

McKay, Matthew, and Patrick Fanning. *Self Esteem*. New Harbinger Publications, 2000.

Middelton-Moz, Jane. *Children of Trauma: Rediscovering the Discarded Self*. Deerfield Beach: Health Communications, 1989.

Middelton-Moz, Jane, and Lorie Dwinnel. *After the Tears*. Deerfield Beach: Health Communications, 1986.

Miller, Alice. *Pictures of Childhood*. New York: Farrar Straus Giroux, 1986.

Nathanson, Donald. *Shame and Price*. New York: W.W. Norton, 1992.

Nietzsche, F. *Beyond Good and Evil*.

_____. *The Gay Science*. Walter Kaufman, trans. New York: Random House, 1966.

Otto, Rudolf. *The Idea of the Holy*. New York: Oxford University Press, 1992.

Sanford, John. *Evil: The Shadow Side of Reality*. New York: Crossroad, 1982.

Satir, Virginia. *Conjoint Family Therapy: Your Many Faces*. Palo Alto: Science & Behavior, 1983.

Scheler, Max. Über Scham ünd Schamgefühl—to French: *La Pudeur*. Paris: Aubier, 1952.

Schneider, Carl D. *Shame, Exposure and Privacy*. New York: W.W. Norton & Co., 1977.

Schore, Allan N. *Affect Regulation and the Repair of the Self. Affect Dysregulation and Disorders of the Self, two volume set*. New York: W. W. Norton and Company, April 2003.

Small, Jacquelyn. *Transformers*. Marina del Rey: Devorss Publishers, 1994.

Smith, Manuel. *When I Say No, I Feel Guilty*. New York: Bantam Books, 1975.

Solovie, Vladimir. *The Justification of the Good*. Nathalie Duddington, trans. New York: Macmillan, 1918.

Stevens, John O. *Awareness*. New York: Bantam, 1973.

Stone, Hal, and Sidra Winkelman. *Embracing Our Selves*. Marina del Rey: Devorss Publishers, 1985.

Subby, Robert. *Lost in the Shuffle: The Co-dependent Reality*. Deerfield Beach: Health Communications, 1987.

Tomkins, Silvan. *Affect, Imagery, Consciousness*. Vol. 2. New York: Sprinter Pub., 1962, 1963.

Viorst, Judith. *Necessary Losses*. New York: Simon & Schuster, 1997.

Wegscheider-Cruse, Sharon. *Choicemaking*. Deerfield Beach: Health Communications, 1985.

_____. *Learning to Love Yourself*. Deerfield Beach: Health Communications, 1987.

White, Robert, and Gilliland. *Elements of Psychopathology: The Mechanisms of Defense*. San Diego: Grune & Stratton, 1975.

Whitfield, Charles, L. *Healing the Child Within*. Deerfield Beach: Health Communications, 1987.

Whyte, David. David is a most extraordinary poet and writer. I recommend everything Whyte has done. (For a catalogue: Avistana@davidwhyte.com. Telephone 360-221-1324.)

Wilber, Kenneth. *No Boundary.* Boston: Shambhala Publications, 1979, 2001.

Wolpe, J. *The Practice of Behavior Therapy.* New York: Pergamon Press, 1973.

Author

JOHN BRADSHAW is the author of the bestselling *Bradshaw On: The Family, Homecoming, Reclaiming and Championing Your Inner Child, Creating Love, Family Secrets* and the Emmy-nominated host of five major PBS series. He's a frequent guest on *Oprah,* CNN, MSNBC and many network news shows. John was selected by his peers as one of the One Hundred Most Influential Writers on Emotional Health in the 20th Century.

John was born in Houston, Texas, and educated in Canada, where he studied for the Roman Catholic priesthood, earning advanced degrees in theology, psychology and philosophy from the University of Toronto. He completed four years of post-graduate work at Rice University in the field of psychology and religion. For decades, he has trained therapists, given intensive healing workshops worldwide, worked as a counselor, a theologian, a management consultant and been a sought-after public speaker. John is married and has three children and three grandchildren.

John gives intensive workshops, lectures and training throughout the world in management, addiction, recovery and spirituality. For more information:

Voice:	713-541-4254
Facsimile:	713-975-8206 or 713-541-4244
Web site:	*www.johnbradshaw.com*
E-mail address:	*youcanheal@aol.com*
Mailing address:	2476 Bolsover, Suite 435
	Houston, Texas 77005

The videotape and audiotape series for John's books, PBS programs, lectures and workshop are available at his Web site or call 800-6-BRAD-SHAW within the United States or 713-771-1300.